VOLUME 560

NOVEMBER 1998

THE ANNALS

of The American Academy *of* Political
and Social Science

ALAN W. HESTON, *Editor*
NEIL A. WEINER, *Assistant Editor*

THE FUTURE OF FACT

Special Editors of this Volume

JEFFREY J. STRANGE
ELIHU KATZ
University of Pennsylvania
Philadelphia

 SAGE Periodicals Press   *THOUSAND OAKS   LONDON   NEW DELHI*

Origin and Purpose. The Academy was organized December 14, 1889, to promote the progress of political and social science, especially through publications and meetings. The Academy does not take sides in controverted questions, but seeks to gather and present reliable information to assist the public in forming an intelligent and accurate judgment.

Meetings. The Academy occasionally holds a meeting in the spring extending over two days.

Publications. THE ANNALS of the American Academy of Political and Social Science is the bimonthly publication of The Academy. Each issue contains articles on some prominent social or political problem, written at the invitation of the editors. Also, monographs are published from time to time, numbers of which are distributed to pertinent professional organizations. These volumes constitute important reference works on the topics with which they deal, and they are extensively cited by authorities throughout the United States and abroad. The papers presented at the meetings of The Academy are included in THE ANNALS.

Membership. Each member of The Academy receives THE ANNALS and may attend the meetings of The Academy. Membership is open only to individuals. Annual dues: $56.00 for the regular paperbound edition (clothbound, $82.00). Add $12.00 per year for membership outside the U.S.A. Members may also purchase single issues of THE ANNALS for $11.00 each (clothbound, $16.00). Add $2.00 for shipping and handling on all pre-paid orders.

Subscriptions. THE ANNALS of the American Academy of Political and Social Science (ISSN 0002-7162) is published six times annually—in January, March, May, July, September, and November. Institutions may subscribe to THE ANNALS at the annual rate: $250.00 (clothbound, $295.00). Add $12.00 per year for subscriptions outside the U.S.A. Institutional rates for single issues: $44.00 each (clothbound, $51.00).

Periodical postage paid at Thousand Oaks, California, and additional offices.

Single issues of THE ANNALS may be obtained by individuals who are not members of The Academy for $19.00 each (clothbound, $29.00). Add $2.00 for shipping and handling on all prepaid orders. Single issues of THE ANNALS have proven to be excellent supplementary texts for classroom use. Direct inquiries regarding adoptions to THE ANNALS c/o Sage Publications (address below).

All correspondence concerning membership in The Academy, dues renewals, inquiries about membership status, and/or purchase of single issues of THE ANNALS should be sent to THE ANNALS c /o Sage Publications, Inc., 2455 Teller Road, Thousand Oaks, CA 91320. Telephone: (805) 499-0721; FAX/Order line: (805) 499-0871. *Please note that orders under $30 must be prepaid.* Sage affiliates in London and India will assist institutional subscribers abroad with regard to orders, claims, and inquiries for both subscriptions and single issues.

Printed on recycled, acid-free paper

THE ANNALS

© 1998 *by* The American Academy *of* Political *and* Social Science

Editorial Office: 3937 Chestnut Street, Philadelphia, PA 19104.

For information about membership* (individuals only) and subscriptions (institutions), address:

SAGE PUBLICATIONS, INC.
2455 Teller Road
Thousand Oaks, CA 91320

From India and South Asia,
write to:
SAGE PUBLICATIONS INDIA Pvt. Ltd
P.O. Box 4215
New Delhi 110 048
INDIA

From the UK, Europe, the Middle
East and Africa, write to:
SAGE PUBLICATIONS LTD
6 Bonhill Street
London EC2A 4PU
UNITED KINGDOM

SAGE Production Staff: LISA CUEVAS, ERIC LAW, DORIS HUS, and ROSE TYLAK
*Please note that members of The Academy receive THE ANNALS with their membership.
Library of Congress Catalog Card Number 98-60538
International Standard Serial Number ISSN 0002-7162
International Standard Book Number ISBN 0-7619-1737-3 (Vol. 560, 1998 paper)
International Standard Book Number ISBN 0-7619-1736-5 (Vol. 560, 1998 cloth)
Manufactured in the United States of America. First printing, November 1998.

The articles appearing in THE ANNALS are indexed in *Academic Index, Book Review Index, Combined Retrospective Index Sets, Current Contents, General Periodicals Index, Public Affairs Information Service Bulletin, Pro-Views,* and *Social Sciences Index.* They are also abstracted and indexed in *ABC Pol Sci, America: History and Life, Automatic Subject Citation Alert, Book Review Digest, Family Resources Database, Higher Education Abstracts, Historical Abstracts, Human Resources Abstracts, International Political Science Abstracts, Journal of Economic Literature, Managing Abstracts, Periodica Islamica, Sage Urban Studies Abstracts, Social Planning/Policy & Development Abstracts, Social Sciences Citation Index, Social Work Research & Abstracts, Sociological Abstracts, United States Political Science Documents,* and/or *Work Related Abstracts, Westlaw,* and are available on microfilm from University Microfilms, Ann Arbor, Michigan.

Information about membership rates, institutional subscriptions, and back issue prices may be found on the facing page.

Advertising. Current rates and specifications may be obtained by writing to THE ANNALS Advertising and Promotion Manager at the Thousand Oaks office (address above).

Claims. Claims for undelivered copies must be made no later than twelve months following month of publication. The publisher will supply missing copies when losses have been sustained in transit and when the reserve stock will permit.

Change of Address. Six weeks' advance notice must be given when notifying of change of address to ensure proper identification. Please specify name of journal. Send address changes to: THE ANNALS of the American Academy of Political and Social Science, c/o Sage Publications, Inc., 2455 Teller Road, Thousand Oaks, CA 91320.

THE ANNALS

of The American Academy *of* Political *and* Social Science

ALAN W. HESTON, *Editor*
NEIL A. WEINER, *Assistant Editor*

––––––––––––––––– FORTHCOMING –––––––––––––––––

EMOTIONAL LABOR IN THE SERVICE ECONOMY
Special Editors: Ronnie J. Steinberg and Deborah M. Figart
Volume 561   January 1999

THE EVOLVING WORLD OF WORK AND FAMILY:
NEW STAKEHOLDERS, NEW VOICES
Special Editors: Bradley K. Googins and Marcie Pitt-Catsouphes
Volume 562   March 1999

THE SILENT CRISIS IN U.S. CHILD CARE
Special Editor: Suzanne W. Helburn
Volume 563   May 1999

See page 2 for information on Academy membership and
purchase of single volumes of **The Annals.**

CONTENTS

BOOK DEPARTMENT CONTENTS

ECONOMICS

PREFACE

These remarks are being written on the Fourth of July weekend, in the virtual space between Jerusalem and Philadelphia. From Philadelphia, it looks as though Jerusalem is full of facts, if not brotherly love, and that Philadelphia has hardly any. After all, facts from the Middle East are on the front page of every newspaper, while Philadelphia hardly makes the inside pages. To worsen matters, Michael Herzfeld tells us that Gary Wills has debunked the famous painting depicting the ceremonial occasion on which signatories of the Declaration of Independence gathered in Philadelphia for the event.

From Jerusalem, however, Philadelphia seems as firmly anchored in fact as the Liberty Bell, while the Middle East is seething with myth and ambiguity. The Palestinian delegation to the United Nations has just been upgraded—but not to the status it was seeking—and both sides are claiming a diplomatic triumph. Not so long ago, an Israeli prime minister announced that there never was a Palestinian people, and the Arab world retorted that Jerusalem was not the capital of Israel. Victory in the Yom Kippur War was claimed by both Egypt and Israel, and Israel is having second thoughts about whether it really won the Six Day War, considering all of the unanticipated problems that have followed in its wake. Facts refuse to stand still, it seems, and that is what this volume is about. Facts are all around us, of course, but they are hard to recognize.

THE CONFERENCE

The conference in which these 14 articles first took form was organized by the Annenberg Scholars Program and took place in February 1997 as the culminating event of a two-year effort to grapple with the status of fact and the role of media in postmodernity. The conferees, and a distinguished audience, met with the two multidisciplinary cohorts of Annenberg Scholars who had spent a year at the University of Pennsylvania deliberating the dilemma of reporting—in journalism, law, history, and the sciences.[1] Both Scholars and conferees were asked to consider that the classical distinctions between facts, representation, and interpretation had apparently broken down. If facts cannot be told without narrators and narratives, and if these inevitably affix imprints of their own, it follows that facts are accessible only through representation, and that representation is tainted with interpretation. As Jerome Bruner puts it, when the classical baseball umpire claims to call balls "like they are," and the modern umpire purports to call them "like I see them," their postmodern counterpart takes issue, insisting instead that "they ain't nothing until I call them."

While these problems are not new, many believe they have reached crisis proportions in recent years. Speaking for history, Peter Novick suggests that the crisis relates to the fragmentation of society into particularisms that command more loyalty than the center and that legitimate the inevitable partisanships of the historians themselves. What then is the relationship between interpretation and fact? we asked. Is one story as good as another— and, if not, how should they be judged? Is the distinction between fact and fiction still tenable? If facts do not speak for themselves, who speaks for them? And who gave these speakers of fact the right to do so?

From the papers presented at the conference, the ones published here can be divided roughly into two groups.[2] The first (Bruner, Novick, Lichtenberg, Margolis, Herzfeld) concentrates on the philosophical problems of constructivism, exploring the embeddedness of facts in the meaning-making contexts of stories and theories, showing how narratives construct facts at least as often as facts constrain stories and theories. The second group of contributors (Ericson; Schwartz and Holyfield; Zaller; McGraw; Kuklinski, Quirk, Schwieder, and Rich; Cowan; Murphy; Johnson; J. Katz) focuses on the social and technological arrangements of storytelling and theory telling; these authors examine the systematic biases that arise from these arrangements and suggest ways in which such bias might be reduced.

CHALLENGING FACTS

Jerome Bruner sets the tone for the first group of articles. In the opening article of this collection, Bruner portrays the essential homelessness of facts. Even after they are noticed, classified, and contextualized, facts long for the company of a welcoming narrative in which they have a function to play. The meaning of a given fact depends on the story in which it is lodged. Bruner suggests that intersubjective understanding depends upon the ability to draw upon a store of common narrative frames. Following Propp, he argues that the stock of story forms is limited and shows a high degree of similarity across linguistic and cultural divides.

Like Bruner, Peter Novick acknowledges the reality of facts—indeed, he thinks they are rather readily gathered and validated—and asserts that historians can tell any number of competing stories without getting the facts wrong, that is, without being more or less untruthful. Abjuring the traditional claim of professional historians to truth and authority—and abetted by the collapse of consensus over the goals of historical scholarship—Novick feels that there is a liberating import to these developments. Historians, he says, should be "exploring and thinking about the past with as much energy and intelligence as we can muster, and then making up interesting, provocative, even edifying stories about it as contributions to collective self-understanding(s)" (37).

In a direct reply to Novick, Judith Lichtenberg contends that fact-finding is very hard work and that Novick underestimates both its costs and its worth. Facts not only serve stories, she insists, but they also place significant constraints on the stories we can tell. While Novick can scarcely distinguish the truth claims of historians and poets, Lichtenberg asserts essential differences in the epistemic grounding these genres require. Over time, she argues, the accumulation of new facts, the falsification of others, the incorporation of more causal factors, and the distancing of partisanship will ultimately, however slowly, make for more truthful accounts.

Philosopher Joseph Margolis and anthropologist Michael Herzfeld each expand Lichtenberg's implication that facts-as-we-know-them have a past. Both, however, stress the thoroughly "languaged" nature of perception and thought and, correspondingly, the inaccessibility (or even nonexistence) of facts in themselves. For Margolis, it is only historically, or after the fact, that humans appreciate the paradigm-contingent nature of (previous) ways of seeing. He does allow for a modified definition of objectivity—anchored in shared methodological practice and consensual validation—but leaves us no hope for neutrality. Herzfeld foregrounds the uses to which claims to factual status are put and emphasizes an awareness of how facts are produced and legitimated. "Recalling the provisionality of all knowledge is the only responsible way of guaranteeing its integrity," he argues.

CHANNELING FACTS

Herzfeld's focus on the who and how of constructing fact leads directly to the second group of articles. Maps, statistical data, holidays are all constructions of various sorts and harbor expressions of power and of interest no less than official pronouncements at a press conference. Thus sociologist Richard Ericson shows how journalists use authorities to establish fact and are very careful before challenging the credibility of a valued source. In effect, authoritative sources exert control over news about themselves. Ericson further illustrates the Durkheimian proposition that by exposing deviance, journalists are constructing the normal. Journalists are also attracted to controversy, Ericson reminds us, and thus, ironically, the resolution of controversy is less likely to be recorded as fact. Indeed, facts that do not fit predominant news frames tend to go unused. More generally—and echoing the first set of articles—fact-as-reported is a product of the communication practices of journalists.

Staging fact, as in the live broadcast of the Nixon funeral, is a further iteration of framing. This is the subject of the article by Barry Schwartz and Lori Holyfield, who show how state rituals promote identification with the collective by mobilizing uniform public action, a process they characterize as "the revenge of emotion on fact." Going beyond Durkheimian analysis, Schwartz and Holyfield argue that state funerals not only integrate the members of a tribe; they also seek to advocate or, in Nixon's case, to bolster the reputation of the deceased by foregrounding merit relative to fault.

Political scientist John Zaller approaches the social construction of political news from the point of view of the "individually rational" choices of the public, politicians, and journalists. Although rational voters do not waste much time on politics, they are attracted by controversy and contest and they do want opposing sides to be heard. Politicians try to manage the news. Journalists—professionally and economically motivated to make their own voices heard—counter attempts at control with critical "negativity." Here Zaller puts to empirical test one of several propositions derived from a theory of news content as the product of interacting self-interests: those of journalists, politicians, and the reading, viewing, voting public.

The rhetoric of politicians also occupies political psychologist Kathleen McGraw and political scientists Kuklinski, Quirk, Schwieder, and Rich. McGraw is interested in the moral claims that politicians use to ingratiate themselves with voters (for example, "I did it for the good of the country"). Under the rules of the game, McGraw asserts, such claims are rarely subject to challenge, making it easy to pass off false assertions as true. Even when motivation to challenge these claims is present, it is difficult to assess the inner states upon which they rest, all the more so in the media, which restricts access to cues that accompany lying.

Kuklinski and his colleagues are also concerned with falsehood, specifically with the misinformation and inaccurate factual beliefs that often accompany social issues. Focusing on welfare policy, they show that inaccurate beliefs (about the amount spent on welfare, for example) are systematically related to policy judgments. They discuss how judgments might be altered by different framings of the same facts (for example, welfare costs "$10 billion" versus "1 percent of the federal budget") and ponder methods for improving the validity, relevance, and usefulness of policy-related information.

Geoffrey Cowan, dean of the University of Southern California's Annenberg School, moves the rhetorical discussion to the level of genre. He reviews the genres in which the media package fact, and he argues that the several genres imply different kinds of contract with audiences concerning expectations about the truth status of propositions. Genres and truth claims need to be properly labeled, says Cowan. Docudramas, for example, represent a particularly thorny problem. And even direct quotes may be used to misinform, as in the alleged neutralizing of Anne Frank's Jewishness and sanitizing of the Nazis in successive versions of the play—presumably for the sake of achieving best-sellership.

The consequences of labeling—as fact or fiction—occupy social psychologist Sheila Murphy. She shows how the presentation of cultural stereotypes and counterstereotypes (about women, for example) in news and in fiction may prime readers' judgments about unrelated public events. She finds interactions between the genre of the text, the gender of the reader, and the stereotypicality of the account. Fictional accounts, for example, may be drawn upon when they support a reader's reference group (for example, males) but ignored as merely fiction when they undermine it.

Marcia Johnson, a cognitive psychologist, analogizes from her work on the mechanisms that individuals employ to distinguish fact and fantasy in their own memories to the means societies use (such as courts, the press) to minimize the passing off of falsehood as fact. She likens the progressive incursion of tabloid journalism, for example, to worsening damage to the frontal lobe, which, in individuals, results in confabulation and delusion. Like individuals, she argues, not only may societies experience such breakdowns; they may also fail to recognize them ("cultural anosognosia"), or they may recognize them yet carry on with blithe indifference.

Finally, communications scholar James Katz turns our attention to the ways in which digital communication is altering the flow of fact. From this vantage point, Katz suggests that the Internet is leveling traditional structures of authority. Anybody can chime in and ask to be believed. Moreover, the threat of cacophony is superseding the hierarchical gatekeeping of yesteryear, Katz thinks, and it is not as yet clear whether public discourse will benefit in the trade-off.

MANAGING FACTUALITY

Three current themes in academic and public discourse underlie this collection of articles. None is altogether new—in fact, some are of considerable age, as our authors point out; it is their convergence that is of particular interest. The first theme is the postmodern turn to constructivism—personified by the umpire who asserts (brazenly? reflexively?) that "they ain't nothing until I call them." The second theme is the allegation that broadcast and print journalism have sold out to infotainment, where fact and fiction are increasingly and maliciously blurred. The third theme is the increasing withdrawal of the public from public affairs, expressed also in mounting discontent with press performance (reporting is described as sensational, biased, or inaccurate) along with precipitous drops in levels of confidence in the press and other institutions.

Our authors take strong positions on these issues, while standing on the shoulders of large bodies of work (including their own). Most of them draw conclusions and offer sensitivity training aimed at both producers and consumers of fact, as well as at those of us who observe them. Beyond the value of the individual articles, however, there is added value in their juxtaposition. While none of them explicitly engages the coincidence that the public is protesting the blurring of fact and fiction just when the philosophers seem to be saying that the distinction is difficult to defend, these themes are implicitly related, and juxtaposition makes this clear.

Thus the articles—especially the first group—struggle with the boundaries of fact and fiction from the point of view of constructivism. The problem begins—although this is not the main thrust—with how to go about establishing fact. Fact-finding is difficult because we do not have direct access to reality—certainly not social reality—and because we are not neutral observers and because the degree of our objectivity is a function of our (always inadequate) methodologies. But even when the facts are agreed on, they do not amount to much in themselves. We hardly notice them, says Bruner, except in the contexts of our need for them: to navigate the world, to tell a story, to spin a theory, to persuade, to adjudicate.

The same facts, however, may serve different—even opposing—stories, and stories cannot be judged for their truthfulness, says Novick. They may be honest, they deserve to be, but they are simply best efforts to put the facts together. They are complex constructions in which facts have been made to work in fictionlike ways. This is the crux of the problem from the points of view of Bruner, Novick, and Herzfeld, even though each concurs that some form of distinction between fact and fiction must be preserved. The mere labeling of fact or fiction, says Murphy, has real-world consequences, and Cowan, likewise, insists on upholding the contractual obligations to readers implicit in the different genres. Lichtenberg repeatedly reminds the others that not only do stories constrain facts but facts constrain stories, and thus stories can be more or less accurate (not just more or less coherent, aesthetically speaking) and stories can be improved, objectively. Johnson concurs, arguing that, in cases such as allegations of sexual abuse, facts are often the crux of the matter. Margolis and Herzfeld advise that a story (or a fact) is more likely to "improve" if the history of its construction is known.

That facts do not speak for themselves is evident not only from the fact that language is required to speak them—even the umpire who calls them "like they are" has to call them—but from the fact that facts have spokespersons. These are, first of all, our professional reporters themselves—journalists, historians, jurists, scientists. But all of these, in turn, have further sources from whom many of their facts originate. In addition, each has technologies by means of which facts are communicated. Even with the best of professional motives and methodological skills, there is a lot of construction going on here, to say the least, and a lot of room for bias—and deception. Our articles—mostly those in the second group—stand also at this intersection.

Michael Schudson (1978) sets the stage for this aspect of our discussion by asserting that the problem of objectivity is not just epistemological but also historical, referring to the rise of public relations practices in the 1920s and the critical culture of the 1960s. "If events are themselves constructed, and constructed by the individuals and institutions with the greatest wealth and power in society, then reporting the news is not just an incomplete approach to the truth but a distorted one" (176).

Establishmentarianism preoccupies a number of our authors. Source bias is a major focus of Ericson's critique of journalism, while Zaller argues that journalists sometimes take revenge on their sources when the latter over-manage the news. The dynamics of self-presentation by the political establishment is analyzed by McGraw as well as by Schwartz and Holyfield in their work on the functions of televised rituals. Johnson considers how the social institutions of truth telling—the courts and newspapers—might do a better job of sorting fact from fiction, truth from untruth, while Kuklinski and his colleagues suggest that the public play a greater role in deciding which facts are relevant to public concerns. Zaller feels that the public is too "rational" to want very much information at all and that it will attend to fact only under special circumstances, mostly when there is a contest.

Genre is another source of bias. Journalists prefer contest and competition to other forms of news partly because the public does, says Ericson. Cowan insists that genre rules need to be better observed— because of the varied promises different genres make—while Murphy suggests that readers' attention to the "this is only fiction" label depends on how well the story fits their needs.

Finally, there is bias in the very technology itself, as McLuhan proclaimed. Television often conceals more than it reveals, says McGraw; the Internet undermines authority, says Katz.

THE UMPIRES STRIKE BACK

The Fourth of July has since passed, and World Cup soccer is putting an end to this preface as Brazil takes on France in the final match. But even now, while the world is watching the players, we find ourselves watching the referees. Like Bruner's umpires, they are there to pronounce on facts. They were put there because contests—one of the primordial genres of play, and the most democratic of them—provide for the role of arbiter. Everyone involved assumes that referees know the rules, are impartial in their judgments, do not take bribes, and strive for objectivity even in the face of pressure from players, managers, fans, and television commentators. When they are challenged, we assume that they have consistent, consensually validated means of defending their calls. Compared to fellow truth tellers, the task of umpires and referees is relatively straightforward. After all, we expect them only to make the calls, not to tell a story. Nevertheless, our expectations—in this genre and others—will sometimes go unmet. If these expectations are repeatedly defied, we may revise them and consider installing a new and improved system of truth telling. For even if we strongly disagree on this call or that, we tend to accept the arbiter's role. Will this role withstand the assaults of new media and postmodern doubt? If the contributions to this volume are an indication, the answer is yes, even though there is a lot to worry about—and improve. For the fact is that we want to believe our truth tellers, if not this time, then the next.

By the way, did France really win?

WORDS OF THANKS

It remains for us to thank the Scholars who designed the conference and, under the sage administration of Barbara Grabias, guided it session by session. We also thank the Annenberg School for Communication of the University of Pennsylvania for the infrastructure and support. Most of all, we thank all those who prepared and presented papers at the conference and, in many cases, went through another round of writing, editing, and rewriting for this volume.

ELIHU KATZ
Jerusalem

JEFFREY J. STRANGE
Philadelphia

Notes

1. The 1995-97 Scholars and their work represented the fields of anthropology, communications, philosophy, political science, psychology, and sociology. For example, anthropologist Ravina Aggarwal explored the construction of ethnographic truth in the context of a case study of a market woman in the Ladakh Himalayas. Other scholars and examples of their theme-related work include David Buckingham, *The Making of Citizens: Young People, Television News and the Limits of Politics* (London: University College London, forthcoming); Gene Burns, *The Moral Veto: Stalemate and Change in American Debates over Contraception and Abortion* (New York: Cambridge University Press, forthcoming); Michael Griffin, Photojournalism and Photographic Icons: From Documentation to Mythologizing War, in *Pictures in the Public Sphere: Studies in Photography, History, and the Press*, ed. Bonnie Brennan and Hanno Hardt (Champaign: University of Illinois Press, forthcoming); Ronald Jacobs, *Race, Media and the Crisis of Civil Society: From Watts to Rodney King* (New York: Cambridge University Press, forthcoming); Hannah Kliger, Communication and Ethnic Identity in Jewish Immigrant Communities: A Sociohistorical Moment, in *The Huddled Masses: Communication and Immigration*, ed. (Cresskill, NJ: Hampton Press, 1997); Tali Mendelberg, Executing Hortons: Racial Crime in the 1988 Presidential Campaign, *Public Opinion Quarterly* 61 (1997); Itzhak Roeh, On the Narration of Facts and Solidarity, *Dvarim Ahadim* 2 (1997); Crispin Sartwell, *Act like You Know: African-American Autobiography and White Identity* (Chicago: University of Chicago Press, 1998); Dona Schwartz, Pictorial Journalism: Photographs as Facts, in *Pictures in the Public Sphere: Studies in Photography, History and the Press*, ed. Brennan and Hardt; Jeffrey Strange with Cynthia Leung, How Anecdotal Accounts in News and in Fiction Can Influence Judgments of a Social Problem's Urgency, Causes, and Cures, *Personality and Social Psychology Bulletin* (in press).

2. We would like to thank the contributors of three papers whose work is not represented in this volume. Media educator and producer Steven Goodman presented research on how New York City teenagers produce and interpret the stories of elites and members of their own

communities in Critical Thinking Through Cultural Practice: The Inquiry Process of Youth-Pro-
duced Social Documentaries. Family therapist Judith Davis delivered a paper on a constructivist
approach to therapy, Rereading Family Facts in Therapy: Evoking a More Hopeful Story.
Communication scholar Justin Lewis argued that television news could benefit from a stronger
emphasis on narrative structure in Reading and Forgetting Fact: How the Absence of Narrative
Determines the Impact of Television News.

Reference

Schudson, Michael. 1978. *Discovering the News: A Social History of American News-
    papers*. New York: Basic Books.

ANNALS, *AAPSS*, **560**, November 1998

What Is a Narrative Fact?

By JEROME BRUNER

ABSTRACT: This article explores the manner in which culturally prevalent narratives lead us not only to interpret facts in a particular way but also to generate those very facts through the acts we perform in consonance with these narratives.

Jerome Bruner is a research professor of psychology and senior research fellow in law at New York University. He has served as professor of psychology at Harvard (1945-71) and Watts Professor at Oxford (1972-81). He has researched and written extensively on the nature and development of thought and language. Along with a handful of kindred rebels against "behaviorist" psychology, he helped spark the cognitive revolution in the 1960s. His most recent book is The Culture of Education *(1996).*

NOTE: This article was presented as a keynote address to "The Future of Fact," a conference held at the Annenberg School for Communication, University of Pennsylvania, 26 February 1997.

F OR my journalist friends, forever wondering where facts end and stories begin, I would like to address the subject of facts, particularly narrative facts. I do so as a student both of narrative texts, what textually constitutes a story, and of the narrative mode of thinking, how we translate our experience of what happened into story form.

But before I start, I should mention my odd professional biases. To begin with, I do not believe that facts ever quite stare anybody in the face. From a psychologist's point of view, that is not how facts behave, as we well know from our studies of perception, memory, and thinking. Our factual worlds are more like cabinetry carefully carpentered than like a virgin forest inadvertently stumbled upon. On the other hand and wearing another hat, I am also a professor in a law school where, under the burden of tradition, we draw a razor-sharp procedural distinction between evidentiary matters of fact and doctrinal points of law, the two officially declared to be utterly independent of each other. Matters of fact are decided upon by juries; points of law, by judges. Even so, lawyers (and judges) know full well that, magisterial rules to the contrary, the two cannot be kept neatly separated—metaphysically and also practically. This often creates problems.

Take, for example, what can count as a fact in torts litigation when the issue is whether somebody is guilty, say, of maintaining "an attractive nuisance" on their property. What facts are probative in deciding whether, say, an unfenced swimming pool behind the house constituted an "irresistible temptation" (or attractive nuisance) to a stranger who fell or jumped into the pool and factually drowned, found by the resident owners at 7:15 a.m. on a specified date? These are facts, all right. Are the homeowners liable? That is a legal fact. Almost certainly they will be found so if the pool in question was factually unfenced, unlocked, and in a thickly settled neighborhood. But there will be a good deal of probative evidence examined in establishing the facts. Precedent will be cited, in an effort to establish whether the present facts of the case are like those covered in precedent cases. For factuality inevitably requires categorization. Do the facts of this case conform to the categories established in the precedents?

Just suppose the swimming pool were located behind a house two miles from the next nearest residence, and the victim of the accident were a "stranger of no fixed address." But now we appear to be dealing with stories rather than facts, as is so typical of the law. What about the facts, the bare facts?

There seem to be two things that make facts malleable or whatever their ephemeralness might be called. The first is that mere facts are not viable until they have been categorized. They are not even facts. Is an unfenced pool way out in the boondocks factually or categorically an attractive nuisance? The second thing is relevance: live facts do not become probative, even once categorized, until they can be shown to be relevant to some sort of theory or story dealing with something more general. Neither law nor life has much room for irrelevant facts; they are immaterial. Besides, irrelevant facts have an exceedingly short half-life, if any at all—not just in the law but even in memory and perception. They scarcely make it to the Lost and Found.

Does all this add up to the charge that storytelling and theory construction bring the very ontology of raw facts into question? Perhaps not, but it certainly makes one wonder what might be meant by *eo ipse* facts, standing free and independent in a place deceptively known as the real world. But even so, in spite of such doubts, any sensible person knows that facts are, in some sense, just like hard rocks: they are there, even if they are also products of our efforts to make sense of the world. Indeed, they are there, like the very rock that Dr. Johnson asked Boswell to kick. That much is plain enough even if we believe that naked facts do not make sense until they are nested in our conception of how the world really is—nested in a theory or story that places them.

To thicken the argument, let us call all such conceptions about the real world fictions, whether scientific or narrative fictions. A fiction is something made up, the Latin root of the word is *fingo, fingere, finxi, fictum*, which means to shape, fashion, form, mold; also to arrange, to put in order; also to represent, imagine, conceive; and also, finally, to feign, fabricate, devise. A neutrino, then, is a fact in certain branches of high-energy physics, one inferred to make theoretical sense of a set of tracks in a cloud chamber in light of a theory about the composition of atoms. But what about facts in a narrative fiction? Nora's marital plight (married to a stiffly conventional husband) in Ibsen's *A Doll's House* seems like some sort of prototypical fact, or a set of conjoined facts that make a plight. Notice, though, that her plight is a fact not only in that remarkable play but also in daily life, where it serves us as a way of making sense of things we encounter. Who is the copycat, life or art? Remember Herman Melville's Captain Vere trying Billy Budd at the drumhead court where he condemns him to hang for striking Claggart dead? Was Melville trying to make sense of his father-in-law, Judge Lemuel Shaw, the ardent abolitionist who nonetheless condemned escaped slaves from the bench to be returned to their owners in the South, perhaps to die? By the Queen's law on mutiny, Billy must hang; Captain Vere says: "An angel must die." Was this Lemuel Shaw, administering the much hated Fugitive Slave Law of 1793? Perhaps when fictions become a culture's windows on the world, facts come to resemble what is expected of them. In classic Athens, when there were no plays by Sophocles, Aristophanes, or Euripides at the theater, citizens would often repair to the law courts for their drama.

MAKING FACTS

Let me begin our serious pursuits with some fanciful philosophy. Socrates, let us say, has been returned to earth to reestablish his famed academy. In preparation for opening day and to become better acquainted with the culture, he is holding a dialogue with three distinguished baseball umpires. "How do you call them from behind the plate?" he asks them. The first says, "I call them like they are." "And you?" he asks the second. "I call them like I see them." The third replies, after a pause: "They ain't nothing until I call them." The classic, the modern, and the postmodern fact in a nutshell! What each of our umpires tells Socrates is true, of course, however incommensurate their accounts may be. But we should know that, when contradicting truths are also true, as Niels Bohr once remarked, they must be Great Truths, for only the opposites of small truths are false. When one encounters such anomalies, Bohr warned, one is almost certainly caught in the dilemma of complementarity, irreconcilable ways of conceiving of the world—like specifying the velocity and the position of a particle at the same time. Let us explore some matters more mundane than particles or balls and strikes to see what we can learn about factuality.

Consider historical facts first. The French Annales school of historians distinguishes between *annales*, *chroniques*, and *histoires*. *Annales* are drawn up from what house-proud historians like to call archival sources—court records, property deeds, birth registers, tax rolls, old newspapers, and other hard-edged stuff. That is where facts are found. But when is a birth register turned to for facts? Say, when a person has a hypothesis that provinces bordering great through roads had more than their share of Black Death. He or she starts examining registers along the Via Emilgia and Via Appia and compares them with ones from towns on back roads. The resources of an *annale* are used after some questions are developed, for questions seem to make facts as well as being answered by them.

Plots and hypotheses lurk in those *chroniques* and *histoires*, prescribing what makes a fact a Fact or, at least, what makes it relevant to the matter at hand. They are guides not only for putting facts together but for determining what facts are worth their salt. *Histoires* simply cover longer periods than *chroniques*, a dynasty's rule rather than a king's, for example. Both provide the connective tissue in the story of factually what happened.

What is found in the archives may sometimes lead to a new interpretation, just as the implicit interpretation in a growing *chronique* may have led to that *annale* in the first place. That bumpy two-way street between interpretation and fact is, of course, the high road into the infamous hermeneutic circle: we justify our choice of bitty facts by appealing to how well they fit into the whole, while supporting our interpretation of the whole by celebrating how well it encompasses the parts. While not fatal, the hermeneutic circle should at least promote a certain modesty about the issue of factuality—relevant factuality.

But facts are facts, one might say (like the umpire who calls them like they are). I would reply, Stop confounding relevance and factuality. I wonder whether one can, so I want to try out a little case study that might help us judge. Here goes. The year is 1997, the 50th anniversary of India's independence. A small industry has already developed exploring what it was that led up to Independence. Let us join it. We will start with a well-documented precursor candidate event: the Indian Mutiny of 1857, when Indian Army sepoys rose against the British in a garrison town near Delhi, gained enough support to move on to Delhi itself, which it took over with the support of its local prince. As the mutiny progressed, it reached a flame point in the city of Cawnpore, where, to cut an ugly story short, several hundred British civilians, mostly women and children, were massacred. What was the Mutiny? Was it a precursor to Independence or not? We will need some facts to determine that. First of all, what precipitated the Mutiny?

Was it the introduction of the Minié cartridge, alleged locally to be lightly coated in a tallow of both cow and pig fat, contact with which corrupted or led to caste loss for Muslim and Hindu, respectively? Bullets literally had to be bitten in those days before being inserted in a rifle's magazine. That is one set of facts, right? Now some more. Was this gaffe just a dumb engineering mistake, or was it a contemptuous gesture of British underlings in the raj? If the former, a mindless mistake, how had things gotten so out of control to have let such a serious mistake happen? Wait, we are drifting off. Let us get back to the facts that might help us determine whether the Mutiny was an early precursor to national liberation.

Some say that the Mutiny was really one of those cruel and naked "racial wars," as evidenced not only by the introduction of caste-demeaning tallow but also by the British forcing Indian prisoners suspected of fomenting the mutiny to eat pork fat before hanging them or blowing them out of the barrel of a howitzer. But there are some other facts, too, which paint another picture, leading one to suspect the Mutiny was a nasty dustup precipitated by the rebellious and intransigent local prince, Nana Sahib, who had had enough humiliation at the hands of the raj to last him all his life, including nonrecognition of the inheritance of his adoptive father's kingdom. Maybe even more realpolitik than that is Lord Dalhousie's introduction of a policy of annexing to the crown any native state whose prince died without natural heir, as with Nana Sahib's father. The princely class had become alarmed enough about this to be interested in a real mutiny, though not so much in the interest of national unity as to protect its princely holdings. For another line of factuality, one can dig up signs of corporate decay: after a century of rule, the East India Company's seniority promotion policy had saddled India with a predictably incompetent collection of Colonel Blimps (Taylor 1995; for a more local account of what happened during the Mutiny, see Ward 1996). I can recommend quite a few more *annales* tracks to explore, but I will stop here.

Start down any one of them and a precursor line from the Mutiny to Independence will begin to take shape—none of them very convincing. What is more interesting, however, is that each effort to find a precursor line will create facts at an alarming rate. So the poor commission established in New Delhi to tell the story of what led to Independence now has more putative facts than they know how to cope with. The irony, of course, is that, likely as not, the official story will have as much to do with how cordial an entente India wants to maintain with Britain as with anything that happened during the Mutiny!

Let us look more technically now at the power of narrative both to govern the selection of relevant facts and to give shape to such facts as are selected. A good place to start is with the great Russian folklorist, Vladimir Propp (1968), although one may well ask what a folklorist, even the greatest in the history of his subject, has to say about fact and factuality. I will come to that in time. Propp's crowning achievement was to show that the underlying form of a folktale, not its surface variations, is what imposes meaning and structure on its parts. That will be clear in a moment. He saw his job as providing a morphology of folktales: how to characterize their underlying structure and how a story's parts are dominated by the whole. One of his first triumphs was to show how to represent these deep narrative structures or forms, and then to show that, once this was accomplished, a wide variety of seemingly different tales could be fit into them, no matter where they came from or in what language. The content could differ, but the form would remain the same. In a way, this was obvious: like proving that a hard-luck story is the same hard-luck story no matter what the flavor of the trouble. His second triumph (related to the first) was to show that varying contents of any particular version of a morphologically basic tale bear what linguists call a type-token relation to the basic tale. I must pause to explain this.

For Propp, a folktale's parts are not just independent facts or events, but functions of its overall structure: they are parts of a story in virtue of playing a specifiable role in the story as a whole. Never mind that these functional constituents comprise such obvious things as protagonists, kinds of situations, kinds of obstacles to achievement, and the like. Their meaning is the role they play in the story. Take, for example, the so-called wonder tale that Propp himself studied—thousands of versions of it, all collected in the famous Helsinki archive. The wonder tale begins with a privileged but still dependent figure being left on his own. He sets out on a quest of some sort and, early on in the quest, meets a mysteriously endowed helper or donor who offers him some sort of magic help in carrying out his quest. The young hero soon encounters his first obstacle, and so on and so forth. That will do to help me explain some of the things that Propp has in mind, like the type-token relationship.

Now each of those constituents in the story has a function in the story as a whole—as, for example, in the quest story. The story requires somebody in want, then some mission, then some obstacles, then some attempted solutions, some resolutions, and so on. These functions must have sufficient generality, must be general types, to accommodate a family or genre of isomorphic tales. A type is like a category; the instances that fit into it are called tokens. The privileged but still dependent figure left on his own may, for example, be a young prince left alone in the family castle; or it may be a young mathematical genius whose mentor has gone off on indefinite holiday; or it may even be poor deserted Nana Sahib, whose adoptive right to the throne has been annulled by Lord Dalhousie (with the complicity of the old peshwa who got an £80,000 annual pension in return). All of these can serve as tokens of the general type of the deserted young man of privilege driven off to a quest.

The fit of facts

Now take the next step. Consider the young man's quest. It will be somewhat (but not entirely) determined by what sort of hero we started with in the first slot. A deserted royal prince might go in search of a maiden who might one day be a fit queen of the realm, but the young mathematical genius might better be searching for a solution to the twin primes conjecture or the three-color mapping problem. Nana Sahib's quest is already given.

Now to the magic gift of the helper or donor. What shall it be—a tireless horse, an endless golden thread, a Cray computer with infinite memory, what? What fits the evolving tale will depend on what has gone before, which means, in reverse, that the further one gets into a narrative, the fewer the options left open. For example, our deserted mathematical genius might perhaps do better with a Cray computer than an endless golden thread. Poor Nana Sahib, by the way, failed to find a magic donor,

though he did send his agent to London looking for someone in the India Office or the Royal Household who might help out. Perhaps his donor, inadvertently, was the mindless Minié who designed the ill-fated rifle requiring the tainted cartridges!

Note that Propp's morphology requires an "arrow of time," a rather fixed sequence unrolling over time. If the sequence is broken, the tale is destroyed—though functions can be deleted with impunity. There need not be an actual donor of the gift, for example, so long as the gift comes to the hero's hand at the prescribed point in the story. Propp's exploration of the Helsinki archive variorum texts revealed, by the way, that some deletion is almost always the rule. A student of mine, Walter Zaharodny, even found that people forget folktales they have heard by leaving out, deleting, but hardly ever by mixing up the order of things.

My purpose here is not to discuss folktales for their own sake. In fact, Vladimir Propp has a very great deal to teach us about facts. But he is not concerned with the verifiability or truth about facts but with their factlikeness, truthlikeness, or verisimilitude. What makes something seem like a fact when one encounters it? That is no trivial question. Verisimilitude does for narrative what verification and verifiability do for science and logic. Something's verisimilitude is the mark of whether the illusion of reality is working. Now, few topics in the history of philosophy have been flogged into more abject correctness than verification and verifiability, and some philosophers, like Richard Rorty (1979), have even urged a moratorium on it. I will spare you the details of the verifiability conditions for establishing the meaning of "an endless golden thread." But there has been precious little written on what makes anything truthlike.[1] Perhaps it defies our analytic, formal efforts at elucidation because verisimilitude is so utterly local and so context dependent, not the elegant stuff of syllogisms, universals, and rules of inference. Yet, when we say of Ibsen's *A Doll's House*, "That's absolutely true to life, Nora walking out on that bastard," it does seem to imply something universal, and so we celebrate the playwright for understanding the human plight.

Which brings us back to Vladimir Propp, for there is something astonishingly systematic about the way in which a lifelike story unfolds its realness. It "fits the pieces together" in the very way we expect truth to do. I want to borrow a term that Derdre Gentner and A. Markman (1997) use in describing how analogy fits a target to its vehicle: they call it the "aligning of systematicity." In what way does Nora's plight match the ideally constructed plight of a sensitive woman with an ambitious, unfeeling husband? The local condition of Nora needs to fit an inherent general condition that we take to be canonical in the world. "Canonical" is a difficult idea. It bespeaks some legitimate expectancy. We seem to learn as much about such legitimate expectancies from the play of narrative imagination as we do from life itself, like the magic donor giving the Cray computer to the abandoned young mathematical genius. Computers with unlimited memory are impossible, but they are a fitting fact for our story.

In a word, facts seem to shape themselves, even at times to be derived from a body of canonical lore (I called them "fictions" earlier) that human beings entertain about how reality really is. What is even more striking is that the very same shaping of facts by a common canonical lore seems to be shared by large masses of people, as in a particular culture but even for humankind in general. If, for example, something of social import happens to us, our first and almost irresistible impulse is to believe that it must have resulted from an act performed by some human agent or agents with some purpose in mind. This conviction or presumption seems to have the power to guide our attention and to shape our experience. It cuts the world up into categories appropriate to it. We look for and often find particulars that fit the requirements of such presumptions to a T. Often we are right; often we are not. Survival depends on being more the former than the latter, and in the main, as we will see in a moment, the presumptions that we acquire or that we are heir to serve us fairly well. Note in passing that these "shaping presumptions," if I may call them that, have a great deal in common with the narrative folklore patterns that Vladimir Propp brought to our attention. Again, as with Propp, they are types that can be instantiated by lots of different tokens—that is to say, they reproduce well locally. Navajos, for example, who entertain strong beliefs about witchcraft, are readier to see injurious acts as being initiated by witch agents with malevolent purposes, and they have developed highly sophisticated procedures for confirming their beliefs (Kluckhohn 1962). Contemporary Americans prefer bureaucrats to witches and are equally adept in confirming their view of the world.

All of this suggests that we as human beings share certain susceptibilities for seeing the world of reality in certain ways—sometimes locally shared in a culture, sometimes virtually universal. There is now a fierce debate in progress among anthropologists, biologists, psychologists, and, of course, philosophers about what to make of all this. Though the debate is too rowdy to sum up, all sides seem to agree on certain things. The first is negative. Nobody believes any longer that "the mind [is] a universal learning device, equally welcoming to any kind of cultural content" (Sperber 1996, 14). The cognitive revolution surely blew that odd notion out of the water; we cannot use our heads just any old which way. Plainly, there are certain ways of perceiving, attending, thinking that come more naturally and easily to human beings than do others. It is also now widely believed that these easy and natural ways reflect something deep in the human being's unique, species-specific cultural adaptation to the world. For example, we are the only species that operates on the belief that others have human minds equipped with intentions, beliefs, expectations (Tomasello, Kruger, and Ratner 1993). How human culture evolved to get that way, what its evolutionary history might

be—these are matters that are still subject to often bitter debate, though the debate gets less bitter as new findings take us beyond the neo–social Darwinism that early flat-out sociobiologists seem to have been peddling.

We can settle for the while for two fairly self-evident claims, both of them neutral where the raging evolutionary issue is concerned. The first is that while representations of the world—what can be taken presumptively as factual—may vary systematically from culture to culture, they do not vary like crazy: the variations themselves seem to reflect certain natural ways of using mind. As Dan Sperber (1996) notes, even so presumably fancy-free a domain as how we represent the supernatural shows amazing commonalities across cultures—perhaps more variability than classifications of, say, the animal kingdom but not astonishingly more so. The second claim is that particular cultural systems for representing reality, if they come easily and naturally, facilitate communication and joint activity within a culture and, in virtue of doing so, become memorable and passed on from generation to generation—in some form or other. That is enough on the evolutionary side!

I would want to add only one point to the immediately preceding thoughts. It relates to what I called internal fit or systematicity—the way the constituents of a realized version of some folktale hang together to make it seem realer than life or truer than true. What is it that grips us about the appropriateness of Iseult lowering her flowing locks from her window so that Tristan can climb up to her? It is not the same as recognizing the intuitive power of Kepler's pre-Newtonian insights into planetary motion—perhaps equally beautiful but compelled by logical necessity. It is not logic but narrative cohesion that makes Iseult's intimate act of bringing Tristan to her arms so compellingly right—and so beautiful. The factuality of that gesture cannot be isolated from the narrative out of which it arises.

Now my final point, and of course it relates to journalists, perhaps to all intellectuals. If what I have been discussing is so, it would be absurd to think of journalism as just an art of fact gathering. If facts are sought after and shaped by the narrative contexts in which they have their life, then the good journalist in the grip of his or her function must be a master of narrative. It is his or her function not simply to cherish the facts that do not yet make sense in anybody's story but also to generate candidate narratives that both handle those aberrant facts and generate new ones. André Gide once said that the novelist's function is to disturb, and that is surely the sometime duty of the journalist. On the other side, the journalist should be a master at recognizing the same old story in new dress, like Propp himself. So I find myself in the rather anomalous, rather old-fashioned position of urging more systematic literary studies for the journalist—though I certainly do not want to talk down politics, economics, and sociology. We have a comparable situation in the law, and in closing I want to offer a legal example where naked fact without its contex-

tualizing story leaves one dizzied. There is a Supreme Court holding of only a few years ago, in *Freeman* v. *Pitts* (118 L. Ed.2d 108 [1992]). It is a ruling on the status of a lower court's earlier desegregation order to the Board of Education of DeKalb County, Georgia. That desegregation order had failed, in its several years of enforcement, to remedy racial imbalance in the county's schools and had, incidentally, led to so-called white flight from the northern part of the county. The majority of the Supreme Court ruled that the lower court's desegregation order should now be terminated on the ground that it was a "demographic change" that had now occurred in DeKalb County, despite the board's best effort, and the Court had no power to remedy "demographic changes." To consider what happened in DeKalb County as a naked demographic fact would be to ignore where facts live. They live in context; what holds most human contexts together is a narrative.

Note

1. The brief entry on verisimilitude in Simon Blackburn's *Oxford Dictionary of Philosophy* (1994) is given over to the verisimilitude of theories and relates to "a theory T . . . [that] implies more truths and fewer falsities than some other theory" (393). In fact, if we take verisimilitude to be the same as believability, its study more properly belongs either in literature (for example, Riffaterre, 1990) or in rhetoric than in philosophy proper.

References

Blackburn, Simon. 1994. *Oxford Dictionary of Philosophy*. Oxford: Oxford University Press.

Gentner, Derdre and A. Markman. 1997. Structure Mapping in Analogy and Similarity. *American Psychologist* 52(1):45-56.

Kluckhohn, Clyde. 1962. *Navaho Witchcraft*. Boston: Beacon Press.

Propp, Vladimir. 1968. *Morphology of the Folktale*. 2d ed. Austin: University of Texas Press.

Riffaterre, Michael. 1990. *Fictional Truth*. Baltimore, MD: Johns Hopkins University Press.

Rorty, Richard. 1979. *Philosophy and the Mirror of Nature*. Princeton, NJ: Princeton University Press.

Sperber, Dan. 1996. Learning to Pay Attention. *Times Literary Supplement*, 27 Dec., 14-15.

Taylor, P.J.O., ed. 1995. *A Companion to the "Indian Mutiny" of 1857*. Oxford: Oxford University Press.

Tomasello, M., A. Kruger, and H. Ratner. 1993. Cultural Learning. *Behavioral & Brain Sciences* 16(3):495-552.

Ward, Andrew. 1996. *Our Bones Are Scattered: The Cawnpore Massacres and the Indian Mutiny of 1857*. London: John Murray.

(The Death of) the
Ethics of Historical Practice
(and Why I Am Not in Mourning)

By PETER NOVICK

ABSTRACT: The ethics of professional historical practice in the United States, as traditionally understood, rested on a consensus about the purpose of historical scholarship, central to which were assumptions about the nature of historical facts, the relationship between facts and truth, and the social functions that factual and truthful historical accounts would perform. Over the past generation, these assumptions have come to be widely questioned, which has entailed the collapse of the consensus that sustained the traditional ethics of historical practice. The author suggests that rather than being deplorable, this represents a welcome development, making possible a more realistic understanding of the nature of historical scholarship.

Peter Novick is professor of history at the University of Chicago. He is the author of The Resistance vs. Vichy: The Purge of Collaborators in Liberated France *and* That Noble Dream: The "Objectivity Question" and the American Historical Profession. *He is currently completing a book on the social and ideological uses of the Holocaust in American society.*

NOTE: I should say something to explain the rather convoluted title. A couple of years ago I was invited to attend a small conference in Uppsala sponsored by the Commission on Historiography of the International Congress of Historical Sciences. I was asked to speak on "the ethics of historical practice," and it was announced that I would do so. When the evil day came when I had to actually write the paper, I concluded that like God, the author, and other good stuff, the ethics of historical practice were dead—a proposition I explicate in what follows.

TO get them out of the way, let me begin with a few matters of definition. In considering here the ethics of historical practice, I am, as is customary in a professional context, using the word "ethics" to describe consensual ethical codes, albeit informal and unwritten: lists of "thou shalts" and "thou shalt nots," violations of which, if known, result in at least professional opprobrium and which, in principle, are grounds for expulsion. These should not be confused with virtues, like high intelligence or a brilliant writing style, which can be thought desirable and can be honored but which can manifestly not be required and whose absence is not an ethical failing. I am taking "historical practice" to include not just scholarly writing, but everything that historians do as historians, whether it is teaching, hiring, refereeing, or participating in public affairs in their professional capacity. Finally, I will be restricting myself to American professional historians, the only ones whose practice I know much about.

My argument can be summarized as follows. Until the last few decades, there was a virtually taken-for-granted consensus about the goals and functions of historical practice, as consensual as physicians' commitment to health. On the basis of that consensus on goals and functions, an ethics of historical practice was equally consensual. This ethics was viable (that is, it seemed both plausible and coherent) for about 80 years: from the beginnings of organized professional historical activity in the United States in the 1880s down to the 1960s. However, as a result of developments within the last few decades, the professionwide consensus on goals and functions, along with other givens of American professional historical practice, has broken down. I take it to be obvious that a coherent consensus on professional ethics can exist only on the basis of consensus on professional goals and functions. (What would happen to medical ethics if promoting health ceased to be the consensual goal and function of physicians?) As a consequence of the collapse of historians' agreement on goals and functions, the traditional professional consensus on the ethics of historical practice has collapsed as well. I will suggest that there is nothing to bemoan about this outcome since it can be viewed as the long-overdue correction of misunderstandings about the nature and possibilities of the professional historical venture. Finally, I will consider some alternative responses to the demise of the traditional ethical consensus.

THE EARLY YEARS

American professional historians' original (and for the most part enduring) conception of the goals and functions of their venture can be roughly divided into their internal and external tasks. Internally, it was to discover and record the objective truth about the past, to cooperatively and cumulatively move ever closer to the perhaps ultimately unattainable but eminently approachable goal of a true and complete picture of the human past. The central ethical norms appropriate to this internal goal were two. First, assiduity in determining and scrupulosity in reporting the facts: their ideal was the man who would "cross an ocean to verify a comma." Second—and this was what would, they believed, most clearly distinguish their work from that of the amateur historians whom they hoped to supplant—freedom from bias, partisanship, "special pleading," preconceived notions, utilitarian purposes, or other interferences with neutrality and objectivity in presenting the facts and revealing their underlying pattern. Their reiterated programmatic declarations make clear that it was these two imperatives, particularly the second, which were at the center of their conception of the ethics of the professional historian. Their evaluative practice repeatedly operationalized it: the most common words of praise were "impartial," "detached," "disinterested," and, above all, "objective"; the most common words of censure were their antonyms. The ultimate accolade was to be acknowledged to have told (or, more modestly, to have closely approached) the truth about whatever episode or process in the past was being considered. The criterion for the relative evaluation of two competing accounts was which one more closely approximated the truth.

The existence of a consensual ethics of historical scholarship firmly grounded on working toward producing the one true story of the past did not mean a total absence of ethical dispute. One recurring disagreement had to do with norms of controversy and criticism. It was a dilemma built into the somewhat oxymoronic notion of academic professionalism, since an academic ethic that mandated ruthless mutual criticism collided with a professional ethic of collective solidarity and a strong sense that it was unethical to publicly criticize a professional colleague. In the early years of the historical profession, cultural norms of gentility and conflict avoidance usually resolved the dilemma by privileging comity. In a broader sense, the venture as a whole, including its core ethical values, was sustained by contemporary cultural norms that took it for granted that truth (as correspondence) was the goal of scholarship.

The ethical obligations of historians went beyond the discovery of truth. Equally important, in some ways more important, was its dissemination (the external function). Professional historians were, after all, employed not primarily to produce scholarship, which they did in their spare time, but to teach. Beyond that, they believed themselves ethically obliged to see to it that sound historical doctrines were promulgated in precollegiate education. In addition, though in the nature of things only a minority of historians with the requisite skills could do this directly, there was a strong sense of a corporate ethical obligation to see to it that sound (disinterested, impartial, objective) historical works, directed to a general audience, replaced the biased, tendentious, and propagandistic works of the amateurs in the literary marketplace. All of this was consistent with the perception by late-nineteenth-century American intellectuals that there was a general crisis of authority in society; that it was urgently necessary to replace (anarchic) mere opinion with (stable) objective knowledge.

At the risk of getting tangled in the analogy, the performance of this public function could be seen—was seen—as "ministering to the health of the body politic," an ethical obligation not totally unlike the corporate ethical obligation of the medical profession to minister to the population's physical health. Most historians of medicine now accept as a commonplace that "health," like "disease," is socially constructed and, in principle, a problematic concept. In practice, 99 percent of all physicians are 99 percent certain that in 99 percent of the cases they confront, they know perfectly well what "health" means. So it was for early professional historians (though I do not insist on the 99 percent). The ideological consensus within the profession in its early years was virtually total. In these circumstances, contemporaries would have been hard-pressed to make a distinction between spreading historical enlightenment (their understanding of what they were doing) and providing ideological legitimation (which is how we would describe it today).

There was one exception to the consensus among American historians, and their manner of dealing with it provides the exception that tests the rule. In the late nineteenth century (and well into the twentieth), there remained deep sectional differences over the great national crises of slavery, the Civil War and Reconstruction. Continuing divisiveness on this issue provided the newly professionalized historians with a magnificent opportunity to both demonstrate their commitment to disinterested historical truth and contribute to the great task of reconciliation. The impartiality to which the historians were dedicated was the opposite of particularism—"loyalty to the part." By producing and disseminating an impartial assessment of the issues, firmly grounded in the consensual scientific racism of the period, historians could bring the sections together. Northern historians became as critical of the abolitionists as they were of "irresponsible agitators" in the contemporary world. They considerably softened their picture of slavery, while their southern colleagues acknowledged that slavery as an institution, as well as secession, were, on balance, wrong. Both sides agreed that Reconstruction, or rather Reconstruction mythologized as rapine domination of the South by freed blacks, was, as one leading northern historian put it, "a punishment so far in excess of the crime that it extinguished every phase of culpability upon the part of those whom it was sought to convict and convert" (Burgess 1902, 297).

The external realm, like the internal, was not totally free of ethical conflicts. Though sectional differences between historians were being reconciled, this was not a process that took place overnight, and there were continued rumblings about fellow professionals who were confusing the public by continuing to propagate an insufficiently impartial account. Ideological consensus was, overall, so tight that the most moderately heterodox opinions were sometimes treated as invitations to anarchy and revolution. In what is a recurring phenomenon of professional ethics, there were occasional conflicts between internal and external ethical imperatives: in the case of historians, potential strain between the duty to the unvarnished truth and the duty to provide legitimation. Occasionally, historians were restive about restrictions imposed by university authorities or by the publishers of textbooks, but for the most part they were not overly bothered. As I have noted, a cultural climate that treated truth and objectivity as unproblematic sustained historians' internal ethos. Similarly, ideological homogeneity within the profession, and congruence between historians' vision of the past and the social order's requirement of an affirming and legitimating historical vision, kept the potential for tension between internal and external ethical obligations very much a hypothetical potential, not an experienced conflict.

THE MIDDLE YEARS

Having dealt very summarily with the first 30 years of the American historical profession (down to 1914), I will be even more summary in treating the following 50 years (down to the mid-1960s) because in what concerns us here—its conceptions of the goal and functions of historiography, and the attendant notions of historical ethics—there wasn't that much change. There was, of course, some.

So far as the (internal) ethics of scholarly inquiry were concerned, there was a decline in the primitive empiricist, no-preconceptions, "let the facts speak for themselves" approach; there was greater (though often nervous) tolerance for explicit

theoretical orientations when approaching the historical record. To this extent, there was a decline in the ethical demand for rigorous "self-elimination." But particularly among those of explicitly social scientific sensibility—and such individuals did not become a visible minority within the profession until well after World War II—these approaches were celebrated for their value neutrality, their efficacy in unearthing the objective truth. The ever widening scope of historical studies (this, too, was a late and slow development) did postpone to an ever more distant future the goal of a final, truthful picture of the entire historical past. But at the same time this very expansion, accompanied by a rhetoric of completeness, indirectly reinforced the old goal. There was a highly ambivalent, and very partial, acceptance of the notion that an historian's values might be a fruitful source of insight. But this acknowledgment was largely negated by a proto-Popperian disjunction of conjecture and refutation. A bright idea might come from anywhere; there could be no logic of hypothesis formation: this was Popper's realistic insight. But the ethical scientist (or historian) would immediately try to see if the facts refuted it: this was Popper's unrealism—what someone called the implausible, not to say perverse, notion of scientists' setting out to murder their children. It became somewhat more common (though still rare) for historians to acknowledge, in prefaces or introductions, their values, but this often took the form of a somewhat shamefaced confession, on the basis of which, as in correcting a compass for magnetic deviation, the reader could find a true north.

Briefly, in the 1930s, there was some discussion within the profession about whether the old "noble dream" of the disinterested search for the objective historical truth could be sustained, a discussion chiefly inspired by the writings of Carl Becker and Charles Beard. But for a variety of reasons—most crucially, anxiety about the way in which it would undercut professional morale and the profession's standing in society—the questioning was rapidly contained. After 1945 these doubts were widely attributed to the doubters' failure of nerve. The so-called "relativist" critique of traditional notions of the profession's goals and function was rejected through partial incorporation. Historians avowed that it was useful to be reminded how social circumstances had shaped historical scholarship in the past. They then proceeded to invoke Hume's riddle of induction: it was illegitimate to infer present social influence on historical interpretation from the demonstration that it was ubiquitous in the past. One prominent historian, recording the profession's rejection of the "relativist" critique, voiced the consensual view in asserting that historians' "awareness of the problem, plus their critical methods, make possible a practicable objectivity" (Gabriel 1961, 16). The cultural climate of the 1940s and 1950s was, if anything, even more insistent on disinterested and objective truth as the prime value of scholarship. Tendentious and ideological scholarship

was the hallmark of the totalitarian enemy; the search for disinterested truth was the distinguishing characteristic of the Free World. Correspondence to the truth about the past remained, as much as ever, the principal grounds in evaluating historical work; fidelity to pursuing and recording that truth remained the principal ethical commandment for historians.

In some ways, the middle years of the American historical profession saw a long-term decline in the relative importance of external ethical obligations. Historians had been massively mobilized for propagandistic work during World War I, and while only a few later expressed active repugnance at the excesses of their labors, it probably left a bad taste in many mouths. In any case, the profession never again avowedly organized itself for propaganda. For the most part, if historians paid less attention to their duties to the broader society, it was because the broader society wasn't much interested. Historians steadily lost whatever small influence they had once had on precollegiate education. With the single exception of Charles Beard, who became increasingly marginal to the profession after World War I, no professional historian ever became a major figure in the culture at large. Particularly after World War II, lower teaching loads and increased research opportunities produced a certain inward turn, with a greater valorization of "scholarship for its own sake," and a turning away from the public arena.

Down through the mid-1960s, there was hardly more ideological diversity (or conflict) within the profession than there had been before 1914. What diversity and conflict could be found, mostly in the interwar years, was largely generational: the reflection of a shift, paralleling changes in the intellectual culture at large, from the consensual moderate conservatism of an earlier epoch to the consensual moderate liberalism that replaced it. Certainly, the turnaround on matters having to do with issues connected to the role of blacks in American society was almost wholly generational: from a set of interpretations based on consensual scientific racism to interpretations grounded on consensual scientific antiracism. With the rarest of exceptions, no published works by American professional historians challenged the conventional wisdom of what Arthur Schlesinger, Jr., called the "vital center." This was not, for most American historians, complacent satisfaction at contemplating static perfection. There were still unresolved social problems, but none was structural or, indeed, all that serious. The "is" was seen as (with a little help) moving ever closer to the "ought." Their satisfaction was, in its way, just as complacent: one could derive pride from the past record of closing the gap between "is" and "ought"; confidence in the future prospect of closing it further. In any case, over this half-century so few delegitimating voices were raised that anything beyond perfunctory gestures toward legitimation was supererogatory.

Conflicts between the internal ethics of pursuing truth and the external ethics of ministering to the body politic were few and muted. Some overtly propagandistic works were mildly disapproved, but, when the writings in question were by senior scholars or, as was almost always the case, they were propagandizing on behalf of values and policies well within the mainstream, indulgence was the rule. When there were explicit calls for a fully and avowedly mobilized scholarship—reminiscent of World War I or uncomfortably close to Nazi or Soviet practice—there were some rumblings in the corridors. But such occasions were few, and the very minor upset they produced hardly ruffled the surface.

Without ignoring the various minor modifications and qualifications introduced over the years to the ethics of historical scholarship, and the ethics of the historian's participation in the public arena, these modifications and qualifications were *very* minor. As of the early 1960s, American historians' sense of their ethical obligation had hardly changed from what it had been in the 1880s. As scholars, it was to approach the objective historical truth; as citizens, insofar as was convenient and necessary (which wasn't much), to disseminate this basically reassuring and upbeat truth to the public in the interest of civic betterment—all of this in the confident conviction that there could be no substantial conflict between the two.

RECENT YEARS

Between the 1960s and the 1980s, far-reaching changes in several realms fundamentally altered the foundations on which American professional historical practice had been based. The first change was political. Gradually, in the course of the 1960s, and accelerating ever since, the broad and deep "vital center" consensus, which sustained historians' conviction of the (approximately) objective and (in the long run) convergent nature of their scholarly work, has been shattered. The political culture lurched sharply left, then right; consensus was replaced first by polarization, then by fragmentation; affirmation was replaced by negativity, confusion, apathy, and uncertainty. For the first time in history, a sizable portion of the American historical profession is hostile to the core values and assumptions of the culture at large; committed to the delegitimation rather than the legitimation of American institutions.

On the left, some see the academy as an arena in which the sort of politics impossible in the public realm can be played out—"the only game in town"; others see it as a secure and convenient home base from which one can launch attacks on the dominant ideology in the wider world, offering a "people's history." A demoralized Right (mostly older erstwhile liberals) is firmly convinced that the Left has taken over the profession and—to the accompaniment of very sympathetic coverage from the mainstream press—is courageously resigned to going down with flags flying. In a perversely symmetrical fashion, both Left and Right are deeply alienated from the existing historical profession: one group because it sees the profession as an irremediably hegemonic institution,

the other because it believes the traditional profession, and its values, has been thoroughly corrupted and undermined.

The point is not that these perceptions are correct, nor that these are, in the aggregate, the views of a majority. Neither is the case. But these are substantial and influential currents within the profession and, though this must be a guess, currents that are likely to be around for some time. Whatever the fortunes of that particular guess, it is all but impossible, barring some turnaround of unimaginable proportions, that the ideological consensus that was the unacknowledged foundation of so much that was central to American historical practice will ever be restored. In any case, what form would it take: what metanarrative would inform it? For globally, there is a crisis of ideological belief unprecedented in the modern age: the (at least temporary) "end of ideology"— though not in the puerile sense advanced in the 1950s by American Cold War ideologists and recently dusted off by Francis Fukuyama. Rather, it is that never since 1789 has such a small portion of the Western intelligentsia been deeply committed to *any* of the major competing worldviews, whether organic conservative, liberal individualist, or collectivist (in either their social democratic or Leninist variants). One can still, to be sure, find some enthusiastic true believers, but they are becoming an endangered species. What is to fill the void?

A related development (dialectically related, since it arose out of the collapse of the leftist activism of the 1960s) has been the rise of "identity politics"—ubiquitous in American culture at large, and nowhere more so than in the historical profession. There has been a dramatic decline in the centrality of a shared American identity and a concomitant rise in the centrality of "essential" particular identities, based on race, religion, ancestors' national origin or language, gender, or sexual orientation. Each (and here is the historian's role, almost always an historian who is a member of the particularity) is in search of its distinctive "roots," the saga of its (systematic) victimization and (occasional) triumphs, the evidence of its uniqueness and unassimilability. Being "essential," these identities generally command greater loyalty than the "contingent" fact of American citizenship, and certainly greater loyalty than that most contingent of all identities, professional historian. There was surely nothing neutral or objective about a framework that prioritized American national identity over that of particular identities—more neutral or objective than a framework that reversed the priorities. But whatever judgment is made about its heuristic or ideological merits, the former framework was integrative and stabilizing in its consequences, both for the larger society and for the historical profession that sought to explain that society, to itself and to the laity. Once again, I am not claiming that this sort of particularism is dominant within the American historical profession: only that it is widespread, apparently growing, increasingly institutionally

accepted and legitimated, and unlikely to go away.

The third and perhaps most significant development of recent decades did not, in origin, have much connection to the first two. It is, of course, the multifaceted cultural phenomenon variously designated as "constructivism," "antifoundationalism," "anti-essentialism," and "anti-objectivism"—most commonly, in the United States at least, lumped together under the (polemical) label "postmodern relativism." There was nothing markedly leftist or countercultural about the most influential American figures in the new thoughtways—Thomas Kuhn, Clifford Geertz, Richard Rorty; nor, for that matter, about its principal historiological representatives, like Hayden White or Dominick LaCapra. It probably *is* true that in a diffuse sense the legacy of the Vietnam war helped to lay the groundwork for the reception of these currents. Continual brazen mendacity by government spokesmen produced a concomitant increase in skepticism about "official truth," and, for some, about truth of any kind—not least the academic. Not all official lying was delegated to those with impeccable scholarly credentials like Professors Schlesinger, Bundy, Rostow, or Kissinger, but enough of it was to destroy the presumption that, in judging veracity, the pronouncements of highly regarded academics should be automatically accepted or even get the benefit of the doubt. A popular Bob Dylan song asserted that you didn't need a weatherman to tell which way the wind was blowing; Americans, very much including academics, did not need Michel Foucault to teach them about the nexus between Knowledge and Power.

In any case, the result has been a broad and deep crisis of what, for want of a better term, I'll call the governing academic sensibility. In one field after another, distinctions between fact and value and between theory and observation were called into question. Postures of disinterestedness and neutrality increasingly appeared outmoded and illusory. Nothing was more revolutionary for thinking about scholarship than Kuhn's suggestion that, in normal scientific practice, "dogmatism" and "open-mindedness" might have to be transvalued. It ceased to be axiomatic that the scholar's (or scientist's) task was to represent accurately what was "out there." Most crucially, and across the board, the notion of a determinate and unitary truth about the physical or social world, approachable if not ultimately reachable, came to be seen by a growing number of scholars as a chimera. With skepticism about that telos, the meaning of progress in scholarship became problematic.

American historians have never been much inclined to systematic reflection on the philosophical underpinnings of their practice, and while this may have changed slightly, it hasn't changed much. Very few have become articulate adepts of the new modes of thought, and almost certainly a majority has so far remained relatively untouched by the zeitgeist. But there is a widespread feeling, particularly among younger historians and including a great many quite respectable and influential figures, that older notions of the nature of historical scholarship are no longer viable.

More than anything else, these people have come to believe that the words "true" and "truthful" were meaningful only when applied to rather narrowly defined "brute-factual" statements, singular or statistical. The words were adjudged quite meaningless when applied to synthetic historical accounts, whose thoroughly constructed, narrativized, emplotted, and, above all, radically selective and perspectival character was increasingly emphasized. And if "true" and "truthful" were incoherent and fatuous as adjectives applied to individual historical works, this was a fortiori the case when it was a matter of making them the goal of historical scholarship in the aggregate. It seemed to follow from this that it made no sense to say of two accounts, assuming neither was filled with egregious misstatements of fact, that one was truer than the other. It also followed from the emphasis on construction and emplotment that while there were undoubtedly some distinctions to be made between history and fiction, the border was much fuzzier than as traditionally represented.

If these propositions, which came to command increasing assent, derived largely from strictly academic sources, other complementary beliefs within this significant minority were at least partially based on the breakdown of ideological consensus. All historical scholarship, save perhaps that small portion devoted to addressing straightforward factual matters (and even here, which ones were addressed and which avoided?), came to be seen as inherently, thoroughgoingly ideological: not a matter of degree but of an inherent dimension, like length or breadth. From this perception, it was just a step to seeing the distinction between history and propaganda as even less clear-cut than that between history and fiction: largely a matter of the unknowable and probably mixed motives of the author, of the author's intended audience, his or her taste for irony and paradox, of rhetorical style, and of the subtlety and sophistication of the propagandist. These two beliefs in turn implied another: that historical scholarship could reasonably be seen as fundamentally an arena of ideological contestation, with no reason to expect convergence, except on limited matters of fact or on the basis of ideological consensus, of short or long duration. And there is, of course, another implication of these views: that the authority of professional historians, individually or collectively, to command assent from the laity is at best extremely limited; probably nonexistent.

A third set of attitudes toward the historical venture within this minority has to do with what for want of a better term I'll call particularism. One proposition that commands very wide assent is that there is no academic reason for privileging the universal over the national, the national over the local or particularist; for favoring an integrative rather than a disintegrative historiography: such judgments are seen as fundamentally political. There is a widespread inclination—in general, endorsed by university administrations—to compensate for past underrepresentation of some groups by giving them preferment in the present; and, in the light of past pretensions of others to speak on their behalf, to give some kind of privilege in representing group experience to members of the group. (In this last realm, the nuances are hotly contested, even among those who agree in general.) Finally, as the United States has come to accept dual and overlapping loyalties and citizenships in the public realm, with their always latent potential for conflict (usually fudged over), in a similar fashion many have come to accept them in the case of the citizen-scholar. They don't see any good reason for giving automatic priority to the scholarly role (particularly if the fudge is kept handy).

FUTURE YEARS

It is not my argument that the attitudes just outlined (is it necessary to add that on the whole I share them?) are, or are likely to soon become, dominant in the American historical profession. I do not think that is the case. It is my (factual) assertion that they are widespread; it is my best guess that they are going to remain widespread—perhaps grow. There can be no doubt that separately, and even more in the aggregate, they challenge the most deeply held beliefs about the nature and ethics of historical practice held by what, I hope not too invidiously, I will call traditionalists.

For those deeply attached—I intend no mockery when I say "religiously" attached—to the traditional code, this is a crisis of disestablishment. As I have reiterated throughout my remarks, a professional code has to be consensual for it to be operative. When more than a handful of dissidents (who can be ignored, marginalized, expelled, or, if one's tastes run in that direction, burned at the stake) repudiate a hitherto consensual and established code, it is disestablished. The old code has the status of a former state religion after disestablishment. It is just as important—perhaps even more urgently important—to believers, but it no longer has coercive power over nonbelievers. Doctrinal commitments that had once been a concomitant of citizenship, coextensive with citizenship, became a matter of private preference.

For those who think as I do, there is no problem—or not much of one. Traditionalists say that the new ways of thinking, insofar as they become influential, mean "the death of historical scholarship as we have known it." I agree but would add that we have known it incorrectly and that the new ways of thinking about history more realistically describe the enduring nature of our venture than the old, whether it is the inapplicability of the word "truth" to historical accounts, the thoroughgoingly and irredeemably ideological nature of scholarship, or the impossibility of algorithmic resolutions to conflicts between scholarly and other loyalties. I am enough of a traditionalist to prefer a realistic to a mythical view.

In my utopian moments, I imagine an ethics of thoroughgoing honesty for the historical profession. The center of that ethics would be acknowledging, to ourselves and, most crucially, to the lay public, that what we are doing is exploring and thinking about the past with as much energy and intelligence as we can muster, and then making up interesting, provocative, even edifying stories about it as contributions to collective self-understanding(s). We would make no greater (but also no lesser) truth claims than poets or painters; no greater (but also no lesser) claims for support from society in this endeavor. Like poets or painters, we would criticize and evaluate each other's work by criteria that are often technical. Like them, we would be evaluated by outsiders on the basis of how well what we offered met their needs. I really do value honesty, would really like to be honest about what I do. My kind of code would allow such honesty. The (in my view) quite deceptive claim to truth and authority that we collectively make, that we have persuaded many outsiders to accept, and in which, as a professional, I am inevitably complicit seems to be dishonest: structural lying.

I would add one other item to my utopian ethical code: professional historians would be obliged to be accurate about straightforward factual matters. On the level of "The cat is on the mat" or "On 7 December 1941, the Japanese attacked Pearl Harbor," which is the sort of thing I have in mind, we wouldn't be allowed to say those things were so unless they were so. I am not fully persuaded that this is a truly ethical requirement. I have a deep-seated feeling that, just as medicine can't be any good unless it tastes bad, so a really *ethical* decision must be painful and difficult. I've always found it a good rule that at any ethical juncture, the thing you least want to do, which is most inconvenient, which works against your selfish interests, is almost surely the right thing to do. Accuracy about matters of fact hardly meets this criterion. It's not hard to do, and it's not at all inconvenient: with minimal ingenuity you can construct a narrative of almost any imaginable shape, drawing whatever moral you wish, without getting facts wrong. And it's always in your selfish interest, because if you deliberately misstate, this is likely to be discovered, and you will suffer penalties ranging from mild embarrassment to total loss of believability. Still, despite its inconsequentiality, I'd include factual accuracy as the second and final item in my utopian ethics of historical practice, because it does serve some purposes. It is convenient and courteous, among professionals, to know that however sterile, wrongheaded, or perverse we find each other's interpretations and conclusions, we can rely on, and confidently use for our own (sterile, wrongheaded, or perverse) purposes, the little bits we find there, which can't be said for the bits we find elsewhere. It is, in a small way, a kind of ritual of solidarity. To a limited but not trivial extent, professional historiography *is* a cooperative venture; it is well to symbolically affirm this. And it probably is useful to maintain *some*

kind of distinction between history and fiction, if only to save librarians a massive job of recataloguing.

Alas, like other utopian visions I've flirted with, the ethics of honesty about what we're doing isn't workable, can't be established. Because just as our colleagues who see the historical venture as engaged in the pursuit of truth can no longer impose their ethic on a profession that includes those of us who don't believe in it, we can't (yet) impose ours on a profession that includes them. Hoist with my own disestablishmentarian petard. So honesty's out. That's a shame. But I'd still keep the ethics of not saying the cat is on the mat when she isn't, for the reasons stated. And so far as I can see, that's the sum total of the ethics of historical practice we're going to have to settle for. Not much, and not my first choice, but if there's no alternative, I can live with it.

But can the antidisestablishmentarians, for whom, to judge by their pronouncements, this is a life-and-death matter? It's not really my problem, but, as I see it, they've got several choices. They can argue with us—try to convince us, depending on which sect of antidisestablishmentarians we're talking about, to repent and go back to the old ethics of historical practice or to join with them in rebuilding consensus around some cosmetically improved variant, thus preserving Western Rationality, the Moral Order, and other good stuff. They *might* succeed (anything's possible), but unless they come up with arguments a lot better than what's been at offer up to now, I doubt it. They could try to expel us, but while their overheated rhetoric about the danger we pose suggests that mere expulsion would be a lenient penalty, that's really not their style—and, anyway, they couldn't carry it off. They could themselves quit in disgust, but I'd hate to see that happen: some of them, despite their retrograde views, often do quite interesting work. Alternatively, they might try an experiment. Let them draw up a list of a dozen recent substantive historical works by American professional historians who repudiate the traditional ethics of historical practice, and a parallel list by historians who subscribe to that ethics. Let them then (objectively, impartially, judiciously—all the things they're good at) consider whether *by their standards* the former works are inferior to the latter. It just might be that the ethics of historical practice does not have a lot to do with practice.

There's another sense in which the ethics of historical practice—professional norms—doesn't seem to me all that consequential. I am thinking of the ethical *impact* of history: its moral, its political, its human consequences.

On one level, the way we do history is a matter of structural and social determination. Generally speaking, dogmatism will govern historical practice in a totalitarian society, openness in a liberal society. A racist society, other things being equal, will have a racist historiography, and so forth.

The more truly liberal and pluralist a society, the less this kind of determinism is operative so far as the content and the moral thrust of the historical work produced are concerned, that is to say, its human consequences. The freer the society, and Western societies are pretty free in this respect these days, the more these become a matter of the visions and values, the hopes and fears, the "propagandistic" purposes and persuasive powers of the individual historian.

I have been in this business for about 30 years and have read a lot of history. I have never been able to find any relationship whatsoever between the professional excellence of a work of history and my estimate of its moral consequences. I'm a firm believer in the importance of two points that Richard Rorty has continually pressed. The first is that, by and large, people change their minds about matters of consequence not as a result of cogent arguments but as a result of persuasive redescriptions. (This is the main reason why I think that the writing of history is so important.) Rorty's second point is that anything can be made to look good or bad by being redescribed. (This is the main reason why I think historical writing, as such, is morally inconsequential.) With the part of me that is a connoisseur of historiography I can appreciate technical brilliance and virtuosity when reading works by professional historians that make things I think very good look very bad and things I think very bad look very good. On such occasions the other parts of me get depressed.

Then I recover and get back to work—writing or teaching—reminding myself that the most effective and persuasive answer to a redescription that points in a direction I don't like is a re-redescription that points to someplace I like better. If the technical virtuoso has followed my minimalist ethic and gotten the little bits right, as most do, I may be able to recycle these bits for my own purposes. If he or she has gotten enough of them wrong, I'm in luck: I'll be able to show that his or her version isn't true.

References

Burgess, John W. 1902. *Reconstruction and the Constitution: 1866-1876*. New York: Scribner's.

Gabriel, Ralph H. 1961. History and the American Past. In *American Perspectives*, ed. Robert E. Spiller and Eric Larrabee. Cambridge, MA: Harvard University Press.

ANNALS, *AAPSS*, **560**, November 1998

The Will to Truth:
A Reply to Novick

By JUDITH LICHTENBERG

ABSTRACT: This article challenges Peter Novick's claims that truth and objectivity are not proper goals for historians to strive after. The author argues that, on the contrary, these ideals are morally and intellectually indispensable. The argument consists of an attack on several fundamental claims Novick makes: that history and fiction are barely distinguishable; that although there are such things as facts, it is easy to get them right and it is possible to construct whatever theory one likes around them; that historians should be honest not in the sense of being faithful to the truth (which, he believes, does not exist) but only in the sense of admitting that what they do is make up stories.

Judith Lichtenberg teaches philosophy at the University of Maryland, where she is also a senior research scholar at the Institute for Philosophy and Public Policy. She is the editor of Democracy and the Mass Media *and has written about philosophical and ethical issues in journalism, as well as about race, nationalism, and a variety of topics in moral and political philosophy.*

PETER Novick does not believe that truth and objectivity are proper goals for historians to strive after, and he is not sorry about it either. In earlier times, he tells us, a consensus existed among professional historians that the aim of history was "to discover and record the objective truth about the past" with the ultimate goal of painting "a true and complete picture" of it. From this lofty goal or "noble dream," as he has elsewhere described it (Novick 1988), two "ethical norms" followed: "first, assiduity in determining and scrupulosity in reporting the facts," and "second, ... freedom from bias, partisanship, 'special pleading,' preconceived notions, utilitarian purposes, or other interferences with neutrality and objectivity" (Novick, this volume, 27-28).[1] But for a variety of reasons both political and philosophical, Novick argues, the consensus has collapsed.

I would not begin to argue with Novick's account of the *history* of the decline of the ideals of truth and objectivity, among professional historians and much more widely in our culture. Indeed, Novick's book *That Noble Dream* (1988) offers much insight into the reasons these ideals have lost their attractions for so many people. (I could say he helps us understand the truth about these developments—although, presumably, he would reject the compliment.) My aim is instead analytical and normative: it is to ask what it means to abandon the ideals of truth and objectivity and whether we can coherently do so. By looking closely at some of Novick's own disturbing pronouncements, and drawing out their implications, I hope to show that these ideals are indispensable both intellectually and morally.

HISTORY AND FICTION

Let us begin with Novick's claim that the words "true" or "truthful" apply only to "rather narrowly defined 'brute-factual' statements, singular or statistical," not to "synthetic historical accounts." It follows, he believes, that it makes "no sense to say of two accounts, assuming neither was filled with egregious misstatements of fact, that one [is] truer than the other" (35).[2]

How, then, do we compare and evaluate historical works? If Novick were right that history and fiction are barely distinguishable—he finds no good reason to separate them except "to save librarians a massive job of recataloguing" (38)—then it might seem that better histories differ from worse ones on purely aesthetic grounds. A better work would be simply a more beautiful, internally coherent work. But Novick argues that what historians are and should be doing is "making up interesting, provocative, even edifying stories about [the past] as contributions to collective self- understanding(s)" (37). In so doing, he suggests that the criteria for evaluating historical works—as well as artworks—are not simply aesthetic but also moral, political, and ideological. An "edifying" history may instruct its readers morally or elevate their sense of themselves; a "provocative" work may challenge their preconceptions.[3]

Now, clearly, we do judge historical works according to such criteria. Other things being equal, a work that "edifies" is better than one that does not; a "provocative" work that challenges old pieties is better than one that reinforces our preconceptions. And who would not prefer "interesting" stories over dull ones?

What is wrong with Novick's view is not the criteria he endorses as much as the one he rejects. In the history-as-fiction model he presents as an ideal, historians "would make no greater (but also no lesser) truth claims than poets or painters" (37). It is here that he runs amok.

Novick is right that, in praising a historical or biographical or journalistic work, we do not ordinarily shower on it the encomium "It's true!"[4] We say instead that it is insightful or that it enhances our understanding or that it sheds new light on the events in question. But to provide insight or illumination is to shed light *on* something. In praising historical works, we mean that they make sense of, explain, fit with *events that happened in the world*. We cannot understand these ascriptions without appealing to the ideal of fidelity to truth.

Now, clearly, poets and novelists also provide insight and illumination. We may say of a novel or a play or a film that it "gets at the truth" about some human condition or that, in depicting a familiar kind of character or situation, it "gets it right." If, as I have admitted, edification and the like can be virtues of history as well as fiction, it might seem that I am agreeing with Novick that the two are barely distinguishable.[5]

But this would be a serious mistake. The truths to which "insightful" or "illuminating" fictional works must be faithful are general truths about "the human condition" or about various human conditions. And it is enough if the individual characters or situations depicted in fictional works, which we may describe as "real" or "realistic," are instances of *types* that exist in the world. We do not assume, however, that the particular individuals or situations depicted in fiction exist in the world, nor is it the case that successful fiction must contain characters or situations that are realistic even in this limited sense. Realism and truth are not indispensable virtues of fiction.

History, however, is different. The characters and situations that form its subject matter are not merely instances of types that may exist in the world; they must themselves have actually existed. Moreover, whereas it seems plausible that in fiction the particular individuals and situations depicted are vehicles—archetypes—for the transmission of general truths, in history it is the other way around: in the end our theories and our explanations are servants to the hard reality of fact.

As a good working historian respectful of the ultimate data of his craft, Novick shrinks from the preposterous conclusions it would be natural to draw from his conflation of history and fiction. He admits what to most of us is obvious: a realm of "brute facts" with which historical accounts must be compatible. Unlike the novelist, the historian cannot simply make up any old interesting or edifying story. Alongside the criteria Novick announces for judging historical works, we must add another criterion that can be called epistemic: fit with the facts. In contrast to fiction, in history the epistemic is the criterion sine qua non.

Yet Novick takes back with one hand what he gives with the other. A realm of brute facts exists to which historians must be faithful, he admits, but the realm is very narrow. Brute facts are obvious facts, it seems, facts no sensible person would dispute. As examples, he mentions "The cat is on the mat" and "On 7 December 1941, the Japanese attacked Pearl Harbor" (37). He singles out two characteristics of being accurate about such matters of fact: "it's not hard to do, and it's not at all inconvenient: with minimal ingenuity you can construct a narrative of almost any imaginable shape, drawing whatever moral you wish, without getting facts wrong" (38).

So just as we might have relaxed, suspecting Novick's wild pronouncements would be tamed by the constraint of facts, he condemns facts as frail, feeble things that are essentially impotent. Facts, he says, are easy to establish. In addition, they are "not at all inconvenient": almost any facts can be rendered compatible with almost any historical account.

Is it so easy to get the facts right? Are facts so accommodating to the stories historians wish to tell? These are the questions that demand answers.

FACTS AND INTERPRETATIONS

It is useful to begin by making explicit a distinction on which Novick's account relies. This is the distinction between a realm of facts (perhaps we should say "brute facts") and a realm of interpretation, which encompasses theories, narratives, stories, and generally the larger accounts that the historian (or other interpreter of events) sets out to tell. Two questions immediately present themselves. One is where facts end and interpretation begins. The second is how interpretations are to be assessed and compared.

That the Japanese bombed Pearl Harbor on 7 December 1941 is a fact. How that fact should be understood, what its causes were, seems to be an interpretation. That millions of Jews and others died in Nazi concentration camps during World War II is a fact. The explanation, or explanations, of the fact—the larger story in which it is embedded—appears to be a matter of interpretation. Novick claims that interpretations are not significantly constrained by facts; thus his belief that the historian can "construct a narrative of almost any imaginable shape . . . without getting facts wrong." The criteria for assessing interpretations, in this view, are aesthetic, moral, and political, rather than epistemic.

Novick would be right if he had said merely that facts *underdetermine* interpretations—in other words, that a given set of facts is compatible with more than one interpretation. This is perhaps tautological, for we might say that an interpretation of a given set of facts just *is* something that is compatible with, but not entailed by, those facts, thus that a given set of facts can support multiple interpretations. Just as clearly, however, facts *constrain* interpretations: not *every* interpretation is compatible with every set of facts, and some interpretations better fit a given set of facts than others.

Here is a simple model for understanding the relationship between facts and interpretations. Imagine a given set of facts F. Imagine also several possible interpretations of F: $Int1, Int2, Int3$, and so forth. Assume that two of these interpretations, $Int1$ and $Int2$, are equally plausible. But now suppose that new facts come to light and are added to the set F. These new facts (we shall assume that the original facts in F have not been discredited) may enhance the plausibility of some interpretations of F and reduce the plausibility of others; perhaps some interpretations can be ruled out altogether. The new set may, for example, render $Int1$ more plausible than $Int2$.

A historical example can flesh out our bare-boned model. With the case of the American Revolution, Raymond Martin has demonstrated how progress in historical understanding can take place. Over two centuries, the two main competing interpretations of the Revolution have been the Whig and the Progressive. The Whigs told the story of the Revolution from the point of view of the revolutionary elite, accepted that the Revolution was fought over principles, and justified the break with Britain. The Progressives, on the other side, emphasized the socioeconomic under-pinnings of the Revolution. Historical accounts on each side developed in a dialectical process: the first Whigs begat the first Progressives, who begat the neo-Whigs, who begat the neo-Progressives.

Each new school of interpretation seems to have taken what it could from the interpretations it superseded, both from those in its own and in the opposing tradition. By the time we get to the "Neo-Progressive" the two schools are so intertwined that it is questionable whether there still are two schools. (Martin 1998, 29)

More generally, Martin argues, we understand the Revolution better today than we did in previous times, for a variety of reasons. A lot more "has become known about early American history." Interpretations have "become more accurate because previous factual and explanatory mistakes have been corrected and the corrections have tended to be cumulative." Interpretations have become more comprehensive and better balanced as "more sorts of causal influences have been taken into account" and more subjective perspectives have been portrayed. Interpretations have become less partisan. They also have become "better justified because the sheer quantity of evidence on which interpretations are based has grown enormously" (27-28).

Returning to our model, Martin's analysis helps us see that the distinction between fact and interpretation is not sharp: it is hard to say where one ends and the other begins. This is a point often made by opponents of truth and objectivity—who like to remind us that facts are "theory-laden"—but the point cuts two ways. Interpretations are also fact laden: the uncovering of new facts renders some interpretations more plausible and others less. Progress in our understanding of the Revolution came about partly because we know a lot more about the Revolution than we used to. Historians have been able to correct "factual and explanatory mistakes"(27) uncovered by other historians, including those with whom they disagreed over interpretation. Later histories have included "more sorts of causal influences" and more "subjective perspectives" of people involved in the Revolution (27).

Some putative facts turned out not to be facts; some new facts came to light. Later explanations benefited from this new knowledge. Having at their disposal the works of earlier historians, as well as a wider range of sources, later histories were able to see events from more points of view, and could subsume earlier historical accounts within their own more comprehensive ones.

Now, of course, Martin examines only one case, and he acknowledges that consensus about how to understand the Revolution is limited in important ways. Two further points are worth noting. First, the goal of painting "a true and complete picture" of historical events is implausible and naive. If earlier historians thought otherwise, as Novick implies, they were misguided. There is not a single Truth or even a single truth about a given set of events. It is obvious, too, that more than one interpretation can explain or illumi-

nate the same events.[6] The point is not that there is only one way to look at the facts, but that some ways of looking at them do not stand up to scrutiny. One can tell several stories, perhaps many stories, about the same set of facts, but some stories will not fly.

Second, interpretational consensus becomes a more attainable goal as time passes and passions and biases subside. We are more likely to agree about the causes of the American Revolution than about the causes of the Persian Gulf war. That means, of course, that many of the historical issues most interesting to us will remain controversial, thereby reinforcing the sense of relativism that Novick describes.

The question, however, is not whether we encounter radically different ways of understanding the same events. Clearly, we do. The question is, rather, what our response to such different understandings should be. Should we simply accept and even embrace the clashing perceptions as the end of the matter, or should we instead try to adjudicate between them? Novick suggests the former. I urge the latter, both as a prescription for what we ought to do and as a description of what we actually do. We would not be disturbed by conflicting perceptions of events in the world unless we believed that some versions are more accurate—closer to the truth—than others. Truth functions for us as an ideal that we must embrace if we are to attain understanding of the world.[7] Compelled by our natures to seek understanding, we experience a will to truth.

NOT ENOUGH FACTS

Another example sheds further light on the relationship between facts and interpretations. Consider the storm of controversy surrounding the publication of Daniel Goldhagen's book, *Hitler's Willing Executioners: Ordinary Germans and the Holocaust*. Goldhagen denies that the extermination of the Jews was carried out by a relatively small number of fanatics or Nazi Party faithfuls, or that it resulted primarily from coercion, peer pressure, or a habit of obedience; he argues that "Germans' antisemitic beliefs about Jews were the central causal agent of the Holocaust" (Goldhagen 1996, 9).

The ordinary person's response to Goldhagen's theory is to ask if it is right. But Novick's view of history does not allow this question. From Novick one would conclude that every imaginable set of facts equally supports Goldhagen's explanation and those of his critics. Of course, historians who disagree with Goldhagen do ask if his theory is right, and they have beliefs about what is relevant to answering it. Ruth Bettina Birn, for example, one of Goldhagen's sharpest critics, argues that Goldhagen's

assertion that German antisemitism was unique can only be made by comparing it to other forms of antisemitism. If one claims that only Jews were treated in a special way, one has to analyse the treatment of other victims; if one claims that only Germans committed certain deeds, one has to compare them to the deeds of non-Germans; if one claims that all Germans acted in a certain way, one has to compare the behaviour of different groups in German society. (Birn 1997, 196)

Goldhagen's interpretation will become less plausible if it is found that many non-Germans treated Jews as badly as did Germans, or that Germans often treated non-Jews as badly as they treated Jews, or that different groups of Germans treated Jews differently. And these propositions can be confirmed or disconfirmed by the uncovering of certain facts.[8]

Novick's denial that facts can be inconvenient suggests that no such comparative data could even be *relevant* to judging the merits of Goldhagen's interpretation. He is right, of course, that facts taken in isolation or even in context do not *entail* a particular interpretation. But Novick appears to maintain that evidence showing that Germans sometimes treated non-Jews as badly as they did Jews, or that some non-Germans treated Jews as badly as did Germans, would have no bearing on Goldhagen's thesis. Such a view is absurd as well as reckless.

The idea that facts constrain interpretations will seem to most people like common sense, but it has a subtler aspect as well. We might put the point by saying that the gap between fact and interpretation is filled partly with undiscovered facts: an interpretation that is plausible given a particular set of facts F will be less plausible or perhaps not plausible at all with set $F + n$, where n comprises certain additional facts. This is just another way of saying that as we learn more, what was once interpretation becomes fact.

Ignorance of facts, then, produces more interpretational disagreement than we in our armchairs, spinning our theories, like to admit. Theories are fine and grand things, we think, with their own internal logic, beauty, and necessity. Facts, on the other hand, are small, contingent, inaccessible, recalcitrant. The past is past and may leave few traces. Evidence is partial, conflicting. The motives of witnesses, as well as chroniclers, may be suspect.

Ignorance of facts is sometimes curable, sometimes not. But one thing is clear: if we had more facts, we would have fewer theories.

TOO MANY FACTS

One problem historians face, then, is not having all the information that is relevant to assessing their interpretations. But the other side of the coin is having much more than they can possibly use. Herein lies a key to interpreting Novick's claim that "with minimal ingenuity you can construct a narrative of almost any imaginable shape . . . *without getting facts wrong*" (38, emphasis added). Novick is almost certainly right. Without ever saying anything false, and never being strictly inaccurate, one can make an implausible view seem plausible if only one leaves out certain crucial facts. It is for this reason that telling the truth and nothing but the truth is not enough: one has to tell the whole truth.

A central task confronting historians, biographers, journalists, and others who chronicle events is the problem of selection: deciding which, among the vast supply of facts out there in the world, to include in their narratives and which to exclude. Earlier, during the research phase of their projects, they must decide which roads to follow—which documents to examine, whom to interview—and which to close off. For these tasks the investigator needs criteria of relevance to sort among the myriad facts actually and potentially available. Clearly, aesthetic and pragmatic criteria play a role here. A work of history must be of finite and manageable length; if it is readable and even pleasurable as well, so much the better. But such considerations must not compromise a work's intellectual and moral integrity. Suppressing inconvenient facts to make an interpretation more pleasing or more plausible violates the standards to which historians, biographers, and journalists are bound. (Novick's denial elsewhere that facts can be inconvenient will come as news to experimental scientists and criminal defense attorneys.)

It is impossible to explain both which facts count as relevant, and why omitting inconvenient (and hence relevant) facts violates widely accepted standards of scholarship, without employing concepts such as fairness, objectivity, and truth. Some facts support a particular interpretation, and others tend to undermine it. To know how good an interpretation is—how well it explains the events in question—we must be aware of the evidence against it as well as the evidence for it. (A criminal lawyer who neglected such guidelines would ill serve his clients.) As John Stuart Mill put it, "Three-fourths of the arguments for every disputed opinion consist in dispelling the appearances which favor some opinion different from it" (Mill [1859] 1956, 44). *Of course* a credible story can be told without getting facts wrong, if those facts that do not suit the theory are left out.

Implicit in the demand for fairness and balance and the acknowledgment of inconvenient facts—demands that we all understand perfectly well—is the idea that there is a reality independent of our interpretations, a reality that our interpretations are aiming to explain or illuminate and to which they must be faithful. As I have argued, it does not follow that there is only one plausible interpretation of a given set of events. But this idea of an independent reality means that our interpretations are not self-contained and that they, and we who do the interpreting, must strive for fidelity to that which they are about.

Of course, every historian, when engaged not in abstract metadiscussions about the nature of historical work but, rather, in the practice of history itself, understands this. Goldhagen passionately believes that anti-Semitic conviction was the central reason ordinary Germans participated in the Holocaust; his critics deny it. That the parties to a historical debate believe there is a truth about the matter does not, of course, mean that there is a truth about the matter. But, as I argued earlier, appealing to Kant, it does mean that people cannot take causal or historical explanations seriously—cannot take interpretations seriously—without a commitment to the existence of truth.

THE HONEST HISTORIAN

Novick wishes to replace the old-fashioned standards historians used to live by—the ones that presupposed the existence of truth and the possibility of objectivity—with a new code of ethics. One element of this new code would require accuracy about matters of fact, which, as we saw earlier, he thinks is easy. (As a result, he says, "I am not fully persuaded that this is a truly ethical requirement," because he thinks that "a really *ethical* decision must be painful and difficult" [38].) The other ethical requirement—the one Novick seems to take more seriously—is honesty.

There is something amusing in Novick's unembarrassed endorsement of honesty after he has dumped truth and objectivity. The ordinary meaning of honesty, after all, is truthfulness. What is it to be honest but to tell the truth as best one can? What is left of honesty if truth is an illusion?

What, then, could Novick mean? He thinks historians would be honest if they admitted that they do not tell the truth and that what they do is make up stories. He deplores the dishonesty he believes is implicit in traditional historians' claims to truth and authority.

Now Novick is right to suspect those who insist on their own objectivity and proclaim themselves as truth tellers. We are wise enough to know, as perhaps our forebears did not, that complete objectivity and freedom from bias are impossible. People who are sure they know protest too much: they are likely to be arrogant, overconfident, or self-deceived. Those who acknowledge their fallibility are often more trustworthy. Certainly we want readers and audiences to approach texts skeptically, aware of the many obstacles standing in the way of knowledge.

But fallibilism—the recognition that we can be wrong, the humility to suspect we might be—does not mean there is nothing to be known or understood. Quite the contrary, it reflects a deep respect for the factuality of the world and the difficulty of penetrating it. It is honest to admit one might be wrong. But claiming there is nothing to be right about is dishonest, unless it is simply dumb. It is honest to acknowledge one's biases, but that is only the beginning. One acknowledges them, and then one tries to overcome them or compensate for them as best one can, knowing that complete success will never be achieved. But to acknowledge one's biases while complacently accepting them—"You're right, I don't like black people, but that's just the way I am"—is the mark of a person who refuses to think.

What would it mean to accept Novick's novel understanding of honesty as the cardinal virtue for historians?: "I am a historian and I don't tell the truth." If we believe the historian's disclaimer, we can discount his version of events. After all, he *told* us historians can make up almost any story out of any facts, so we need not take him seriously unless his story happens to suit our purposes. If we do not believe him, his disclaimer has no effect, except perhaps to bolster our confidence in someone so honest as to tell us he is not.

There is another way to understand Novick's commitment to honesty, one that confirms our suspicion that even a sophisticated postmodern historian cannot deny the reality out there to which his interpretations must be as faithful as they can be. I believe that part of the reason Novick uses the old-fashioned term "honesty" is because he values old-fashioned honesty. The reason he values it is that no nonfiction writer worth his salt can manage without it. He can *say* he does not believe in truth and all that, but he cannot *mean* it. If he dismisses values like truth out one door, he will just have to admit others, like honesty, that serve the same function: to ensure the distinction between fact and fiction. Honesty—fidelity to truth—might be the best policy for a novelist. For a historian, nothing else will do.

Notes

1. Citations to "(The Death of) the Ethics of Historical Practice (and Why I Am Not Mourning)" are given by page number in parentheses. For extended discussion and defense of the concept of objectivity, see Lichtenberg 1996.

2. Novick makes his case against truth and objectivity coyly, not by direct argument but as a putative historical account of the development of their declining fortunes. Thus he speaks of the belief of "people" that the words "true" and "truthful" applied only to narrow "brute factual" statements, and he writes that "it seemed to follow" (to these people) that it made no sense to say that one account was truer than another. Only well into the article does he acknowledge what is, of course, obvious: that these beliefs are his ("is it necessary to add that on the whole I share them?" [36]).

3. Interestingly, in this view, a valuable work can be one that makes its audience feel good (the work that enhances a group's identity) or one that makes its audience feel bad (the one that challenges its preconceptions). Indeed, the same work is likely to enhance the image of one group while demoting another: by challenging conventional historical accounts, it may "afflict the comfortable and comfort the afflicted," to use a phrase journalists sometimes employ to describe their role. This is, of course, precisely what happens when new historical accounts tell stories from the point of view of previously marginalized groups.

4. Novick focuses on historical works, although much of what he says applies to biography, autobiography, journalism, and more broadly to the realm of what used unproblematically to be considered nonfiction. In general, I shall use the example of history, although the same points often apply to these other genres. Of course, there are also differences between them.

5. Novick, after all, has said that historians should "make no greater (*but also no lesser*) truth claims than poets or painters" (emphasis added). For all we know, he thinks novelists' claims are chock-full of truth value. Arguments that X (history) is like Y (fiction) are always ambiguous: is X more like we thought Y was, or is Y more like we thought X was? Clearly, Novick means to downgrade the truth-content of history, but just how far he intends to empty history of truth depends on how truth-full he believes fiction is.

6. There are two kinds of cases: first, where we have multiple incompatible interpretations of the same set of events; second, where we have multiple yet compatible interpretations. The second kind of case poses no problem: we can imagine two historians, say, looking at the same set of events from different points of view and highlighting different aspects. Here we might think in terms of the meaning or significance of a set of events; it is plausible to think that meaning and significance are relational concepts that make reference to individuals or groups *to whom* events have meaning or significance. (See Martin 1998 and Lichtenberg 1996 for some suggestions along these lines.) Can there be multiple incompatible interpretations? Clearly, there can be in one sense; the question is only whether the equal plausibility of more than one interpretation is a function only of our lack of information. In that case, if we knew more, one of these interpretations would become less plausible. The alternative is to countenance some ultimate indeterminacy or ambiguity in the world. I do not deny that there is such indeterminacy or ambiguity in humanistic studies like history; I claim only that this view is a last resort to be admitted only when all avenues to truth have been exhausted.

7. Kant called such ideals "regulative principles." They "supply reason with a standard which is indispensable to it, providing it, as they do, with a concept of that which is entirely complete in its kind, and thereby enabling it to estimate and to measure the degree and the defects of the incomplete" (Kant [1781] 1965, 486 [A569 B597]).

8. Not possessing adequate evidence, I make no claim here one way or another about the merits of the debate between Goldhagen and his critics.

References

Birn, Ruth Bettina. 1997. Revising the Holocaust. *Historical Journal* 40:195-215. Reprinted, with additions, in Norman Finkelstein and Ruth Bettina Birn, *A Nation on Trial: The Goldhagen Thesis and Historical Truth* (New York: Henry Holt, 1998).

Goldhagen, Daniel Jonah. 1996. *Hitler's Willing Executioners: Ordinary Ger-*

mans and the Holocaust. New York: Alfred A. Knopf.

Kant, Immanuel. [1781] 1965. *Critique of Pure Reason.* Trans. Norman Kemp Smith. New York: St. Martin's Press.

Lichtenberg, Judith. 1996. In Defense of Objectivity Revisited. In *Mass Media and Society*, ed. James Curran and Michael Gurevitch. 2d ed. London: Edward Arnold.

Martin, Raymond. 1998. Progress in Historical Studies. *History and Theory* 37:14-39.

Mill, John Stuart. [1859] 1956. *On Liberty.* Indianapolis: Bobbs-Merrill.

Novick, Peter. 1988. *That Noble Dream: The "Objectivity Question" and the American Historical Profession.* New York: Cambridge University Press.

Objectivity as a Problem:
An Attempt at an Overview

By JOSEPH MARGOLIS

ABSTRACT: Objectivity has become a contested notion. The chief contending models, which may be conveniently abstracted from Thomas Kuhn's *Structure of Scientific Revolutions* and Ludwig Wittgenstein's *Tractatus*, may be termed, respectively, constructivism and objectivism. There are difficulties, but of different sorts, confronting each. Objectivism is now seriously challenged, but constructivism is not yet cast in any canonically compelling way. There is an increasing tendency, now, to construe knowledge as a construct of historical experience and to challenge any principled disjunction between objectivity in the natural sciences and in the human sciences and practical life. To favor these themes is, effectively, to deny any privilege or hierarchical order of knowledge favoring the natural sciences.

Joseph Margolis is currently Laura H. Carnell Professor of Philosophy at Temple University in Philadelphia. He has authored somewhat more than 30 books. His most recent book, What, After All, Is a Work of Art? *is to be released shortly.*

IT is noticeably difficult, now at the end of the century, to grasp the full import of the original reception of Thomas Kuhn's *Structure of Scientific Revolutions* ([1962] 1970). I mean its impact not only on the analytic philosophy of science but, beyond that, on the general intellectual orientation of all forms of responsible inquiry. I was once told by a senior editor at the University of Chicago Press that the sale of Kuhn's book came close to rivaling the sales of several of the lesser Bibles. Yet, by the end of the century, shortly before his death, Kuhn had reversed himself and had given more than polite encouragement to the canonical doctrines that *Structure* had, as we now realize, so innocently challenged. I find it entirely fair to say that the central pronouncement of the book—namely, that the attempt to ensure the "fixed and neutral" standing of sensory experience "through the introduction of a neutral language of observation now seem to me [Kuhn] hopeless" (126)—was much more startling and more profound in its effect on Western thought than all the postmodernist and post-structuralist pronouncements that, since the book's appearance, have come to rest on the problematic standing of such notions as those of fact, objectivity, and neutrality.

Kuhn was unable to sustain or strengthen his own thesis, I am afraid. He actually fell back from his important challenge, under considerable pummeling from the academic community that he had implicitly attacked. The result, at least in English-language philosophy, has been the nearly total eclipse of Kuhn's official influence and of any sustained close interest in his original argument. Still, what Kuhn drew to our attention (under the nose of the *International Encyclopedia of Unified Science*, which sponsored the publication of *Structure*—a miraculous event, if one thinks about it) continues to nag. We are in a conceptual limbo now: we no longer believe in the ensured accessibility of neutral facts, but we also lack a proper replacement for such facts, under Kuhn's important change of vision. What is remarkable about Kuhn's influence—perhaps not easily isolated from the ongoing contemporaneous influence of the Wittgenstein of the *Philosophical Investigations*, late pragmatism, Heidegger, the Frankfurt Critical school, such pop figures as Derrida and Foucault, self-styled postmodernists like Lyotard and Rorty, and an army of lesser presences who have used up all their dry powder by this time—is simply that, as beneficiaries, we no longer find it problematic to concede the coherence (even the viability) of viewing facts and objectivity as artifacts of history. We often view facts as socially constructed, subject to endless revision under the critical pressure of discovering (always after the fact) that whatever we may have posited *ante* (as reliable forms of objectivity) inevitably generate, in their turn, logical paradoxes, methodological impasses, epistemic embarrassments that we would rather replace than continue to support in our routinized inquiries.

That was the undeniable lesson of Kuhn's notorious insistence on "paradigm shifts" and conceptual "incommensurabilities." Kuhn's failure—for that is what it was—to legitimate his own intuition is now irrelevant to its prospects at this late hour. Kuhn was largely right, I am convinced; more than that, he was incomparably better at collecting compelling illustrations for his own brief than most of the other theorists who questioned neutrality. What Kuhn demonstrated was nothing less than that the closed rational system of validating the progressive enlargement of objective science was no such system at all. I also believe that all those who are now genuinely committed to an objectivist scruple secretly worry about what we ought to mean by "fact" and "objectivity," now that we realize we can no longer pretend to recover, by criterial means, any imagined changeless norms of inquiry that, in past canonical accounts (or fresh replacements), might match the "independent" world our would-be neutral "facts" once represented (or were a part of).

In the *Tractatus*, which circulated in the 1930s, in manuscript, among the members of the Vienna Circle, Wittgenstein had set down the following propositions as the first two of his famous tract: "(1) The world is all that is the case [*der Fall*]" and "(1.1) The world is the totality of facts [*Tatsachen*], not of things." There is, of course, no theory of knowledge in the *Tractatus*, but the theory Kuhn contests is usually thought to be presupposed there. That is certainly the way the positivists read Wittgenstein. Between the 1930s and the early 1960s, therefore, the intellectual climate in the West changed so radically that Kuhn's denial of neutrality came to be accepted as an unexceptional option, even among those who supposed it was dead wrong. No one now, reading Kuhn for the first time, would raise an eyebrow.

You may not agree with my sense of the story. But I think you cannot deny that, now, at the end of the century, fact has become a problematic notion. Deep down, it had nearly always been construed (when equated with truth) as that which results from the neutral adequation of truth-bearing assertions about the world and the independent world, or, in Wittgenstein's idiom, that in or of the world (disjoined from truth) to which true propositions correspond. Once Wittgenstein discovered that he must construe "the world" as the totality of "facts" (not of "things" [*Dinge*]), to make his own way of capturing objectivity logically snug, he obliged us to pay attention to the double lesson: (1) that if the world were composed of "things," the correspondence theory of truth and fact would, on any reading, require an interpretive *tertium* to have any point at all, and (2) that there simply were no straightforward readings in which the world is composed of "facts." The post-Tractarian Wittgenstein realized that he had cast the classic doctrine in such a way that it could never be convincingly resurrected, and so he moved on (in the *Investigations*) to identify only the social conditions under which the question of truth arises, not any criteria that could replace whatever, empirically, might have been thought to be the Tractarian view. The objectivity of fact remains, of course, but what does it now entail?

Objectivity is needed to signify, at least, the cognitive standing we accord the concepts of certain scrupulously pursued inquiries. I put the point as thinly as I do to indicate the genuinely subversive import of what Kuhn achieved, as well as what, as I see matters, Wittgenstein came to believe in the *Investigations*. Yet, of course, both thinkers—otherwise so utterly different—paid their respects to the natural discipline of saying what is true, relative to practices in which such loyalties have point. Certainly, Kuhn believed in an objective science. Certainly, Wittgenstein did not abandon either science or the genuine (if unnoticed) rigor of the quotidian inquiries of ordinary life; it is only that he came to see that the picture he had held—which was implicitly endorsed by all the reigning philosophers of science and logic— must have been completely misguided. Yet, moving on from the *Tractatus* to the *Investigations*, Wittgenstein nowhere presumes to recover neutrality or objectivity as such.

By contrast, if you read the postmodernists, you see that, for them, to concede the loss of the kind of neutrality Kuhn was willing to give up (or Wittgenstein or Dewey or Heidegger)—to remind you, by an aside, of Richard Rorty's version of the tale—would signify that there was nothing left of objectivity at all! How so? you ask. To work, they say (very archly), it must be assured in the Cartesian or Kantian or Aristotelian or some such way and, now, it simply can no longer be so assured. Ergo, if strict neutrality fails, all philosophy fails: there is no possible way to legitimate any one notion of objective fact over any other. Nonsense!

Are, then, the labors of science, you wonder, all for nothing? No, of course not, Rorty answers (ditto Lyotard, though in his different way): science remains, but only as a "conversation" (Rorty) or as a labor lacking all legitimative "metanarratives" (Lyotard). Still, the postmodernists neglect to add—perhaps slyly, perhaps innocently—that if the sense of a reasonably disciplined or "successful" science continues, then they will not have eliminated so-called second-order questions about fact or objectivity: they will only have confirmed that objectivity need never have been obliged to claim indubitable sources in Descartes's sense, or transcendental sources in Kant's, or anything of the sort. In short, they saw the need to disjoin "neutrality" and "objectivity," to reject all forms of the first and to redeem the second as a critical artifact revised again and again under the pressures of historical experience. The role of fact then shifts: it no longer signifies what is discernibly independent of our inquiries but only what, in inquiry, is posited as independent. That is what Kuhn saw clearly but failed to capture in any explicit way and what Wittgenstein had no interest in formulating.

I can put the lesson in an unpleasantly glib way: first-order fact without second-order objectivity is blind; objectivity without facts is empty; and the distinction between first-order and second-order inquiry is itself a second-order distinction. In effect, the postmodernists were indeed making legitimative pronouncements (false ones) when they pretended to discover the end of legitimation. The truth is that, at the same time the canonical picture of a changelessly rational system of objective inquiry was being cast in conceptual cement, the doubters were busy exposing the inherent informality, the constructed nature, of reason itself. Regarding the analysis of science, you will find the evidence, long before Kuhn's *Structure,* in Ludwik Fleck and Gaston Bachelard and, in the political world, more ambiguously, in the Frankfurt Critical movement.

The answer to the puzzle about objective fact—no more than a clue about any pretended answer—is that fact is an artifact, not a fiction but a continual reconstruction of prior reconstructions of prior reconstructions. Except mythically, fact is not in accord with the objectivist canon, as by way of recovering some primeval match between thought, or speech, and world—which, of course, can never be recovered, because it was never there. I find this very close in spirit to Derrida's wild joke about Lévi-Strauss's trudging through the Amazon jungle in search of the Nambikwara, in the vain hope of getting as close as possible to the original form of truth-bearing discourse. But there is no possibility of approximation there: no possibility of approaching the phantom of neutrality. You can imagine Lévi-Strauss's excitement only if you can imagine the lure of coming upon a perfect guide in the wilderness, apt for all seasons of discovery. That is what Kuhn had disorganized in the mythic assurances of the most honored sciences. That is all gone now, though the melody lingers on. You can find the tepid uses to which the old claims are still being put, in the small piety that says, for instance, that "there is no scientific evidence that smoking causes cancer." There is indeed no (such) evidence because there never was a science like the one supposed to decide tobacco's fate. There never was a neutral science, a science that could escape the contingencies of mortal confidence. But to grasp that much is to begin to fashion a viable sense of objectivity. It is not causality that is discarded but only an ersatz assurance that observation and experiment do actually glimpse a changeless and necessary order of causes. Hence, science is not put at risk, except for claims of modal necessity; but the interpretation of what science can accomplish will have been considerably sobered.

What we dismantle, in honoring Kuhn (and Wittgenstein) at least, is not science or objectivity but an utterly indefensible, false model. You must finally come to see that it is both empirically necessary and conceptually possible to separate objectivity from neutrality, if the second is meant to secure the first. All of the old canons favored neutrality in that sense. It is not enough to say that the claim is not true. That would be a little like saying that Platonism was false, that there was no heaven of eternal Forms. No, someone is bound to come along and claim to have a privileged inkling of the Platonic heaven. The point is rather that there is no way to fix neutrality neutrally: every would-be effort produces a vicious regress. The claim is not only false; it is impossible to pursue or confirm—except to save your prejudice or mine. It is not that Platonism is false; it is that we have no idea of how to gain the slightest access to any such sources.

Objectivity is quite another matter: we can secure the objective facts, despite our dreadful prejudices. They need not interfere. That is what needs explaining. To oversimplify—but not to err: all that is needed is that we share (in a suitable sense of "share") an established practice, open to all the usual sorts of first- and second-order challenge. That is all that Kuhn and Wittgenstein were saying. Hardly enough, I grant, but not actually wrong. Objectivity—fixing the facts—is mortal enough, but neutrality is Olympian. The objectivists—those who believe in strictly neutral knowledge about the independent world—do have Olympian pretensions: certainly, the positivists and the unity-of-science crowd did; certainly, the strict constructionists about the American Constitution; certainly, the Romantic hermaneuts about literary meanings; certainly, the Ideal Observers and the Disinterested Judges; certainly, the revelationists about God's Word. But for the rest of us, neutral inquiry is not a skill anyone can acquire by any known labor. To insist otherwise is to invite the postmodernists to enjoy their revenge.

OBJECTIVITY AND NEUTRALITY

What remains? What, finally, are objective facts—in the second-order sense? My first pass at answering will be as useless as it is useful. (There is some demolition to be done, you see.) We could say—as indeed the would-be canons do—that fact is "that about the world to which true propositions correspond." That is certainly the familiar formula. It is also a piece of ordinary philosophical cant: everyone knows there is no settled or separable sense of proposition and fact—or truth and correspondence, for that matter—by appropriating which we could ever fix facts criterially. The answer betrays the ultimate futility of the *Tractatus*. Wittgenstein himself came to realize he had been had: there is no neutral place from which to look at propositions first and then at facts and then check to see whether indeed they matched one another. The whole idea was suddenly seen to be an academic hoax. There is the marvel of the *Tractatus*: "Whereof one cannot speak . . ." becomes its own *reductio*! Of course, we cannot literally speak of correspondence.

I have an improbable suggestion to make. I am convinced that the entire Western philosophical tradition—more or less up to the French Revolution—knew in a dim way that it lacked resources enough to secure the objectivity of inquiry. It had to pretend that true science had a touch of divinity about it. It needed to assure itself that the vagaries of human belief could, finally, come to rest in a secure reality. It needed a cognitive competence that would never be lost among the passing appearances of the things of the world. I find the signs in Descartes's "natural light of reason," in Kant's transcendental labors, in Aristotle's "*nous*," in the theory of Forms and medieval Universals, in Parmenides's Way of Truth. These are all inventions for guaranteeing neutrality by impossible means—recovering what is changeless and necessarily true in the very flux of the world. Among the sciences themselves, divinity takes the form of the Principle of Induction, matched (on the propositional side) to the nomological necessities of causal order. But there is no heavenly inductive Logic. It is as much a mundane artifact of entrenched practices as is objectivity. Certainly, there is no fixed canon to observe, nothing remotely like Mill's Methods, for instance, nothing like Reichenbach's necessities of reason, nothing like Frege's "laws of the laws of nature." Induction is a patchwork of ceteris paribus clauses that can never be completed; or, where they are thought to begin to approximate to completion, they fall back to natural-kind fixities or essences or universals or nomological necessity. (Divinity again.)

The reference to the French Revolution is not as far-fetched as it may seem. At that moment in history, the West found it possible, for the first time, to link objectivity to the actual collective practices of viable societies. From Hegel on, at least—certainly not yet from Kant—through Marx (I should say), through the discontinuities of history that Nietzsche correctly but extravagantly affirmed, down to Kuhn and Wittgenstein in the most dampened and conservative way possible, objectivity came to be captured (not perspicuously, it is true) in terms of the sheer tacit consensual tolerance of mortal practice.

You cannot, prior to the work of the post-Kantian Idealists, find a firm expression of the idea that the norms of truth and right conduct must be distilled (in some way) from the habituated practices of actual human inquiry and social life. No doubt the vestiges of divinity resist demotion. You find them lingering in Hegel and Marx, of course, just as you find them in Reichenbach and the Wittgenstein of the *Tractatus*. They are not in Nietzsche, it should be said, nor in Dewey (as opposed to Peirce), nor in the early Frankfurt Critical figures (as opposed to Karl-Otto Apel and Jürgen Habermas), nor in Foucault (as opposed to Rorty), nor in early Kuhn (as opposed to late Kuhn).

If you must reclaim the doctrine in correspondentist terms, then bear in mind that the conceptual bridge between world and language—the totality of facts—antecedently requires the constituting mediation of a human framework indissolubly symbiotized between the two, between subjects and objects: language, we may say, is always "worlded," and the world, already "languaged." Propositions, or asserted statements, abstracted from that indissoluble relationship, answer only to what is similarly abstracted as the facts to which they answer.

The French Revolution ushers in the single most important conceptual innovation the modern world has added to the armamentarium of the whole of ancient and medieval philosophy, namely, the idea that the intelligible world—not the prior pristine world but only what we human inquirers are consensually prepared to count as that (the Big Bang, for instance)—is itself a historicized construction made within the same conceptual space in which we constantly reconstruct our sense of our own capacity for fixing facts. The shock of this innovation, now fully 200 years old, is still terribly difficult to concede. It explains the reception of Kuhn and Wittgenstein, however, at the end of our century.

The official reason given for resisting the innovation is the falsity of idealism: the physical world—reality in the most robust sense—cannot (one hears it said) possibly be composed of beliefs or mere ideas. But that is a dodge, for a world that is not linked in any way to our cognizing powers is simply an unknown (unknowable) world; and a known world is not, for that reason alone, composed of mental elements of any kind. Also, more tellingly, to say what is true about a world independent of so saying is to admit that *its* independence is, epistemically, a posit that depends on our capacity to so speak! There is no escape from such encumbrances. Kuhn and Wittgenstein were not idealists. The analysis of the conditions of knowledge is not the analysis of the world we claim to know; but you cannot have the one without the other.

I admit all this is strenuous—I admit that it invites implacable resistance. But there remains one absolutely essential innovation, tethered to the French Revolution, that dissolves the puzzle: the historical practices in which the idealized constructions of fact, truth, reality, knowledge, and reason are embedded are constitutive of the epistemic standing of facts. That was never rightly perceived before the end of the eighteenth century, possibly never perceived in a similar way anywhere else in the world. I think it is the key. Because not only are the

norms of truth and fact embedded in societal life (in our *Lebensform*, as Wittgenstein would say; in our "paradigms," as Kuhn would say), but they are also historicized, made hostage to variable and diverse convictions, never fixed criterially but only consensually, hardly more than tacitly or tolerantly implicit in the fluency of societal life. In that sense, the intelligible world is a construction answering to our inquiries; the independent world, a construction answering to our ontic posits relative to the other. Ultimately, they are one and the same.

I do not say that that is all there is to it: that, as the occasional Hegelian extravagance has it, what is is simply what ought to be, that what appears (through history) is (in its own secret way) what the world ineluctably is. But Hegel was surely right to suppose that whatever we posit as true or right, in the second-order sense, cannot fail to be projected from our first-order practices. We begin, we must begin, with our customary practice, whatever its persuasion: our best norms can never be derived in any straightforward way from that. Wittgenstein barely notices the historical drift of our practices, though, after all is said and done, he does take notice: his traditionalist soul turns away from history, though not from social construction—hence, not entirely from change. Kuhn, however, was a frank historicist. It is the deeper meaning of his shallower philosophy that finally brings him and Wittgenstein together within the interpreted clearing of the French Revolution. That is what is now risked again at the end of our century.

Late-twentieth-century thought is, by and large, the continuation of eighteenth-century thought irrelevantly distracted by nineteenth-century speculations about historicism and constructivism.

If you grasp all this, you grasp as well that history is blind. To say the concept of fact is the concept of a social construction subject to the contingencies of historical experience is not to suppose that we ever learn, by history, what fact is. We learn only, retrospectively, that whatever we provisionally posit as the marks of fact will be forever less than what will be needed thereafter, at some later turn of history. Both truth and reality are criterially inoperative; they are no more than what we construct, epistemically, as the systematic fit between language and the world on the strength of our current conceptual scheme. We cannot exit from that scheme, any more than we can exit from language—any more than we can find our true nature buried in whatever, within that scheme, we judge our nature to be. We cannot escape our worlded language or our languaged world. You may think we can; but the immense labor that opens with Galileo and Descartes and closes with Hegel identifies the forms of skepticism we must avoid if we are not to make a hopeless muddle of the human condition. That is what we must retrieve. If you mean to argue otherwise, you must prepare an alternative account of the history of the entire theory of knowledge from the early seventeenth century to the early nineteenth century. Ignorance of our lore is no excuse.

Our thought, our reason, our science, and our sense of reality and ourselves are grounded in a conceptual framework whose boundaries we cannot finally fathom. Through history, we begin to see how parts of our conceptual scheme may be beneficially altered—enlarged, adjusted, replaced, as new discoveries and new problems require. The paradoxes of classical mechanics, for instance, dawned only in the twentieth century: all the fixities of inductive reasoning were threatened by a stroke by that discovery. On that account, physics needed to revise its sense of fact. The postmodernists pretend there are no such difficulties, but there are. We improvise as we can, but we must forever improvise. Physics is no different from law and politics: for example, regarding whatever may prove to be justice in the matter of abortion or in the way of respecting multicultural values. We are forever forced by the puzzles of a dawning history to concede questions akin to Kuhn's.

We know that our picture of the facts must go askew from time to time, because we are continually confronted by small-scale epistemic crises that never arose before. The facts about X-rays, for instance, began to dawn when the phenomena their admission eventually collected and reinterpreted had produced sufficient conceptual noise *ante*, affecting the rest of our physics, that we could no longer marginalize them as minor failings in the precision with which we studied other phenomena. The discrepancies—the break in the fluency of our standard explanations—

obliged us to change our picture of the facts and, more profoundly, our picture of how we ever come to know the facts. Now, that is pure Kuhn: a form of pragmatism, I should say, that forces even the stolid pragmatism of Wittgenstein's *Investigations* to make good sense well beyond what Wittgenstein would ever have admitted. But none of that could ever have surfaced were it not for the post-Kantians' reflection on the meaning of the French Revolution! There's a conceptual leap for you. It is in that sense alone that we can speak of the future of fact.

PRAGMATISM

Did you know that there is no possible criterial or algorithmic basis for fixing reference, or the reidentifiability of whatever has been referred to, in natural-language discourse? We have only informal, heuristic, rule-of-thumb solutions. If that is so, then, interestingly, there cannot be a computational model of the human mind (as opposed to artificial intelligence simulations); a fortiori, there cannot be an algorithmic rule for fact. Facts cannot be discerned, in the second-order sense, in any other way than in accord with the collective tolerance of our viable practices.

Facts are not historicized, any more than truth is; to say they are produces intolerable paradox. But determining what the facts are, like determining what is true, is indeed subject to the vagaries of history. Small wonder that truth and fact have no methodological function: we deal only with assigning truth values, with fixing what we believe to be

true—that is, the counters of the intelligible world. Lacking privilege and fixity, there is no other way to proceed.

In this sense, pragmatism is the doctrine of the hour: not by way of first-order assurances of what merely works, but of second-order conjectures regarding what might favor the first-order results that meet our needs. Some think that that is a vulgar doctrine, but it is not. (It was, I admit, originally mismanaged by William James and therefore trounced by Bertrand Russell—the same Russell, I remind you, who deftly misled Wittgenstein for a very short season. Russell eventually relented, and James improved his formulation. And the collapse of objectivism proved inevitable.)

It would not be appropriate, here, to pursue the technical details of the problem of reference—or predication, for that matter, or the problem of context regarding either, or the meaning of meaning. I ask you only to bear in mind that the inherent informality of fact and objectivity is of a piece with these more familiar notions. The objectivists—those, roughly speaking, who believe in the criterial accessibility of the correspondence between propositions and facts—are obliged to neutralize the effect of all these difficulties. They have done so in the most extraordinary way: regarding reference, for instance, they simply insinuate that predication under suitable constraints can do all the work of reference. Leibniz had already glimpsed the impossibility of proceeding thus, but the objectivists have either never addressed Leibniz's problem (W. V.

Quine, for instance), or if they have they have done so by embracing Platonism (Russell, for instance). Platonism, however, has never been shown (can never be shown) to be humanly accessible.

Now, if reference and predication are inherently informal—hence, also, the fixity of context, meaning, individuation, reidentification, evidence, confirmation, legitimation—then it is quite impossible that fact and objectivity should elude the same conceptual traps. Only a constructivist picture of objective inquiry could possibly work: only the admission that our second-order conjectures are historicized in the same way our first-order beliefs are. But that is hardly a philosophical—or scientific—disaster.

Let me, for just a bit, pursue the advantage of what I am now saying. Strange as it may seem, we never fix the referents of our discourse, or, perhaps better, we fix them in a story-relative way. I say to you, for instance, that I am referring to the same man I mentioned a moment ago, but, for the life of me, I cannot pick him out uniquely from all the things (or creatures) in the universe that anyone might have mentioned. I never have to, of course; I fall back on the consensual fluency of ordinary discourse. You understand that I am not referring to some twin Earth in a distant galaxy that might falsify a claim of mine about a unique feature of the man I am now referring to. (This is a hothouse matter, I do not deny, but it is pertinent to the fate of fact nevertheless.)

When I refer, in a passing moment, to Pope John Paul, how do you know whether I am referring to the first or the second John Paul? Under suitably ephemeral conditions, you do not—and it does not matter. When it does, you appeal to context or to distinctive properties under the constraint of context. But how do you know how to fix the right context? You say that you do that under the constraints of an even more inclusive context! But if you think that the universe is the context of all contexts—hence that you cannot make truth claims about that (but only, as we say, about what falls within the universe, which, trivially, is everything)—you see that you must rely on something more immediate and incomparably more modest to ensure referential success at all. I say, as you may guess, that discourse always works like that. Referential and predicative success is never more than consensual, never criterial, always subject to the historical drift and informality of practice. Wittgenstein's *Investigations*, I am suggesting, gives us the slimmest picture of how that works: criteria, truth claims, conversational exchange all come to rest in our "form of life." So seen, Kuhn clarifies the additional need to change, from time to time, our paradigms, our exemplars, our rules of thumb, theories, conceptual schemes, logics, notions of truth and reality and fact and objectivity.

There is where the puzzlement arises. Everyone is bound to wonder how we could possibly change what, in second-order terms, we regard as the marks of true theory or genuine fact. Where are the grounds for such revisions? they ask. The answer is simplicity itself: they are in the same *lebensformlich* practices on which first-order truth claims rest; there are no privileged resources to fall back on. When we change our orientation—say, from Aristotle to Galileo, on pendulums; or from Priestley to Lavoisier, on oxygen—we change our picture of a large part of the universe, all the while we eat and sleep and chatter to one another as we always have. We cannot change our theory of the pendulum, Kuhn says, without changing our picture of objective fact. (Priestley and Lavoisier "lived in different worlds," remember.) Alternatively, I should say, without changing ourselves—our cognitive capacities. What Kuhn says here is profoundly true, but it baffled him as well as his readers. There is reason to believe he never got the hang of what he himself said! But the answer is already glimpsed in Wittgenstein, who never addressed Kuhn's puzzles.

We bring our discursive innovations under the receptive tolerance of collective practice. Where we depart too radically from established practice, communication breaks down. (One hears it said, for instance, that the Fauves had had a similar effect on the art world. Perhaps.) Where our conceptual innovations are deliberate but very grand, we must be patient in providing the mediating meanings of the change. We are perhaps (still) at such a point in making sense of quantum physics: we use quantum mathematics, but we are not entirely clear about the right relationship between quantum and classical physics—or, better, about what the quantum picture of the macroscopic world comes to.

We cannot leave things there, of course. What looked like fact in the space of classical mechanics cannot now be such, in the space of quantum physics—or so it seems. We live, apparently, "in a different [Kuhnian] world," but we are not clear about what that world is like. If you see that the change in objectivity and fact is a change in the intelligible world, not necessarily in the independent world—which we distinguish, you remember, as the epistemic and ontic faces of one and the same construction—then no paradox need arise, though we change our constructions as we must. Our sense of fact and reality remains grounded as before in our form of life: what we change are the explicit conceptions we choose to honor within that space, which, then, gain their aptness and fluency by being similarly grounded.

There is no paradox there. The last wrinkle to admit is that all this takes place within the drift of history. If you think that human selves (and entire societies) are socially constituted—say, by the historically changing processes of enculturation (in learning a first language, as infants, at different stages in a society's history)—then you can imagine that, over a span of time, innumerable changes in conceptual imagination will occur without their being tethered to any truly large changes like those involved in adopting the theory of the pendulum. The spread of our informational technologies, for instance, has surely changed our moral and political possibilities, not merely local values but the conditions of moral objectivity itself.

History remains blind, as I say, but, at different stages in the historical process, we reconsider (differently) how the world appeared before—to the denizens of an earlier world. Foucault's genealogies are the most familiar exemplars of such retrospective labors. They are, as I have been hinting, Nietzscheanized versions of the Hegelian vision. They bring in their wake a final paradox affecting fact. If you look at Foucault's work, you will see that the concept of truth is used equivocally: in the double sense of tracing the truth about genealogical change itself, from one paradigm (let us say) to another, and of fixing the sense of truth, now or in some imagined past ("archaeologically," as Foucault says), at which inquiry proceeds in its ordinary synchronic way.

In the objectivist's idiom, they would produce insurmountable paradox; fact and objectivity would become instantly incoherent. But if objectivism is no longer defensible, then we need to understand Kuhn's and Foucault's innovations more congenially. The solution is straightforward enough. Truth-bearing discourse is always synchronic (or benignly diachronic within the conceptual system that we assume to be in place). It is never construed historically, that is, as changing, epistemically, in the very process of use.

Our epistemic practices change, it is true; but we identify them, in second-order terms, always synchronically. The "system" of fact that might have been in place in the seventeenth century was, according to Foucault, replaced by another "regime" of truth in the eighteenth century—which Foucault duly reports in the second half of the twentieth. That is, he reports it in accord with the implicit *episteme* in which he himself works. He realizes, of course, as we must as well, that, in time, his own would-be *episteme* will be genealogically reconstructed from the vantage of an even later and (then) more inclusive frame of reference. We theorize systematically (and inclusively) at the historical moment we inhabit: we reconstruct the facts of the historical past from that present vantage; in time, as we realize, that same construction will be reconstructed from another vantage that will also take the inclusive universe for its space and will therefore diminish the topical space of every prior such labor. In that way, paradox is avoided, but realism remains constructive.

Any other scheme would produce unwanted paradox. To treat truth or fact historically—in a historicized way—would signify that truth (or fact) would change with history. The world may change, but truth and fact cannot (be seen to) change: not because the world has a changeless structure (as Aristotle holds) but because the logic of the notions of truth and fact make sense only timelessly.

I acknowledge that we are quite unable to fix truth timelessly. But we need not bother to try, for truth and fact are never criterially operative. They play only a connecting role in our theory of science and reality. In practice, we always fall back on the assignment of truth values and on beliefs (believings-true). Fact is problematic, only because canonical theories of fact are impossible to defend in direct cognitive terms. But theory is itself a form of practice fitting the practice of inquiry, and there, there are no deep difficulties about fact in the second-order sense. That is, there are no difficulties if we agree to abandon the old canons of objectivity and neutrality. Still, you know as well as I that the champions of professional turf will never yield gracefully.

Reference

Kuhn, Thomas. [1962] 1970. *The Structure of Scientific Revolutions*. Enl. ed. Chicago: University of Chicago Press.

ANNALS, *AAPSS*, **560**, November 1998

Factual Fissures:
Claims and Contexts

By MICHAEL HERZFELD

ABSTRACT: Claims of factuality are assertions that rest on effective performance. What constitutes a good performance may vary culturally and according to social context. A comparative perspective, moreover, shows that distinctions between fact and judgment may not be universally clear and may themselves be culturally determined, but that inserting our own claims to factual precision into that perspective strengthens rather than weakens them because it broadens the empirical basis of assessment.

Michael Herzfeld is professor of anthropology at Harvard University; he previously taught at Vassar College and Indiana University, Bloomington. His seven books include The Poetics of Manhood: Contest and Identity in a Cretan Mountain Village *(1985);* Anthropology Through the Looking-Glass: Critical Ethnography in the Margins of Europe *(1987); and* Cultural Intimacy: Social Poetics in the Nation-State *(1997). Awarded the J. I. Staley Prize of the School of American Research in 1994, he has served as editor of* American Ethnologist *(1994-98).*

S AYING that something is a fact is like saying that it is self-evident. The listener is asked to suspend disbelief. Yet the claim of factuality is itself not subject to tests of factuality. To say that "this *is* a fact" is the simplest kind of what J. L. Austin (1962) dubbed a "performative utterance," that is, a kind of utterance that creates meaning instead of merely reporting or stating it. Moreover, as Austin implied, in the social world there is in effect no *other* kind of utterance: everything we say gets its meaning through the effects that it produces on the sensible world. These effects may include belief or at least acceptance of what has just been said, or they may actively *constitute* the truth (as in a judge's verdict of not guilty, which may not reflect what actually happened since one is not guilty until proven innocent). Thus facts *are* made up. And that *is* a fact.

Now read what I have just written. You will see that virtually everything there is declarative. I have made what passes for a statement. By ironizing the paragraph, however, I have also conducted a rather self-conscious kind of performance. I have—implicitly but unmistakably—raised questions about the good faith of my own words. But perhaps, in so doing, I have been demonstrating another kind of good faith, one that does not permit me to let a potentially misleading declaration pass. But is faith really the issue?

Anthropologists have long contended that it is impossible to make authoritative statements about psychological inner states such as belief.

Most notably, Rodney Needham (1972) has argued that statements to the effect that a people believes in something fail to persuade because they generalize from the psychological state of one individual to the assumed complicity of the tribe; because even the thoughts of the individual are known to us only through their externalization as utterances, which are indeed performances and as such are social rather than psychological phenomena; and because the act of translation from one culture or language to another cannot fully convey the etymological associations of a word like "belief" and must therefore lose much of the largely unspoken penumbra of meaning that such a word possesses for its users.

Even those who have argued for a recognition of internal psychological states in the way that anthropologists describe social and cultural life now almost always recognize this difficulty. They may examine such states as representations. Following Cohen (1994), who has made an especially strong case for looking at novels in this regard, I have argued that the critical reaction to novels marks the range of culturally acceptable representation in a particularly accessible way (Herzfeld 1997b). This is an interesting problem for anthropologists, who, it seems, can represent empathy only by using a novelistic mode of description that in effect invites readers to suspend disbelief (see Leavitt 1996)—a dramatically double-edged illustration of the extent to which our willingness to acknowledge or deny factuality always ultimately rests on conventions associated with belief. Indeed, some anthropologists have simply confined themselves to describing native psychologies, that is, the social conventions governing the description, in various cultures, of states of mind (Heelas and Lock 1981; Rosen 1995).

This is important because, as my opening paragraph shows, claims of factuality depend on the presupposition of belief. (If a person asserts a fact in which that individual does not believe, what status could I possibly accord it?) Such claims are therefore irreducible to empirical demonstration independent of either the social contexts in which they are made or the ultimately inaccessible minds of the social actors who make them. This is what Giambattista Vico (1744) meant by his famous dictum that "the truth is constructed." But if fact is indeed—in fact—constructed (*factum*), as even its etymology tells us, why do we so strenuously resist that insight?

There are, I suggest, two fundamental reasons. One has to do with the inert logical properties of classification; the other is a matter of political activity. In this brief essay, I shall suggest that anthropologists can help explain that resistance. But the relative exclusion of anthropologists from debates about current affairs may itself be diagnostic of both these basic causes of the current popular understanding of what makes a fact.

The idea of an ethnographic description of intellectual life in the late twentieth-century industrial world is itself often seen as a contradiction in terms, despite the vigorous defense of such an approach by Geertz (1984, 155). As Andrew Lass (1997, 722-23) so clearly puts it, "It is anthropology's aim to make of the particular a case of generalized importance, that is, to come up with *theories of practice*. The study of cultural production, specifically the study of European conceptual thought, provides it with the opportunity to gain insight into the *practice of theory*" (italics in original). Anthropologists are no longer inclined to confine their attention to the tribal peoples of the world or, at most, to extend their purview only to peasants who live in the margins of industrial states. The popular view of what anthropologists do, however, has not caught up with this new reality. Their increasingly common refusal to play their stereotypical role as explorers of the exotic and the marginal frequently draws into the open the racist line between "them" and "us," the studiable and the studying, that so often lurks in the most liberal discourse.

Conversely, even within anthropology, the suggestion that peasants and hunter-gatherers may develop their own varieties of social theory sometimes provokes considerable irritation. I am tempted to attribute that reaction to the fear of seeing a professional mystique demystified. So we should not be surprised that the larger world of political pundits and media experts should find the idea of becoming the subjects of ethnographic analysis to be discomfiting in the extreme. It violates a deeply held conviction in the commonsense basis of all claims to factuality. More technically, but perhaps more revealingly, it violates a key principle of the way members of Western industrial societies classify the world.

This is crucial to understanding the predicament of fact for the two reasons already mentioned. Let me detail each reason with some care. The first concerns the relationship between factuality and classification itself. When we understand that decisions as to whether something is a fact or not depend on a prior cultural convention—classification—we also see why the idea of a factual bedrock is illusory. If common sense consists, as Mary Douglas (1975, 281-83) has argued, in the arbitrary system of classification peculiar to a given society, and if all claims to factual status are predicated on a notion of common sense, the distinction between fact and fiction ceases to be one of ultimate reality and becomes instead a question of how reality is construed. Common sense is like the Holy Roman Empire, which was, as Voltaire famously pointed out, "neither holy, nor Roman, nor an empire" (1773, lxx). For its part, what people call common sense is neither common to all other cultures nor particularly sensible from the perspective of most of them. Even within "our culture"—itself a notoriously preemptive notion (see Handler 1985)—disputes that some regard as questions of fact, others treat as merely questions of belief, as though factuality were, in some ultimate fashion, independent of belief. The solution proposed by F. Allan Hanson (1979)—in effect, to accept the statement that "God has a body" as true for those who believe it—may not satisfy those of scientistic bent, but it does at least demon-

strate the practical difficulty of trying to dispense with questions of belief altogether. That we cannot accurately describe or define belief does not mean that we should simply discount its role in calibrating individuals' assessments of factuality to the social phenomenon of collective representation.

The second factor that makes the issue of classification so important is that, properly pursued, it forces us to break with the common assumption that "we" possess a subtle knowledge of reality itself, whereas the peoples studied by anthropologists still live in a benighted world dominated by strange belief systems and mediated by arcane symbolism—amusing and perhaps even interesting for academic purposes but possessing no value to the real world of today. Anthropology has itself contributed to this misapprehension. Invented in the context of the colonial project, of which it was a part, it has tended to represent its object as the remnants of a distant time in the history of human evolution; ironically, this bias flourished, as Fabian (1983, 33) notes, because practitioners were afraid "that their reports might otherwise be disqualified as poetry, fiction, or political propaganda"—in other words, as lacking in factuality.

But this is an outdated view of anthropology, and it should be forcefully resisted: the idea that "we" are more rational and have a better grasp of fact is itself a reflection of our classification of humanity. As such, it must take its place among the vast array of such classifications, of which no one system is either more or less "rational," whether it be Linnaeus's natural history or Nuer classifications of the social order; all, our own included, share the key feature of asserting the moral superiority of insiders over the rest of the world. Indeed, if we examine the segment of Linnaeus's taxonomy that specifically classifies human beings, we rapidly discover that it has a great deal to do with prejudices about the alleged capacities of the world's peoples to exercise self-discipline as revealed in their type of clothing, and very little to do with science as we now understand it.[1]

We can take this insight right into the heart of the project called modernity, for taxonomy is central to what Weber saw as the ultimately modernist and rationalist project: bureaucracy. Don Handelman (1981) has argued that all bureaucracy should be studied as a form of operationalized classification. Mary Douglas, whose justly famous *Purity and Danger* (1966) did so much to expose the workings of taxonomy in everyday life, derived her analysis from a substantial range of apparently obscure topics from the Abominations of Leviticus to the taboos of African and other non-Western peoples. But she has also applied these insights to modern institutional decision making (Douglas 1986). Her work has inspired others to see in modern institutional relations and practices the world over some of the same taxonomic principles she identified in Leviticus (see French 1995; Herzfeld 1992a; Malkki 1995).

In all these works it becomes clear that symbolism is not some arcane miasma hanging over the benighted heathen. What anthropologists have studied in far-flung corners of the world they can also study at home: the rational itself is a system of symbols, and the premise of factuality ultimately depends on the conventions governing the expression of belief. These conventions are grounded in modes of classification, which are cultural and therefore technically arbitrary. That may be relatively inconsequential when we are trying to establish why some people view pork as unclean, for example (although it is a highly serious matter for them). But such attitudes can become materially much more consequential when they are relocated to the temporal sphere; the trick is to recognize the logical principle as the same in each case.

Note, for instance, the Balkan or British bureaucrat's contempt for Gypsies as "matter out of place" because they do not have a fixed address and thus violate the cartographic sensibility of the deskbound (see Okely 1987); the Canadian authorities' wartime rejection of Jewish refugees on the grounds that a country defining itself as frontier farmland did not want representatives of the urban morass (Abella and Troper 1982, 54-55); or the extraordinary plight of a stateless Iranian now stranded for literally two decades in Charles de Gaulle Airport in Paris for want of papers that would equip him with a "real" identity.[2] What does not fit in does not "exist" and may be consigned to perdition with impunity.

Facts are the external shell of classifications. They are brought into being by fiat—religious dogma, educational inculcation, or bureaucratic intransigence. Arguing that facts do not exist does not help and indeed is self-contradictory (it is a factual statement). But asking about what it means to recognize their existence is another matter. The ontology of facts—whatever is encapsulated in those deceptively short words "be" and "exist"—cannot be separated from questions of power and control.

Neither infinite regress nor scientistic assertion offers much purchase on experience. (They are also very much alike in their solipsistic self-satisfaction, although each usually denies any resemblance to the other.) Infinite regress manifestly ducks the key questions. What of its alleged opposite, scientistic reductionism? A surprising amount of science fares very badly as soon as it is subjected to its own criteria of validity. The real gauge of its success is public acclaim, not getting results. In economics, for example, some failures have been catastrophic. Yet failure does not seem to have discredited economists any more than it has discredited meteorologists, diviners, or even the prophets of doomsday in their respective spheres of expertise. Indeed, in a performative view of the world, one might argue that in any society a high rate of unpunished failure is perhaps the clearest mark—and thus also one of the most potent sources—of real power.

If prediction entails cosmological notions about chance, it thus certainly need not succeed particularly often. Fact, too, may falter, and its weaknesses may similarly confirm its basic unchallengeability. When Garry Wills (1978, 341-42) demonstrated that no signatory to the U.S. Declaration of Independence actually signed it on 4 July and that it was not signed by all the signatories on any one occasion at all, he revealed a fissure between the signifiers—John Trumbull's painting of the signing among them—and the signified (a unified history with a single point of origin). And this, for all that it seems consequential in that it challenges a national myth, has not upset the annual Fourth of July celebrations in the least. On the contrary, through performance, they constantly re-create the factuality of a myth.

Fact has semiotic properties; it is itself a signifier. If the signifier—here the documentary evidence of a painting and numerous texts—can be used to perform reality to such a successful degree, it is because its outer form—a date—is so stable. By that token, we should be especially suspicious of the more positivized forms of factual representation: statistics, maps, photographs, charts of various kinds, dictionaries, and government records. We do not have to ask questions of belief and motive (although contemporary attributions of motive are always interesting) to identify the particular kind of semiotic sleight-of-hand by which facts are invested with a relatively unimpeachable authority. To put the matter in more anthropological terms, these representational devices are especially effective tools of classification, generating versions of common sense that should be the precise object of ethnographic investigation—that is, an investigation into both their taxonomic properties (the inert aspect) and the uses to which those properties are put (the political dimension).

Some work along these lines has already proved highly revealing. Although he was not an anthropologist and did not write in particular theoretical terms, H. R. Wilkinson, in a work he called an "ethnographic cartography" of the Balkans (1951), effectively deconstructed map-based claims about ethnic boundaries. In a similar but more directly anthropological vein, Jacqueline Urla (1993) has tackled the uses of statistical data in the construction of Basque identity. The critical analysis of scientistic forms of representation shows how contingent the very idea of factuality usually is.

Note again that I am not arguing here that there is no such thing as a fact. Such a claim is logically self-defeating, since it relies on ontological certainty (implied in the word "is") to refute the very possibility of such certainty. Nor am I suggesting that ethnographic writing is a form of fictional writing indistinguishable from the novel. It is useful, as I have argued (1997b, 23), to preserve the distinction between ethnographic and novelistic writing not because the division between them precisely reproduces an empirically verifiable distinction between fact and fiction but because the pragmatic purposes respectively served by these two genres are significantly different from each other. One consequence of that difference, moreover, is that novelists usually leave implicit those details of ethnographic exegesis that the eth-

nographer feels obliged to spell out (Bateson 1936, 1).[3]

If today some anthropologists appear more interested in emphasizing the kinship of ethnography with fiction or travel writing, one should ask, in pursuance of a serious (as opposed to self-indulgent) attempt at reflexivity, why they find it useful to point up this superficially rather disreputable relationship. Again, I see little profit in arguing about whether ethnography should be considered a form of fictional representation; its practitioners declare its intentions to be otherwise and have never argued—in contrast to fictional writers—that its realism is a form of verbal trompe l'oeil. That it possesses common ground with fiction—as, for example, does historical writing—does not mean that it must share the ontology of fiction; and in practice a substantive difference does separate the two genres, however "blurred" (Geertz 1984, 19-35) they may now be. What we must always remember, however, is that this insight is no less provisional than the epistemological and institutional configurations that currently make it so. "All is flux"—but flux has a temporal ontology.

There is thus considerable profit to be had in training the ethnographic gaze on fact construction itself, viewing it, in accordance with current practice, as a process. That is, in effect, what Wills did with the Declaration of Independence. Those who persist in reading my argument as a rejection of the very notion of fact will respond by pointing out that Wills simply displaced one piece of supposedly well established but actually flawed piece of knowledge with a better one—that he was still committed, in short, to a realist notion of factual precision. That objection simply misses the point, which is not to deny the existence of factuality but to historicize its ontology by asking how it comes into being—a different procedure altogether.

Vico long ago understood the difference. The irony is that the subsequent fate of Vico's ideas—which were either held up as the precursor of a powerfully literalist form of European nationalism or rejected as foolishly subjectivist—illustrates his own argument extraordinarily well: that, while humans indeed construct the facts of their past, the best defense against the potential for total regress and anarchy that this insight threatens to unleash remains a full recognition of the power to corrode knowledge posed by malicious gossip, totalitarian authority, and the march of time toward oblivion. The issue is one of accountability: recalling the provisionality of all knowledge is the only responsible way of guaranteeing its integrity.

This is clearly discomfiting to many scholars and writers. It is especially galling to those who have identified their interests with repressive sources of power. (Vico specifically noted the parallel between nationalistic and scholarly forms of vanity.[4]) Thus, for example, the Greek colonels who came to power in 1967 sought to censor literature through a literal-minded edict that required all book titles to reflect the contents precisely. The regime's principal critics responded by publishing a set of one poem and 17 satirical stories under the title *Eighteen Texts*.[5] This clever move beautifully illustrates Vico's thesis that crass literalness is a form of self-deception exactly parallel to pretensions of absolute power since both literalism and tyranny blind their bearers to the degree to which they depend on the experienced world of ordinary people and things.

So the argument is decidedly not a rejection of facts. It is, rather, a cautionary tale about the dangers of treating facts as something other than representations—a common instance of the fallacy of misplaced concreteness. I follow Vico in proposing that those who appeal to the authority of preconstituted fact are, ironically, unrealistic. Their claims are no less rhetorical than what they seek to refute, and their success may be measured precisely as the degree to which they have succeeded in obscuring or disguising the historical processes through which the facts (and their expression in language) have come into being.

The rhetoric of factuality may vary considerably in scope and style. One scientistic idiom that serves the interests of totalitarian regimes, nationalistic ideologies, and predatory politics dismisses ethnographic data as trivial or anecdotal—trivial when it concerns populations deemed unimportant by those in power, anecdotal when it concerns those who actually wield the power. Those who dismiss as unscientific, for example, the data of an ethnographer who relies on coffeehouse gossip also thereby reproduce their own rhetoric of science—a science no less popularized than the coffeehouse data.[6]

In other words, they do exactly what they claim the ethnographer is doing: they judge the reliability of data in terms of everyday categories and criteria masquerading as scholarly ones. Now, there would be nothing objectionable in that procedure were it evenhanded. I am quite prepared to dissolve the scientific-everyday distinction. But our critics will have none of it—and wisely so, from their point of view, for it exposes their own vaunted rationality as itself a cultural construction.

Instead, they dismiss the data as atypical. In debates about the alleged mistreatment of ethnic minorities in Greece, for example, one often hears nationalist claims that these groups are too small to be significant or that they are treated better in Greece than are minorities, including the Greeks, in other Balkan lands. We might even agree about the latter argument. But can one logically defend the purported absence of ethnic minorities by saying that they are numerically few? Who decides the proportional size at which we can recognize a group of people as typical or significant? And what is unrepresentative or "mere" about gossip and anecdotes, given that these report the very fabric of the taken-for-granted, made palpable in the breach (and repeatedly made palpable by the frequency of the gossip)? It is not, then, only in the use of grand statistical analyses that we find the signifiers of factuality to be deftly manipulated. The same process takes place, far more pervasively and thus far more significantly, in the unreflexive everyday uses of the language of certainty: "it's typical," "that's a fact,"

"they all do it," "they are only a handful in number." The informality of this discourse ensures its seepage into the vast stratum of submerged knowledge far more effectively than any deliberate propaganda. And then it is easy for those who know the more sophisticated cant of scientific precision to add legitimacy through the skilled use of an appropriate rhetoric of science.

Those anthropologists who work with Third World peoples, groups that are often politically and economically marginalized within their own encompassing nation-state structures, encounter a large-scale version of this attitude: that tribal populations have nothing to do with modernity, so that studying them is a luxury that should not be allowed to interfere with the march of development (see Ferguson 1990). Those of us who work in the industrialized West, however, often encounter the converse objection: when we do turn our ethnographic techniques loose in the laboratory or the business office, our accounts are seen as necessarily unserious in relation to the scale and importance of the culture on which we work. We are, in short, accused of trivializing the business of modernity by daring to compare it to exotic savagery.

Yet there is special pleading here. Such critics want to be seen as representing "their" cultures; so why should they fear the ethnographer's scrutiny? That they dislike the analytic attention suddenly paid to their management of factuality may be understandable. On the other hand, they can hardly respond that the views and actions they find thus described are atypical. To do so would be to undermine their own authority to speak for "their" cultures.

What clearly galls these critics is to be treated "like natives." But anthropology can hardly make good on its stated intentions of rebutting racism unless it also repudiates its own colonialist underpinnings, and that necessarily entails treating global and local elites as grist for the ethnographic mill—as no less appropriately subjected to the interrogatory stare of anthropological research than were the "natives" of yore. Today, for example, anthropologists have increasingly begun to study wealthy and sophisticated elites with views on the power of inherited character—the "dynastic uncanny" (Marcus 1992, 173-87)—no less cosmological than similar phenomena reported by Malinowski or Evans-Pritchard. Ethnographic accounts of science itself, as well as of such scholarly pursuits as archaeology and history, have proliferated. As a result, factuality in turn looks more and more vulnerably contingent. Factuality merges with authenticity, and the assessment of authenticity increasingly smacks of arbitrary judgmentalism.

Questions of judgment may themselves not be claimed as matters of fact, and the political and ideological criteria on which they rest are sometimes openly admitted. Questions of authenticity, on the other hand, are a very different matter: so much is at stake that, for example, Andalusians of today may tell an anthropologist who has known their community for several decades that what she remembers of their grandparents' culture is not authentic—because it had not yet undergone the "purification" from Castilian elements that Andalusian separatism now requires (Collier 1997, 207-12). Other people, for similar reasons, insist on defining what is authentic in their culture in highly specific terms, in order to create forms of resistance to a dominant population (see Jackson 1995). Midway between these positions come assessments of ability, from the politically overdetermined assessments of "talent" among music students (Kingsbury 1984) to crudely scientistic measures of "intelligence" (see Gould 1996).

What this list makes apparent is that the distinction between judgments of taste and questions of fact is not absolute but forms a continuum embedded in social realities. Issues that may appear to some as a matter of aesthetic judgment will strike others as incontrovertibly about fact. In this context, questions about the status of minority populations, the origins of national culture, or the authenticity of cultural emblems are allowed as little ambiguity, as little interpretative space, as a railroad schedule.

Nowhere is the contingency of fact more apparent, or more strenuously denied, than in the management of the past. Here, we must address at least two layers of obfuscation. Not only is there the relatively obvious notion that claims of factuality are filtered through political interests; there is also the realization, much more hardly won, that fact in Western, literate, industrial society is no less subject to the relativity of political allegiance than it is in so-called tribal societies—the latter simply have different views about the necessity of concealing the social basis of fact building.

That is what Henry Kingsbury (1984) tried to demonstrate in his analysis of the concept of talent in a New England conservatory. It might be argued, however, that he was dealing with a matter of "the judgment of taste" (Bourdieu 1984) that had very little to do with fact at all—that, indeed, his analysis shows how important it is to distinguish between fact and judgment. But this, once again, would miss the point. The filtering of news stories through our own highly factionalized media is as subject to the imperatives of allegiance as are the "tribal" narratives underlying some forms of Arab nationalism, for example, a discourse in which the very possibility of a truth beyond the social is denied by all the contesting factions even while, and indeed because, they consider it imperative to denounce each other as liars (see Shryock 1997, 312-14). I have found in provincial Greece, for example, that the factual reporting of nationally significant events—notably, the government's long-delayed attempt to redistribute church-owned lands among the peasantry—varied significantly according to the political allegiance of particular newspapers (Herzfeld 1992b). This was a clear instance of the social refraction of fact, no less specifiable than the refraction of supernatural or ideological entities through the perceived divisions of the social world.[7] Uncontested history is only possible under totalitarian rule.

In exploring the relationship between fact and fiction in a contemporary novelist whose preferred genre is the realist historical novel and who often marvels at the stranger-than-fiction quality of real life, I have suggested (Herzfeld 1997b) that the blurred quality of the distinction reflects the merging of different ideas about what is important: the normative cultural detail in the ethnography, the recognition of common human problems in the novel. As I have noted earlier, it is useful to keep the distinction between ethnography and novel in mind if only because we bring different criteria of veracity to bear on each. Lest readers also be tempted to insist on a distinction between scholarly writing and small-town newspaper reporting on the grounds that the latter is more obviously motivated by political interest, let me reply that this obviousness is the only difference. Besides, some famous recent scholarly debates have no less clearly betrayed their grounding in the politics of identity. Consider, for example, the argument between Obeyesekere (1992) and Sahlins (1995) on what Captain Cook's death really meant to the Hawai'ians or between Bernal (1987) and Lefkowitz (1995) on where ancient Greek culture originated. The local anger vented against the novelist about whom I was writing, Andreas Nenedakis, partly arose from his incorporation into his historical novels of newspaper clippings from the very town in Greece in which I conducted the research on media treatment of the church property debate: such touches of realism blurred the lines between fiction and fact and upset the living kin of recognizable characters. This provincial Greek tempest reflects larger—even global—developments. The genres are *all* blurred today; all are refracted through a restless social actuality. It becomes increasingly difficult to sustain the idea that facts exist independently of the social world.

Scientistic diehards will insist that there is a difference—and that, with the advantages of science on our side, we can tell that difference—between fact and fiction; and they will contend that not all writers are motivated by the politics of identity. But such assertions fail on the objectors' own criteria: they are not evidence but simple declarations of belief.

But what, in the end, is wrong with that? How is it more objective to ignore the grounding of factuality in collective representations of belief—in the cosmology of scientism, an idea that seems less of an oxymoron when it is placed in the broader perspective of a comparative ethnology? To be factual logically means to recognize the contextual character of fact. Moreover, that comparative perspective reminds us that those exotic peoples who are supposedly still in thrall to their own strange and wonderful beliefs manage to live effectively in their world. Does this not then suggest that they, too, possess ways of provisionally positing a distinction between fact and fiction, ways that work in their experiential universes as well as our similar distinctions work for us in ours? If we shrug our shoulders and say they were merely lucky, what does this say about the

alleged freedom from bias, cosmological dogma, and social context of our own notions of rationality? And what future does it augur for fact? In a scientistic world, factuality would itself cease to be open to question, and fact, deprived of its past, would also have lost its future.

Notes

1. For a more detailed discussion of the Linnaean schema and its implications, especially with regard to the symbolism of clothing, see Herzfeld 1987, 96-101.

2. A refugee, he was robbed of his papers; "as he had no official documents, there was no country to which he could be deported" (Patton 1998).

3. The anthropologist and poet Michael Jackson has made a very similar observation to me (personal communication; see also Herzfeld 1997b, 24).

4. On the implications of Vico's insight here, see Herzfeld 1987, 189-90.

5. See Van Dyck 1997, 19-20, for the colonels' treatment of *Eighteen Texts*, and passim for an outstanding account of their horror of figurative language in general.

6. Note that the anthropologists' use of pseudonyms to protect their informants sometimes earns them the charge of substituting fiction for science and that this brand of scientism often supports the literalizing claims of nationalist ideology (see also Herzfeld 1997a, 171-72).

7. On this use of "refraction," see Evans-Pritchard 1956, 121, 196.

References

Abella, Irving and Harold Troper. 1982. *None Is Too Many: Canada and the Jews of Europe, 1933-1948.* Toronto: Lester & Orpen Dennys.

Austin, J. L. 1962. *How to Do Things with Words.* Cambridge, MA: Harvard University Press.

Bateson, Gregory. 1936. *Naven: A Survey of the Problems Suggested by a Composite Picture of the Culture of a New*

Guinea Tribe Drawn from Three Points of View. New York: Cambridge University Press.

Bernal, Martin. 1987. *Black Athena: The Afroasiatic Roots of Classical Civilization*. New Brunswick, NJ: Rutgers University Press.

Bourdieu, Pierre. 1984. *Distinction: A Social Critique of the Judgement of Taste*. Trans. Richard Nice. Cambridge, MA: Harvard University Press.

Cohen, Anthony P. 1994. *Self Consciousness: An Alternative Anthropology of Identity*. New York: Routledge.

Collier, Jane Fishburne. 1987. *From Duty to Desire: Remaking Families in a Spanish Village*. Princeton, NJ: Princeton University Press.

Douglas, Mary. 1966. *Purity and Danger: An Analysis of Concepts of Pollution and Taboo*. London: Routledge & Kegan Paul.

———. 1975. *Implicit Meanings: Essays in Anthropology*. London: Routledge & Kegan Paul.

———. 1986. *How Institutions Think*. Syracuse, NY: Syracuse University Press.

Evans-Pritchard, E. E. 1956. *Nuer Religion*. Oxford: Clarendon Press.

Fabian, Johannes. 1983. *Time and the Other: How Anthropology Makes Its Object*. New York: Columbia University Press.

Ferguson, James. 1990. *The Anti-Politics Machine: "Development," Depoliticization, and Bureaucratic Power in Lesotho*. New York: Cambridge University Press.

French, Rebecca. 1995. *The Golden Yoke: The Legal Cosmology of Buddhist Tibet*. Ithaca, NY: Cornell University Press.

Geertz, Clifford. 1984. *Local Knowledge: Further Essays in Interpretive Anthropology*. New York: Basic Books.

Gould, Stephen Jay. 1996. *The Mismeasure of Man*. Rev. ed. New York: W. W. Norton.

Handelman, Don. 1981. Introduction: The Idea of Bureaucratic Organization. *Social Analysis* 9:5-23.

Handler, Richard. 1985. On Dialogue and Destructive Analysis: Problems in Narrating Nationalism and Identity. *Journal of Anthropological Research* 41:171-82.

Hanson, F. Allan. 1979. Does God Have a Body? Truth, Reality and Cultural Relativism. *Man* 14:515-29.

Heelas, Paul and Andrew Lock, eds. 1981. *Indigenous Psychologies: The Anthropology of the Self*. London: Academic Press.

Herzfeld, Michael. 1987. *Anthropology Through the Looking-Glass: Critical Ethnography in the Margins of Europe*. New York: Cambridge University Press.

———. 1992a. Segmentation and Politics in the European Nation-State: Making Sense of Political Events. In *Other Histories*, ed. Kirsten Hastrup. New York: Routledge.

———. 1992b. *The Social Production of Indifference: Exploring the Symbolic Roots of Western Bureaucracy*. Oxford: Berg.

———. 1997a. Anthropology and the Politics of Significance. *Social Analysis* 41:107-38.

———. 1997b. *Portrait of a Greek Imagination: An Ethnographic Biography of Andreas Nenedakis*. Chicago: University of Chicago Press.

Jackson, Jean E. 1995. Culture, Genuine and Spurious: The Politics of Culture in the Vaupés, Colombia. *American Ethnologist* 22:3-27.

Kingsbury, Henry. 1984. *Music, Talent, and Performance: A Conservatory Cultural System*. Philadelphia: Temple University Press.

Lass, Andrew. 1997. The Role of Europe in the Study of Anthropology. Pp. 721-23 in Provocations of European Ethnology, by Talal Asad, James W. Fernandez, Michael Herzfeld, Andrew

Lass, Susan Carol Rogers, Jane Schneider, and Katherine Verdery. *American Anthropologist* 99(4): 713-30.

Leavitt, John. 1996. Meaning and Feeling in the Anthropology of Emotions. *American Ethnologist* 23:514-39.

Lefkowitz, Mary R. 1995. *Not out of Africa: How Afrocentrism Became an Excuse to Teach Myth as History*. New York: Basic Books.

Malkki, Liisa. 1995. *Purity and Exile: Violence, Memory, and National Cosmology Among Hutu Refugees in Tanzania*. Chicago: University of Chicago Press.

Marcus, George E. 1992. *Lives in Trust: The Fortunes of Dynastic Families in Late Twentieth-Century America*. Boulder, CO: Westview Press.

Needham, Rodney. 1972. *Belief, Language, and Experience*. Oxford: Basil Blackwell.

Obeyesekere, Gananath. 1992. *The Apotheosis of Captain Cook: European Mythmaking in the Pacific*. Princeton, NJ: Princeton University Press.

Okely, Judith. 1987. Fieldwork up the M1: Policy and Political Aspects. In *Anthropology at Home*, ed. Anthony Jackson. London: Tavistock.

Patton, Susannah. 1998. Red Tape Confines Man to Airport. *Baltimore Sun*, 11 Mar.

Rosen, Lawrence, ed. 1995. *Other Intentions: Cultural Contexts and the Attri-bution of Inner States*. Santa Fe, NM: School of American Research Press.

Sahlins, Marshall. 1995. *How "Natives" Think: About Captain Cook, for Example*. Chicago: University of Chicago Press.

Shryock, Andrew. 1997. *Nationalism and the Genealogical Imagination: Oral History and Textural Authority in Tribal Jordan*. Berkeley: University of California Press.

Urla, Jacqueline. 1993. Cultural Politics in an Age of Statistics: Numbers, Nations, and the Making of Basque Identity. *American Ethnologist* 20:818-43.

Van Dyck, Karen. 1997. *Kassandra and the Censors: Greek Poetry Since 1967*. Ithaca, NY: Cornell University Press.

Vico, Giambattista. 1744. *Principij di scienza nuova*. Napoli: Stamperia Muziana.

Voltaire, [Jean François Arquet de]. 1773. *Essai sur les moeurs et l'esprit des nations; et sur les principaux faits de l'histoire, depuis Charlemagne jusqu'à Louis XIII*. Rev. ed. Neuchâtel.

Wilkinson, H. R. 1951. *Maps and Politics: A Review of the Ethnographic Cartography of Macedonia*. Liverpool: University Press of Liverpool.

Wills, Garry. 1978. *Inventing America: Jefferson's Declaration of Independence*. Garden City, NJ: Doubleday.

How Journalists Visualize Fact

By RICHARD V. ERICSON

ABSTRACT: Fact is a product of the communication practices of journalists. Journalists rarely have the resources or access to penetrate their sources' informational worlds to establish facts independently. Moreover, the norms of objectivity in journalism often preclude efforts to establish facts independent of sources' accounts. Therefore, journalists visualize the fact value of a story on the basis of a source's face value as an authoritative, normative witness to events. While television visuals offer a greater capacity for believability, the need for an orderly visual narrative leads to staged news events, retakes, reenactments, use of stock footage, and other fakes. These communication practices blur distinctions between fact, value, information, and knowledge and have literary properties. Like literary fiction, news requires the willing suspension of disbelief in order to have its knowledge accepted. This important literary character of news may be fading as the news institution breaks down into segmented markets and specialized information services.

Richard V. Ericson is principal of Green College and professor of sociology and law, University of British Columbia. During the 1998-99 academic year he is visiting fellow, All Souls College, Oxford University. A coeditor of the Canadian Journal of Sociology, *his books include* The Ordering of Justice *(1982);* Reproducing Order *(1982);* Visualizing Deviance *(1987);* Negotiating Control *(1989);* Representing Order *(1991);* Making Crime *(1993); and* Policing the Risk Society *(1997).*

COMMUNICATION does not stand apart from reality. There is not, first, reality and then, second, communication about it. Communication participates in the formation and change of reality.

VISUALIZING FACT

Fact—defined simply as that which is accepted as reality—is an artifact of communication practices. People use communication media (Thompson 1995; Altheide 1995), language (Meyrowitz 1994), trust (Luhmann 1979; Mistzal 1996), and institutions (Ericson 1991, 1994) to make facts, understand, organize experience, and take action. They produce facts, information, and knowledge as a capacity for action (Stehr and Ericson 1992).

There is no real distinction between facts, information, and knowledge. They are all a result of interpretation through communication practices that give them meaning in the contexts of their use. This view differs sharply from statements such as the following one by Bell (1985):

Information is news, facts, statistics, reports, legislation, tax-codes, judicial decisions, resolutions, and the like, and it is quite obvious that we have had an "explosion" of these. . . . But that is not necessarily (or even usually) knowledge. Knowledge is interpretation in context, exegesis, relatedness, and conceptualization, the form of argument. (17)

News and other "information" designated by Bell are indeed knowledge, in his own sense that they have been interpreted in context and given particular meanings. They may be given different meanings as they are transformed and used in additional contexts, but that does not make them knowledge in the additional contexts as distinct from information or fact in the original context. They are knowledge in all contexts, in the sense of being given an objectivated, real meaning that is used in action and has social consequences.

Visualizing is a concept that captures the communication practices of journalists as they make facts. Through the accounts of journalists and their sources, facts are made visible in the minds of audience members even if they are not visible to their eyes. News accounts visualize what happened, why it happened, what it was like to be involved, what should be done about it, and whether any or all of this is good or bad.

The focus on what is good or bad means that a great deal of what journalists visualize is deviance: the behavior of a thing or person straying from the norm. Deviance is a defining characteristic of what journalists regard as newsworthy and, as such, becomes inextricably linked with their communication practices. Deviance and control are not only woven into the seamless web of news reporting but are actually part of its fiber: they define not only the object and central character of news stories as morality plays but also the methodological approaches of journalists as they work on their stories (Ericson, Baranek, and Chan 1987).

In visualizing deviance, journalists inevitably blend fact and value. The norm is a factual standard established with the help of science, such as a risk threshold regarding environmental pollution or a dangerous offender. But the norm is also a powerful ethical constraint, so that any declaration of a factual standard also bears the imprint of moral evaluation. Journalists are perpetually making up normal people and normal events as a touchstone for evaluating the human condition, using "a power as old as Aristotle to bridge the fact/value distinction, whispering in your ear that what is normal is also all right" (Hacking 1990, 170).

The journalist proceeds like a fiction writer, imaginatively construing the facts as they fit the communication practices of news. His or her main task is to quote sources' accounts of events, behaviors, and documents that are not made visible otherwise. This is the case even in television, as journalists and their sources mainly give talking-head accounts of the facts rather than being everywhere as an eyewitness to reality as it happens (Glasgow University Media Group 1976; Ericson, Baranek, and Chan 1991). The journalist-as-novelist imagines typical demands on organizations and their key actors on a particular occasion, and then proceeds through questioning or listening to choose interview quotations and to construct factuality. The story is told in terms of his or her sense of what the sources represent in the roles in which they have been socially cast, carrying on the ancient tradition of Thucydides as enunciated in the *Peloponnesian War*:

It was in all cases difficult to carry [speeches] word-for-word in one's memory, so my habit has been to make the speakers say what was in my opinion demanded of them by the various occa-sions: of course adhering as closely as possible to the general sense of what was said.

In summary, journalism has a set of communication practices that blur the distinction between fact, information, and knowledge, collapse fact and value, and have literary properties. Examination of specific communication practices in journalism reveals the fact of fiction in news but also how fiction nevertheless provides knowledge as a capacity for action.

CREDIBLE SOURCES

Journalists establish factuality by using credible sources who make statements that can be quoted as fact without further investigation. The journalist rarely has the time, material resources, or access to penetrate the source's back region informational world to establish the facts independently (Fishman 1980; Schlesinger 1987; Ericson, Baranek, and Chan 1989). Moreover, as will be addressed, the peculiar norms of objectivity in journalism often preclude efforts to establish facts independent of sources' accounts. The journalist must establish the fact value of a story on the basis of a source's face value as a normative witness to events.

The credibility of sources is established through institutionalized forms of authority and knowledge. Sources are typically predetermined as authorized knowers by the source organization itself, within its own hierarchy of credibility. The source organization selects the best person to represent its interests in the news event, regardless of whether that person is in the best position to know the facts of the matter. Journalists also turn to those with expert knowledge and experiential knowledge in the field in question, and to official bodies without a direct stake in a conflict. As a result, news represents political power as residing in formal institutions, such as electoral politics, legislatures, and law enforcement agencies. This emphasis tends to erase other powerful groups, such as private sector corporations that wish to stay out of the news (Golding, Murdock, and Schlesinger 1986), and marginalizes oppositional groups as at best theatrical and at worst irrational and illegitimate (Gitlin 1980; Hackett and Zhao 1996).

QUOTATION AND VERIFICATION

Journalists also produce factuality through their peculiar means of making the accounts of sources seem objective. Facts are clearly attributed to official sources, often in point-counterpoint format. These attributions make the journalists seem to be operating in a detached, impartial, independent, fair, and balanced manner. News production is a perpetual process of authorizing facts through official sources. Official authorization provides the orderly world of news accounts in contrast to the chaos of rumor, innuendo, mudslinging, and lawsuits.

Journalists follow the institutional grooves of authorized accusation. For example, a source's allegation against another person or organization is not treated as fact unless the allegation is officially deemed fact by law enforcers or other constituted authorities. This practice is, of course, guided in part by the law of defamation and libel, which is in effect the law of authorized accusation. However, it is guided more routinely by the official organization of the process being reported on.

For example, court reporting is organized to display the formal legal rationality of the courtroom process rather than the fish market rationality of the plea bargaining process (Chibnall 1977; Drechsel 1983; Ericson, Baranek, and Chan 1989). There is a preference for obtaining quotations from the accused, witnesses, and victims who are testifying under oath rather than through separate interviews outside of the courtroom. On the other hand, many facts are accepted from the prosecutor without attribution or independent checks, in part to save time and in part because it is important to the journalist's own authority as a narrator to appear to be in command of some basic facts. Thus it would be peculiar for the journalist to report, "According to the prosecutor, the accused is 27 years old and charged with robbery," because to name the prosecutor as authority in this context is to raise doubt about the prosecutor's authority and thus the validity of the facts. On the other hand, the journalist would most likely name the prosecutor if he or she referred to the accused as "a known con artist" because the journalist would not want to be seen as making that attribution without further knowledge of the accused's actual record.

Ethnographic research reveals that verification practices vary by the power of the sources the facts are about (Ericson, Baranek, and Chan 1987). A story involving a powerful source facing a serious allegation requires two or three independent checks from other reliable sources. If a less powerful source is involved, one such check will do. When the source is a marginal member of society, no such checks are required, although the journalist should know where to obtain a credible verification if called upon to do so.

News that is already published or broadcast has credibility as a source of verification. This was institutionalized in the former two-agency rule of the British Broadcasting Corporation: "No report should be treated as adequately confirmed if it had not appeared independently on the tape of two news agencies" (Schlesinger 1987, 90). There is also a hierarchy of credibility among news outlets regarding reliable sources. Newspapers of record, such as the *New York Times*, or news agencies of repute, such as Reuters, are assumed to be factually accurate. In routine news production, materials from other news outlets are lifted and reproduced verbatim without attribution. For example, many local broadcast outlets are known as rip-and-read operations that take stories from newspapers and broadcast them as simply the facts without reference to the source (Ericson, Baranek, and Chan 1987).

Verification through access to documents of the source organization being reported on is relatively rare. In spite of regular protests from journalists that they do not have enough freedom of access to information,

they have much more access to sources' documents than they take advantage of (Ericson, Baranek, and Chan 1989). Journalists shy away from documents for two main reasons. First, documents require interpretive work that is troublesome because the journalist lacks expert knowledge that would help to interpret them and because there is always room for error in interpretation. Second, factuality for journalists is in any case grounded in having a source person in the know say it is so. Indeed, probing documents for the discovery of competing facts can soften the hard facts of source quotations and may even lead to the conclusion that there is no story to report because the documentary evidence settles the conflict.

Journalists frequently operate within a binary-opposition format of allegations from one source and the counterpoint response of the other source. Within this format, there are many situations in which journalists choose not to forgo their story by obtaining an accessible document that will disconfirm one side and result in no story (Ericson, Baranek, and Chan 1987, 258-64).

Since a correspondent is required to present contrasting points of view, even if he finds the views of one side to be valid and those of the other side to be false and misleading . . . any attempt to resolve a controversial issue and find "the truth" can become self-defeating. (Epstein 1974, 68)

Thus what journalists regard as objective can undercut both what is truthful and what is ethical (Hackett and Zhao 1996). As indicated by the following remarks of a television news producer, journalists end up reporting what should be the facts of the matter.

The *final* test is to go and ask the opinion of the institution or the individual that's had the statement made about him, . . . to get their side of it. Because there are some statements that are in dispute. A statement that's in dispute is a fact, but you don't know what side of it is a fact. (Ericson, Baranek, and Chan 1987, 291)

FRAMING

Journalists must tell their story within a narrative framework that has salience in popular reality (Goffman 1974; Hartley 1996). While a journalist may work hard to establish a frame and to relate it to an ongoing theme or issue, once the frame is established, there is a strong disinclination to consider information or alternative frames that do not seem to fit into the picture. Potentially relevant facts are routinely ignored because they would make the story too complicated; the journalist already has his or her story; and/or the journalist is disinterested in the possible story that might be derived from the additional facts.

Research on news accounts of crime waves has demonstrated how journalists frame facts (Cohen 1971; Fishman 1980; Pearson 1983; Voumvakis and Ericson 1984; Orcutt and Turner 1993). An illustration is provided in an ethnographic account of how a crime wave story was handled by a local television outlet (Ericson, Baranek, and Chan 1987, 173-78).

An assignment editor handed a reporter a newspaper story about a significant increase in thefts from pleasure boats in the city's harbor, and asked her to produce a second-day lead for the story. However, in spite of her best efforts, and with concern about expending valuable camera crew resources without producing a story, she was unable to verify that thefts from boats had increased. Police officials denied the problem, and a visit to seven marinas and yacht clubs along the waterfront failed to yield one source who believed there was a problem. The assignment editor did not heed the reporter's early indication that there was no problem and asked her to persist because, in the words of the reporter, "Around here, as I'm sure you've learned, newspapers are everything—they think if it is in print it must be accurate." In this case, the only frame possible was an increase in thefts from boats, indicating a serious problem that required more intensive control remedies. Normal crime is not news; only abnormal crime is. If there is no deviance, there is no story.

There was one possible source of deviance in this story that was not pursued. There was no perceived possibility of reporting on the newspaper journalist's deviance in reporting doubtful facts. Police documents on thefts from boats and a systematic survey of boat owners were not imagined as possible sources to correct the facts of the matter. To have pursued a frame critical of the newspaper account would have exposed the everyday fact of fiction in news reports in too blatant a manner. As the television station producer remarked about the questionable newspaper facts, "I mean, that happens so frequently that it's something we're not going to get into, unless it becomes a major concern" (Ericson, Baranek, and Chan 1987, 176).

As opposed to direct criticism, correction, or contradiction, accounts found wanting are ignored or a story with improved information is published without specific reference to the faulty account in the other news outlet. Of course, this is also usual practice in other fields, such as science, where "publication in a journal in no way establishes that a claim has been accepted by the scientific community. . . . claims which are found wanting are seldom publicly refuted. They are usually ignored instead" (Mulkay 1979, 57).

TELEVISION VISUALS

The visual capacity of television news gives it greater believability than newspapers and radio news (Robinson and Levy 1986; Meyrowitz 1991). Television visuals offer strong validation of the context of the story, and a more direct reading of the moral character and authority of sources. They also offer a sense of immediacy and seem to be in real time or present tense. Combined with the redundant and simplified scripts of television news items, they require little imaginative work by the viewer. Nevertheless, the believability of television news is a strategic accomplishment of the journalists involved. Their news stories are staged productions, complete with props and a cast of journalists and sources as actors. A news producer's manual for the national broadcasting corporation in Canada directs simply to "treat news as theatre" (Cayley 1982, 136).

The theatrical production of television news includes the staging of sources' authority in highly controlled contexts. The news conference is the most controlled context, with authorities who are preselected and preened stating in a matter-of-fact manner what appears to be the case. When a source is interviewed individually, care is taken to visualize the authority of his or her office. Various props are used to sustain the dominant cultural impression that good people work hard and use all available technologies to be knowledgeable and efficient: computers are at hand, books appear in the background, and documents are piled on the desk. If television crews are allowed inside private space to convey what goes on there, it is still in the terms of public cultural expectations of how authority should appear.

Television journalists also help to stage authority in the midst of conflict and chaos. Demonstrations by social movement activists are typically staged rituals in which they, for example, burn figures in effigy, spray paint in bright colors, carry colorful placards, and block transportation routes in order to be pictured under arrest by police. Even riot coverage is contained by the police arranging for television cameras to be positioned behind their lines in order to show that they are invincible, that they are indeed the thin blue line between order and chaos (Holloran, Elliott, and Murdock 1970; Tumber 1982).

Television news staging is inevitable for a number of reasons. There are problems with crew timing and availability. Technical difficulties arise with respect to lighting, sound, and focus. There is the need to appear normal and natural, which is far easier to accomplish through staged events, retakes, reenactments, and the use of stock footage than through simply letting the camera roll as cinema verité.

What journalists term fakes—retakes, reenactments, and the use of stock visuals—help enormously with the flow of the visual narrative in face of the pragmatic problems in producing daily television news. Fakes come in handy when the reporter faces a distant event, an event that has already occurred, an event occurring in a private space that cannot be penetrated, or an encroaching deadline. For example, in reporting on the release of a local government report concerning domestic violence, a journalist did not have time to obtain shots of local police and therefore used five-month-old stock footage of a domestic response team in a distant foreign city (Ericson, Baranek, and Chan 1987, 278). Even ethnographers studying television news production get used as actors in the staging of those productions (91). The only concern of journalists in using such material is to avoid any indication that things are staged, for example, obvious inconsistencies regarding seasons, dress, and signage, or repeated use of the same stock clips.

While visuals are important, they are usually secondary to the script in the visualizations of television journalists. The visual material can become paramount when it is exceptionally dramatic, immediate, and/or exclusive. A shot of a person leaping from a building that is engulfed by flames may speak for itself. However,

most visual material comprises talking heads of people speaking for themselves, more like the newspaper photograph that pictures sources who are part of the printed text (Ericson, Baranek, and Chan 1991, 221-23).

Most often, visuals contribute to factuality by picturing events that support the scripted narrative (Ericson, Baranek, and Chan 1987). Thus, in covering a fire in a high-rise apartment building, a reporter included a shot of a woman looking up fearfully at the fire, with a voice-over that relatives were waiting anxiously to learn the fate of their loved ones. The fact was that this woman was worried about her cat still being in her apartment. Another journalist was doing a story on fear among women, in the context of a reported series of attacks on women. She decided to take shots of a secluded area in a park where a woman had been raped while sunbathing in her swimsuit. On location, there were approximately one hundred men, women, and children in the area. The journalist had the cameraman isolate two women in swimsuits sitting on a bench, with no other people in the background. This clip was later used in the story, suggesting that even after the rape there were women foolhardy enough to be in this presumably secluded area of the park wearing only scanty clothing.

THE FACT OF FICTION

The same television network that directed its journalists to "treat news as theatre" also provided a policy book that said journalists must ensure that

what in fact results from selection and editing is a compression of reality, a slice of reality—which must nonetheless reflect the essential truth without distortion. . . . Production techniques may not be used to distort reality nor to have the effect of producing editorial comment. (Canadian Broadcasting Corporation n.d.)

A mandate to dramatically reflect the facts may seem contradictory, but it is not if we appreciate the fact of fiction in journalism. Every use of language, every classification has an element of fiction because it is not the thing itself. As Nietzsche observed, "What can be thought of must certainly be a fiction." Fiction is bound up with our ways of imaginatively construing the world, of visualizing what something is in order to know it and act upon it. Organized life depends upon acting as if things are as they have been imaginatively construed. The law requires legal fictions to take and justify action. Rhode Island was once declared a peninsula to settle a legal case (Fuller 1967; Scheppele 1988). Historians require regulative fictions, "the imposition of plot on time" (Kermode 1966, 43). Quantitative social scientists use dummy variables to fill in the facts, while ethnographers tell stories that are fashioned within their own narrative frames (Geertz 1973; Clifford and Marcus 1986). The same holds for the practices of physical and natural scientists (Knorr-Cetina 1981).

In the case of literary fiction, to which news is most akin, the essence is what Coleridge once termed the "willing suspension of disbelief" so that the material can be engaged as if it is reality. Literary fictions are "consciously false" (Varhinger 1968) and hence not intended to deceive. In this light, perhaps the best analogy for news is that it is like the Victorian novel: fiction that functions to report facts about the world. Indeed, explicitly fictional entertainment programs can sometimes do more to report the facts than the news itself. Schlesinger, Murdock, and Elliot (1983) found that in the face of U.K. government legal restrictions on journalists interviewing Irish Republican Army terrorists, the reality of the terrorism was more accurately portrayed in fictional entertainment programs.

There is no distinct genre of literary journalism, in spite of efforts to make it distinctive (Kerrane and Yagoda 1997; Sims and Kramer 1995). All journalism is literary in that it employs fictions to discover and apprehend the world. Fictions give order to the world and are essential to the creation of an orderly world of fact. We experience events with a sense of randomness, except when we attend to them closely and analyze them as patterns. News provides analysis in this sense, using fictions to order its products and how those products depict the world. "The randomness of events occurring daily around the world is presented by the daily newscasts as a structured, artistically contrived unity" (Pietropaolo 1982, 53).

Like the novel, news is also a fantasy. As with fiction, fantasy does not mean that it is all made up with whim and fancy or that it is intended to deceive. Rather, it is grounded in fact, reality, a way in which people both make sense of their experiences and make their social worlds. Fantasy is also a method for

> the imaginative and creative interpretation of events that fulfills a psychological or rhetorical need. The Greek root is *phantaskikos* and means to be able to present or show to the mind, to make visible. A fantasy theme is a way for people to present a show to the group mind, to make visible (understandable) a common experience and invest it with an emotional tone. (Bormann 1983, 99-122)

Metaphors, tropes, and other figurative language are important means of accomplishing this imaginative and creative work. Fires *rage*, communities are *battlefronts* over planning and zoning decisions, and elections are reported using boxing metaphors. It is not only that one news picture is used to say a thousand words but also that one news word can visualize a thousand others.

> In metaphor one has, of course, a stratification of meaning, in which incongruity of sense on one level produces an influx of significance on another. As Percy has pointed out, the feature of metaphor that has most troubled philosophers is that it is "wrong." The power of a metaphor derives precisely from the interplay between the discordant meanings it symbolically coerces into a unitary conceptual framework and from the degree to which that coercion is successful in overcoming the psychic resistance such semantic tension inevitably generates in anyone in a position to perceive it. When it works, a metaphor transforms a false identification . . . into an apt analogy. (Geertz 1973, 210-11)

Neither the visual fakes of television journalists nor the figurative language of all journalists should be seen as deception or forgery. They are simulation devices that add unity, coherence, plausibility, and order to the news. Figurative language is a creative means of making news items recognizable in terms of the presumed common sense (Shearing and Ericson 1991). It gives meaning and flow to events in the recognizable terms of news discourse.

THE FUTURE OF FACT

Fact has a strong future. However, its power or capacity for action perpetually shifts between different institutions as they struggle to maintain the power of their respective discourses.

Hard facts continue to have a prominent role in governing modern society. The hard facts of the sciences of probability determine risk thresholds, provide the basis of legal regulation, and help people to tame chance and take risks (Hacking 1990). The hard facts of consumer marketing, credit cards, and police surveillance systems allow institutions to govern at a distance and to include or exclude people as they see fit (Gandy 1993; Turow 1997; Slater 1997; Ericson and Haggerty 1997).

Perhaps the news and other literary discourses are not faring so well in this orderly world of hard fact. News inevitably falls down when it is held up to the hard facts of normal science. Consider the prevailing research methodology for studying news content. The facts of news are compared with other measures of reality, for example, asking whether crime in the media reflects the reality of police statistics and crime victimization surveys (Sherizen 1978; Ditton and Duffy 1983; Sacco 1995). Of course, discrepancies are found, with the mass media overrepresenting murder and other forms of serious violent crime and underreporting burglary and other forms of property crime. But why would anyone expect the cultural products of the news media to reflect other facts about crime? Police statistics themselves do not mirror the reality of crime but are cultural, legal, and social constructs produced by the police for organizational purposes (Kitsuse 1964; Ericson 1993). Each institution has a peculiar discourse for rendering and valuing facts.

The news institution itself is breaking down into specialized information services that feed the reflexive frenzy of other institutions and individuals who demand facts about risk for their own instrumental purposes. Market segmentation of print media and narrowcasting of broadcast media create knowledge-based inequality that is "breaking up America" (Turow 1997; Schiller 1989; Webster 1995).

There is a need to appreciate news for what it is, a form of literary fiction that provides valuable facts about the human condition. There is a parallel need to ascertain the relative position of the news institution in comparison to other institutions as a producer of valuable facts. Such knowledge may well lead us to worry that the literary powers of journalism are losing ground in a society that is increasingly governed through the utilitarian morality of probability statistics and actuarial justice. The morality plays that result from how journalists visualize fact remain vital to the mentalities and sensibilities of modern society.

References

Altheide, David. 1995. *An Ecology of Communication: Cultural Formats of Control*. New York: Aldine de Gruyter.

Bell, Daniel. 1985. Gutenberg and the Computer. *Encounter* (May):15-20.

Bormann, Ernest. 1983. Symbolic Convergence: Organizational Communication and Culture. In *Communication and Organizations*, ed. Linda Putnam and Michael Pacanowsky. Beverly Hills, CA: Sage.

Canadian Broadcasting Corporation. n.d. Internal policy manual.

Cayley, David. 1982. Making Sense of the News. *Sources* (Spring):126-28, 130-33, 136-37.

Chibnall, Steven. 1977. *Law-and-Order News*. London: Tavistock.

Clifford, James and George Marcus, eds. 1986. *Writing Culture: The Poetics and Politics of Ethnography*. Berkeley: University of California Press.

Cohen, Stanley. 1971. *Folk Devils and Moral Panics*. London: Paladin.

Ditton, Jason and James Duffy. 1983. Bias in the Newspaper Reporting of Crime News. *British Journal of Criminology* 23:159-65.

Drechsel, Robert. 1983. *News Making in the Trial Courts*. New York: Longman.

Epstein, Edward. 1974. *News from Nowhere*. New York: Vintage.

Ericson, Richard. 1991. Mass Media, Crime, Law and Justice: An Institutional Approach. *British Journal of Criminology* 31:219-49.

———. 1993. *Making Crime: A Study of Detective Work*. Toronto: University of Toronto Press.

———. 1994. An Institutional Perspective on News Media Access and Control. In *Controlling Broadcasting*, ed. Meryl Aldridge and Nicholas Hewitt. Manchester: University of Manchester Press.

Ericson, Richard, Patricia Baranek, and Janet Chan. 1987. *Visualizing Deviance: A Study of News Organization*. Toronto: University of Toronto Press; Milton Keynes: Open University Press.

———. 1989. *Negotiating Control: A Study of News Sources*. Toronto: University of Toronto Press; Milton Keynes: Open University Press.

———. 1991. *Representing Order: Crime, Law and Justice in the News Media*. Toronto: University of Toronto Press; Milton Keynes: Open University Press.

Ericson, Richard and Kevin Haggerty. 1997. *Policing the Risk Society*. Toronto: University of Toronto Press; Oxford: Oxford University Press.

Fishman, Mark. 1980. *Manufacturing the News*. Austin: University of Texas Press.

Fuller, Lon. 1967. *Legal Fictions*. Stanford, CA: Stanford University Press.

Gandy, Oscar. 1993. *The Panoptic Sort: A Political Economy of Personal Information*. Boulder, CO: Westview Press.

Geertz, Clifford. 1973. *The Interpretation of Cultures*. New York: Basic Books.

Gitlin, Todd. 1980. *The Whole World Is Watching*. Berkeley: University of California Press.

Glasgow University Media Group. 1976. *Bad News*. London: Routledge.

Goffman, Erving. 1974. *Frame Analysis: An Essay on the Organization of Experience*. Cambridge, MA: Harvard University Press.

Golding, Peter, Graham Murdock, and Philip Schlesinger. 1986. *Communicating Politics*. Leicester: University of Leicester Press.

Hackett, Robert and Yuezhi Zhao. 1996. Are Ethics Enough? "Objective" Journalism and Sustainable Democracy. In *Journalism Ethics in a Changing World*, ed. Valeria Alia, Brian Brennan, and Barry Hoffmaster. Halifax: Fernwood.

Hacking, Ian. 1990. *The Taming of Chance*. New York: Cambridge University Press.

Hartley, John. 1996. *Popular Reality*. London: Arnold.

Holloran, James, Philip Elliott, and Graham Murdock. 1970. *Demonstrations and Communication*. New York: Penguin.

Kermode, Frank. 1966. *The Sense of an Ending: Studies in the Theory of Fiction*. New York: Oxford University Press.

Kerrane, Kevin and Ben Yagoda, eds. 1997. *The Art of Fact: An Historical Anthology of Literary Journalism*. New York: Scribner.

Kitsuse, John. 1964. Social Reactions to Deviant Behavior: Problems of Theory and Method. *Social Problems* 9: 247-56.

Knorr-Cetina, Karen. 1981. *The Manufacture of Knowledge: An Essay on the Constructivist and Contextual Nature of Science*. Oxford: Pergamon.

Luhmann, Niklas. 1979. *Trust and Power*. New York: John Wiley.

Meyrowitz, Joshua. 1991. The Questionable Reality of Media. In *Ways of Knowing: The Reality Club*, ed. John Brockman. New York: Prentice Hall.

———. 1994. Medium Theory. In *Communication Theory Today*, ed. David Crowley and David Mitchell. Stanford, CA: Stanford University Press.

Mistzal, Barbara. 1996. *Trust in Modern Societies*. Cambridge: Polity.

Mulkay, Michael. 1979. *Science and the Sociology of Knowledge*. London: Allen & Unwin.

Orcutt, James and Blake Turner. 1993. Shocking Numbers and Graphic Accounts: Quantified Images of Drug Problems in the Print Media. *Social Problems* 40:190-206.

Pearson, Geoffrey. 1983. *Hooligan: A History of Respectable Fears*. London: Macmillan.

Pietropaolo, Dimitri. 1982. Structuring "Truth": The Uses of Drama in "Information" Radio. *Canadian Theatre Review* 36:52-56.

Robinson, John and Mark Levy. 1986. *The Main Source: Learning from Television News*. Newbury Park, CA: Sage.

Sacco, Vincent F. 1995. Media Constructions of Crime. *The Annals* of the American Academy of Political and Social Science 539(May):141-54.

Scheppele, Kim. 1988. *Legal Secrets*. Chicago: University of Chicago Press.

Schiller, Herbert. 1989. *Culture, Inc.: The Corporate Takeover of Public Expression*. New York: Oxford University Press.

Schlesinger, Philip. 1987. *Putting "Reality" Together: B.B.C. News*. London: Methuen.

Schlesinger, Philip, Graham Murdock, and Philip Elliott. 1983. *Televising Terrorism*. London: Comedia.

Shearing, Clifford and Richard Ericson. 1991. Culture as Figurative Action. *British Journal of Sociology* 42: 481-506.

Sherizen, Sanford. 1978. Social Creation of Crime News: All the News Fitted to Print. In *Deviance and Mass Media*, ed. Charles Winick. Beverly Hills, CA: Sage.

Sims, Norman and Mark Kramer, eds. 1995. *Literary Journalism: A New Collection of the Best American Nonfiction*. New York: Ballantine.

Slater, Donald. 1997. *Consumer Culture and Modernity*. Cambridge: Polity.

Stehr, Nico and Richard Ericson, eds. 1992. *The Culture and Power of Knowledge*. New York: Walter de Gruyter.

Thompson, John. 1995. *The Media and Modernity*. Stanford, CA: Stanford University Press.

Tumber, Howard. 1982. *Television and the Riots*. London: British Film Institute.

Turow, Joseph. 1997. *Breaking up America: Advertisers and the New Media World*. Chicago: University of Chicago Press.

Varhinger, Hans. 1968. *The Philosophy of the As If: A System of the Theoretical, Practical, and Religious Fictions of Mankind*. New York: Routledge.

Voumvakis, Sophia and Richard Ericson. 1984. *News Accounts of Attacks on Women*. Toronto: University of Toronto, Centre of Criminology.

Webster, Frank. 1995. *Theories of the Information Society*. New York: Routledge.

ANNALS, *AAPSS*, **560**, November 1998

Nixon Postmortem

By BARRY SCHWARTZ and LORI HOLYFIELD

ABSTRACT: Cultural theories of communication and media events transcend naive ideas about the media as mere transmitters of information; however, they attend insufficiently to information itself. Richard Nixon's eulogists outraged his critics as they tried to bring the moral, emotional, and informational aspects of the funeral into balance. Placing the Watergate scandal in the context of Nixon's progressive administration, the eulogists not only affirmed national values and the dignity of the presidency but also provided positive information about Nixon that would have had less impact if communicated outside a symbol-laden state funeral setting. Thus, the Nixon funeral shows why the informational function of media events must occupy a more central place in communication theory.

Barry Schwartz is professor of sociology at the University of Georgia. His current work on memory as a cultural system includes a book on Abraham Lincoln's emergence as a national idol during the Progressive Era. He is also investigating Lincoln's diminishing relevance during the postmodern decades.

Lori Holyfield is assistant professor of sociology at the University of Arkansas. Her recent research concerns white-water rafting and the construction of adventure; her current research focuses on leisure, tourism, and emotion management.

RECENT work on state ritual includes analyses of inaugurations, coronations, holidays, parades, festivals, rallies, pilgrimage, drama, and music (for recent examples of this massive literature, see Hobsbawm and Ranger 1983; Spillman 1997; for a summary, see Gusfield and Michalowicz 1984). As mass communications increase exposure to these kinds of events, new questions arise about their role as integrative forces in society.

Impressed with Emile Durkheim's treatment ([1915] 1965) of the symbolic order, which "operates not to provide information but confirmation" of the underlying scheme of things, James Carey ([1975] 1989) regards news watching and reading less as as a means of learning about the world than a means of affirming it. News works as high drama (19-21). Along this Durkheimian line, Roger Silverstone (1988) construes television as a focus for the "mobilization of collective energy and enthusiasm" and "palaeosymbolic meanings" (25, 43).

Nowhere can Carey's "cultural approach to communication" be applied more usefully than to death and funeral rites. In this perspective, funeral rites are understood as ways of draining off emotion, sustaining morale in the context of loss, promoting consensus and solidarity, imposing upon the public's notice the fact of a death that it might otherwise minimize, or affirming the dignity of the status occupied by the deceased. But Carey's approach, like Durkheim's ([1915] 1965; see also Hertz 1960; Warner 1959; Greenberg and Parker

1965; Metcalf and Huntington 1991; Schwartz 1991), is too pat, for the consequences of communication, in Clifford Geertz's words, "seem adventitious, the accidental byproducts of an essentially nonrational, nearly automatic expressive process initially pointed in another direction" (1973, 206). Communication's envisioned consequences, on the other hand, carry their own mysteries and warrant examination.

The cultural approach to communication embodies the revenge of emotion upon fact. Cultural communication theorists, while seeking to disclose the symbolic components of public events, have never denied the significance of their contents, nor have they denied that factual particularity can impassion just as emotion can enhance factual relevance. Their emphasis, however, moves us from naive ideas about the media as mere transmitters of information to a cathectic conception that gives information less emphasis than it deserves. A cathectic conception of ritual focuses too sharply on what Edward Sapir (1930) termed "condensation symbols"—emblems and ceremonial forms that reach deep into the nonrational, emotional levels of consciousness—and disposes of "referential symbols" (492-93), representing objective knowledge, including knowledge conveyed by ritually framed speech acts, as being peripheral to rituals' ostensibly true (self-affirmative) function. The present study, using President Richard Nixon's funeral as a vehicle, addresses this less clarified aspect of state ritual and seeks to achieve a more balanced understanding by broadening, not abandoning, the cultural approach to communication.

MEDIA RITUAL AND REPUTATION

The American people's assessment of Richard Nixon's presidency (January 1969–August 1974) is too differentiated to be based on nonrational sentiment alone. Between 1976 and 1983, 11 Gallup surveys showed Nixon's positive rating increasing from 30 to 43 percent. In 7 Harris surveys from 1976 to 1988, he was compared to presidents since Franklin Roosevelt, and on the management of foreign policy he ranked first in all but one. In June 1994 the Hart and Teeter survey asked respondents whether Nixon's presidency was, on balance, good or bad for America. Sixty-six percent responded good; 20 percent, bad; 6 percent, mixed; 8 percent expressed no opinion. The July 1994 Yankelovitch survey showed 12 percent of adult Americans rating Nixon as one of the greatest presidents; 32 percent, a good president; 36 percent, average; and 15 percent, poor. Five percent had no opinion (Roper Center 1997).

On the other hand, the 1976 Harris poll revealed 63 percent of the respondents as naming Nixon the most immoral postwar president. In 1988, the percentage designating Nixon the least moral dropped to 48 percent, but it was still far higher than the percentage naming any other president. In 1995, the Michaels poll showed 57 percent believing Nixon's influence on American moral values to be negative; 17 percent, positive. In the same year, 1995, the CBS Poll showed 2 percent of the respondents naming Nixon as the best of all American presidents; 19 percent, as the worst (Roper Center 1997). Thus, by the time Richard Nixon died, the American people had come to imagine him a technically competent but morally imperfect man, one who had served his country well but had set the wrong moral example.

Public opinion of Nixon was affected not only by his achievements but also by the activities of "reputational entrepreneurs" (Fine 1996), including the Nixon presidential library and museum staff. Leaving aside Nixon's adversaries as well as supporters, however, our concern is to know how his mourning rites might have enlarged or made more relevant the positive aspects of both his character and his presidency.

The Nixon funeral was at best a mini-media event, for it possessed none of the emotional resonance of grand funerals like President Kennedy's and Princess Diana's; still, it was a serious affair warranting front-page headlines and special comment in both the visual and printed media. Media events, whatever their scope, exploit an "anthropology of ceremony" (Dayan and Katz 1992, 1-2) to construe public events as articulators of consensus (197; see also Dayan and Katz 1988). The televising of such events interrupts the rhythm of mundane life, creates vast audiences, affirms moral ideals, creates fellow feeling, connects the center and periphery of the society, and defines its moral boundaries. Focusing on the unintended consequences of events, Dayan and Katz (1992, 188-217, esp. 195-98) exemplify Philip Elliott's earlier (1982) claim that "irrationalism is a general feature of popular journalism which is to be found in particularly striking form in these [media] rituals" (129; see also Edelman 1988).

Since oratory is a constituent of media rituals—from presidential inaugurals to holiday observances and official mourning—Michael Gilmore's conception (1978) of the eulogy informs and extends the cultural approach to communication. Funeral eulogies, as instances of ritual speech, are, according to Gilmore, symbolic biographies: "By treating the dead as a kind of cultural ideal, the eulogist seeks to compose the collective biography of an entire people. Thus the true subject of the eulogy [is] the speaker and his community rather than the character and career of the person nominally portrayed" (131).

A PROGRESSIVE PRESIDENCY

Eulogies may be screens on which representatives of a community project their own needs and concerns, but they also provide standpoints from which people are exposed to otherwise inaccessible information about the deceased. If eulogies are necessarily biased, they cannot be spun out of thin air. Pro-Nixon eulogists drew on facts to "de-romanticize evil" (Ducharme and Fine 1995, 1326-28)—to make him a lifelike man rather than a larger-than-life demon.

Richard Nixon had distinguished himself as an effective congressman before serving as Dwight Eisenhower's vice president from 1952 to 1960. He then ran against John Kennedy in November 1960 and was defeated in one of the closest elections in history. After suffering a second defeat as candidate for governor of California, he ran for the presidency again in 1968, defeating Hubert Humphrey narrowly. In 1972, after the Watergate break-in, Nixon beat George McGovern in a landslide. Two years later, after unsuccessful efforts to conceal his Watergate role, he resigned the presidency.

Foreign relations constituted the most visible arena of Richard Nixon's presidential achievement. Most Americans, opposing George McGovern's characterization of the Vietnam war as a national sin, supported Nixon's effort to end it honorably, that is, without "divisive recrimination" that would "scar our spirit as a people" (Morris 1996, 216, 217). Although Nixon's delay in terminating the war was controversial, he was admired for establishing regular relations with China, improving relations with the Soviet Union, and forming evenhanded Middle East policies, even while facing down the Soviet Union and supplying Israel directly during its perilous Yom Kippur War (when every European nation denied the United States access to its airfields).

On domestic matters, Democratic Senator Daniel Patrick Moynihan asserts, Richard Nixon led the most progressive of all postwar administrations (Wicker 1991, 144; see also

Barone 1990; White 1982). In the context of severe economic problems, most acute during his second term in office (inflation, an oil embargo, and a weakening stock market), Nixon broke with conservative tradition by establishing the Environmental Protection Agency, and he initiated legislation to control noise, protect scenic rivers, expand national parks, improve water quality, maintain coastlines, and prohibit ocean pollution.

Nixon had reduced and eliminated many of Lyndon B. Johnson's programs, but his goal was to fine-tune, not abolish, the Great Society. He doubled the food stamp program from $340 million to $640 million during his very first year in office. The amount of Aid to Families with Dependent Children tripled from 1970 to the end of his presidency. The Nixon administration also started the War on Cancer, increased public health and occupational and consumer product safety, increased supports for subsidized housing, and expanded aid to the blind, disabled, and aged. Nixon's total social service budget grew from $55 billion in 1970 to $132 billion in 1975, and, while increasing the Social Security tax, he also increased domestic spending generally from 28 to 40 percent of the gross national product while decreasing defense spending from 40 to 26 percent. When the economy turned downward, he rejected advice to allow the market to regulate itself and instituted wage and price controls.

Nixon also instituted federal supports for elementary and secondary education, quadrupled federal support for the arts, established the National Student Loan Association for students from low-income families, the Career Education Program for community colleges, and the National Endowment for the Humanities.

Nixon gave Native Americans unprecedented assistance, from the establishment of legal rights and favorable economic legislation to material relief. In addition, he strengthened measures against school segregation and sex discrimination by increasing the staff of the Equal Employment Opportunity Commission from 359 in 1969 to 1640 in 1972. During this same period, 1969-72, set-aside contracts for minority businesses rose from $8 million to $243 million. Grants, loans, and guarantees to minorities and women increased during this same period from $69 to $472 million. (See Aitken 1993; Burke and Burke 1974; Hoff 1994; Whitaker 1976, 1997.)

The policies of a Democratic president, specifically Hubert Humphrey and George McGovern, would likely have been more liberal than Nixon's. However, the Nixon administration, although acting in its own political interest (as Schuman et al. [1997], among scores of others, have noted), was fundamentally compassionate, concerned for the well-being of the nation, and attentive to issues of social justice as well as the production and distribution of wealth. President Nixon had violated his oath of office and was capable of private cruelty, but he acted on his statements about political adversaries infrequently. Nixonian discourse, even when preserved dramatically on tape, was less significant than Nixonian practice (Swidler 1997).

FUNERAL AT YORBA LINDA

The meaning of practices is not always straightforward. This is why Emile Durkheim's belief that mourning is obligatory ([1915] 1965, 443) is an insufficient starting point for a theory of funeral practices. It is well to say that mourning is a social obligation when the deceased is one whose death is regretted or even accepted with indifference, but what of cases in which the object of mourning can be treated with neither indifference nor grief? What if the deceased is a man whose crimes against the people are widely known and condemned? Moreover, what if this same man is too important and his impact on his nation and on history too significant to ignore? What kind of duty does the group then impose? What values would public mourning then affirm? How, then, does a nation ritually embrace the deceased leader it has decisively expelled.

Richard Nixon's funeral was a neutralization ceremony consisting of the ritual repair of wounds induced by semi-religious censure and degradation (Alexander 1988). Nixon himself understood the identity-conferring power of ritual. Designing parts of his own funeral rites, he omitted their highlight: the Capitol visitation ceremony. No political figure can receive a greater national honor than to be placed in state in the U.S. Capitol Rotunda, but Nixon knew the press would compare him with the unpopular president—Johnson—and contrast him to the popular presidents—Kennedy and Eisenhower—who had lain there. He therefore arranged for his body to be taken directly to the Richard Nixon Library and Birthplace in Yorba Linda, California.

The funeral at Yorba Linda took place on Wednesday, 27 April 1994, at 4 p.m. Pacific time and appeared on television in the east at 7 p.m. So scheduled, it did not interrupt prime-time television viewing. All major networks carried the ceremony live; some repeated it later in the evening. Three-quarters (73 percent) of the adult population, according to a post-funeral survey, followed the event closely. Most of these viewers understood its anomalous character, for 91 percent correctly identified Nixon with the "Watergate scandal" (Roper Center 1997). However, this funeral's symbolic display and eulogical oratory recontextualized the scandal, put it in a broader and clearer light. The impressiveness of Richard Nixon's funeral rites was instrumental in making viewers receptive to the information his eulogists were about to deliver.

The funeral, following Defense Department protocol, began with the bearing of the president's coffin to its catafalque by a military honor guard. Henry Kissinger, National Security Council adviser and secretary of state under Nixon, Senate majority leader Robert Dole, California governor Pete Wilson, and President Bill Clinton delivered the secular eulogies. The Reverend Billy Graham, representing the family, delivered the religious eulogy. As each man approached the podium, he stopped, faced the coffin and bowed slightly. The statements were generous and conciliatory, and after each the Navy chorus performed selections from its patriotic repertoire.

After the choir's singing of "America," the honor guard lifted the presidential coffin and stood at attention for the playing of the national anthem. A few moments of silence followed, then the faint sound of aircraft, then the thundering flyover salute. At last, the honor guard, accompanied by the band's solemn rendition of "America," bore the coffin to the other side of the white frame house where Richard Nixon had been born and reared. The contrast between majestic symbols of state and humble symbols of middle America sharpened as viewers followed the coffin to its burial place. The incumbent president, four former presidents, and the highly decorated pall and flag bearers, representing each of the armed forces, led the procession.

Close-up television pictures made the emotional texture of the event more moving to home audiences than to the people actually in attendance. It was the camera that revealed best the emotion of eulogists Henry Kissinger, whose voice trembled and lower lip quivered as he read his address, and Robert Dole, whose face contorted as he wept at the end of his statement. It was the camera that showed family members, like the hundreds who came to pay respects, standing at attention for the national anthem, their patriotic allegiance overriding their private grief. Close-ups disclosed the aging of former presidents and their wives and brought future presidential funerals to mind.

As television cameras followed the proceedings, they interspersed images of national power with the deceased president's two daughters and their husbands, his grandchildren, brother, and friends. The effect was a sense of the presidency as a remote yet familiar institution—an office beyond comprehension yet filled by an ordinary man and family. The dignified demeanor of this family, on the other hand, amplified eulogists' portrayals of the dignity of the deceased.

EULOGIES

Richard Nixon's funeral eulogies are distinguishable from their classical precedents. A eulogy, as Thrall, Hibbard, and Holman (1960) define it, is "a formal, dignified speech or writing, highly praising a person or a thing" (189). Eulogies marking the deaths of earlier presidents, including George Washington and Abraham Lincoln, were written in elegant prose at the invitation of municipal or religious bodies. They were composed according to a classical model with a view to teaching virtue and persuading imitation; required an hour for delivery; and were printed for distribution (McManamon 1989; Schwartz 1986, 1991; Theroux 1997). The Nixon eulogies, like all eulogies now broadcast to a mass audience, were shorter, lasting no more than several minutes; written in simple rather than formal prose; and summarized in local newspapers. These eulogies were nevertheless the funeral's centerpoint. In a eulogy, Gilmore (1978) claims, the concrete details making up the life of a particular person are neutralized by the didacticism of the genre itself. "The deceased appears less as an individualized figure than as an emblem or symbol contrived for the purpose of instructing an audience" in the standards of its culture (131). Is this really so? Every eulogy must appeal to cultural values to praise the dead, but can it be reduced to those values? Were Nixon's eulogists not also showing the deceased president to be a more complex individual than critics assert?

Official eulogists addressed separate themes, almost as if there had been a division of labor among them. Henry Kissinger emphasized the president's foreign policy triumphs. He announced that Richard Nixon, a "seminal president," had supervised America's transition from world "dominance" to world "leadership." He had ended the Vietnam war and the draft, as he had promised to do; had established a permanent dialogue with China; had improved relations with the Soviet Union; and had contained the conflict in the Middle East. Kissinger added that Nixon had made human rights an international issue, thus laying the moral foundation for Cold War victory. He also asserted that Nixon's Quaker background, with its emphasis on peace and reconciliation, had moved him powerfully on matters of foreign policy, so much so that he ignored reelection prospects and even long-term friendships in favor of his convictions.

Robert Dole opened his remarks by asserting that the second half of the twentieth century would be known as the "Age of Nixon." Portraying Richard Nixon as the personification of democracy, Dole pursued the second theme of the day. Born in the house his father had built, young Nixon had raised himself by hard work. "How American!" Dole exclaimed at this and other points in his delivery. Suffering as many defeats as victories, Nixon had sympathized with the plight of common people. He was "truly one of us," truly the man to recognize the dignity of middle America and the merit of the working man. This, according to Dole, is why domestic programs were crucial features of his presidency. Strengthening of environmental and nutritional programs, committing the government to a massive war against cancer, establishing revolutionary health care and welfare reforms that made more resources available than ever to the deserving poor—these measures could only have been inspired by profound love for the people. Richard Nixon was indeed the people's president—the pride of what he had called "the silent majority."

Pete Wilson enlarged on Dole's points as he emphasized Richard Nixon's moral character. He recounted the president's kindnesses to him while he was a young man breaking into politics. Just as Nixon had aided the new generation of politicians, he unselfishly had advised veterans as they managed the nation's affairs. He had been so unselfish, Wilson said, that he had chosen not to challenge his 1960 presidential election defeat, despite conspicuous irregularities, because it would have undermined the integrity of the presidency and the election process. "He so loved his country that he refused to risk its being torn apart by the constitutional crisis that might ensue." Where did this man acquire his generosity, his devotion to family and nation, his capacity for hard work and willingness to take risks? Where did he get his "heart"? Governor Wilson's claim that President Nixon found his virtues in the mores of Orange County, California, may or may not have been accurate, but to most television viewers the possession of these virtues was more important than the source.

President Clinton summarized the previous speakers' points before coming to his own: Richard Nixon's life must be judged comprehensively. "Today is a day for his family, his friends, and his nation to remember President Nixon's life in totality. To them, let us say, May the day of judging President Nixon on anything less than his entire life and career come to a close."

The Reverend Billy Graham, too, referred to the totality of Richard Nixon's personal qualities: his bravery in the face of death, how difficult he had been to get to know despite the many kind deeds he had anonymously performed, how much compassion he had felt for the luckless and suffering. Above all, Graham noted, he had regularly prayed in the privacy of the White House, where his piety was known to God alone.

So short were the testimonies that they hardly seemed like eulogies at all, yet even a cursory examination shows they contained the traditional elements: an exordium (introduction), recitation of "external goods" (birthplace, family, education), and "goods of the soul" (including the cardinal virtues of prudence, justice, courage, and temperance, all of which had been established through recordable deeds [McManamon 1989,

20]). By articulating the unusual achievements of an ordinary man, the eulogies showed that consensual narratives (in this case, America as a setting where virtuous people rise from obscurity to fame) remained relevant to the integration of a postmodern society. The eulogies were not summaries of what everyone liked about Nixon but selective commentaries designed to convince a 1994 audience that one event, Watergate, could never summarize Richard Nixon's life or presidency.

The eulogies finished, the funeral entered its final phase. Pallbearers, moving in perfect unison, placed Richard Nixon's coffin over his grave, removed the flag, stretched it, as a canopy, above the coffin during the final sequence of gestures: the playing of taps, the long 21-gun salute, the rifle squad's briefer three-round salute, and prayers by the Reverend Graham. At last, the flag shielding the coffin was folded to the sound of the "Navy Hymn" and delivered to Tricia Nixon Cox, the older surviving child.

The final scene was ironic, for the officer delivering the flag to Mrs. Cox was one of the Americans her father allegedly despised—an African American. As the officer delivered his words of consolation and extended the folded flag to the president's daughter, she placed her white gloved hand on his and, visibly moved, looked up and thanked him. The bearing of Julie Nixon Eisenhower, the younger child, was slightly less self-possessed. Her head dropped tearfully as she took the prefolded flag from the compassionate officer while David Eisenhower, her husband, thanked him with a warm and grateful look. Nixon's brother Edward, too, acted graciously, although he appeared inconsolable. As the funeral party left the grave site, it seemed that a selfish, racist president could not be part of such a decent and patriotic family, could not be loved by daughters so deferentially polite and indifferent to color, could not be so deeply mourned by a brother. The demeanor of Richard Nixon's family had affirmed eulogists' claims about Richard Nixon's character.

COUNTER-EULOGIES

The day after Nixon was buried, his funeral rites and eulogies were detailed in American newspapers by straight reporting and by special commentaries; almost all of the latter were hostile. If Michael Gilmore (1978) were right and the eulogies were only nominally about Richard Nixon, these commentaries would make no sense. If *Radical History Review* had believed that eulogies were merely symbolic statements about society, its special section "Counter-Obituaries for Richard Milhous Nixon" (1994) would have been superfluous, as would have been the scores of biting critiques appearing in American newspapers.

The critics' discourse claimed to reflect the true foundations of the president's character, to gloss situational limits and unmask the villain as evil "in the first place," "fundamentally," "from the very beginning," "all along" (Garfinkel 1956). Nixon, according to *Time* magazine correspondent Otto Friedrich, was the master of slurs and "symbol of the politics of anger" (1994, 43). Hunter Thompson, writing in *Rolling Stone* (1994), informed his readers that "Richard Nixon was an evil man—evil in a way that only those who believe in the physical reality of the Devil can understand. . . . It is Nixon himself who represents that dark, venal and incurably violent side of the American character that almost every country in the world has learned to fear and despise" (44).

Critics also attacked the eulogies by characterizing Nixon's positive actions as coerced, accidental, incidental, "shamelessly magnified," or by making them symptomatic of moral imperfection. Certain aspects of the president's sense of humor, for example, betrayed "his incessant anger and resentment at its core" (Chapman 1994), while his refusal to give in to adversity expressed malicious stubborness. The expression "He's baaack!" summarizes the negative meaning of Nixon's "heart" (see, for example, Cheakalos 1997). Some critics denied the conventions of eulogy by criticizing authors for ignoring villainous episodes in Nixon's life and for failing to make his crimes understandable (Broder 1994; Semple 1994).

Nixon's antagonists disparaged him by discrediting his eulogists' motives as well as their words. Joe Queenan's "Gag Me with a Eulogy" (1994) tells the reader, beneath a cartoon of a weeping crocodile, that Kissinger spoke at Nixon's funeral in order to congratulate himself for foreign policy triumphs; Dole and Wilson, to exploit free television coverage for their respective political agendas; and Clinton, in order to minimize his draft evasion, marital infidelity, and Whitewater troubles (see also Broder 1994; Goodman 1994). Other critics disparaged Nixon by deprecating the people attending his funeral. David Gergen, presidential adviser, "worked a row of mourners like a ropeline," as did the remnants of Nixon's old staff. The official delegation representing the U.S. Congress, too, used the funeral for a "flurry of politicking" (Von Drehle 1994). Also, the thousands who passed by Nixon's flag-draped casket were described as "largely working class, Mr. Nixon's kind of people" (Margolick 1994).

The most indignant mocked the very observance of Nixon's death. In the *Washington Post*, Jonathan Yardley (1994) wondered what kind of day would follow the National Day of Mourning for this "psychological basket case," "moral pygmy," and "unconvicted criminal." A postal holiday for John Dillinger? A national moment of silence for Lizzie Borden? The American Civil Liberties Union (ACLU), for its part, distributed a memo announcing it would close down nationally—for 18 and a half minutes (the length of the famous tape deletion). The memo proved to be a hoax. The ACLU did not close at all. One of the *Boston Globe*'s commentators noted the special day by portraying the dead president in his coffin proclaiming in rap-style verse: "The name's Tricky Dicky and it's plain to see,/The flags are flying half-staff for me./The flags are flying half-staff for me" (English 1994). Finally, critics conceived the positive content of the eulogies as sympto-

matic of the diminished state of society, for which Nixon was responsible. Watergate was the beginning of not only a new series of government scandals but also a new tolerance of scandals that made Nixon, in retrospect, seem less menacing (Apple 1994; Emery 1994).

RITUAL AND BELIEF

Without reminders of President Nixon's crimes against the government—whether overblown or not—American society could not maintain its morality, for it is on public occasions that the boundary between right and wrong is dramatized (Erikson 1966). On the other hand, if there is no forgiveness for a president's offenses, then the authority of the presidency itself erodes (Schwartz 1979). Whether Richard Nixon's offenses were forgivable depended on the credibility of what his supporters, including his eulogists, asserted.

There can be no agreement on objects of moral assertion. Robert Dole, Elliott Richardson, Spiro Agnew, Bill Clinton, and George McGovern assembled at Richard Nixon's funeral despite disagreement between them as to what kind of president he had been. Yet, "what often underlies people's political allegiances," David Kertzer (1988) has observed, "is their social identification with a group rather than their sharing of beliefs with other members" (66). Ritual (including televised ritual) builds cohesion through uniformity of action rather than similarity of belief. Indeed, it is the gathering together of political and personal enemies that defines the significance and power of the funeral ritual. Thus Kertzer is reiterating the key premise of the cultural approach to communication: that facts are mainly vehicles for thinking about other matters, like national identity, solidarity, history, and destiny.

Kertzer's weak point, like the weak point of culture of communication scholarship, is to have underestimated the relevance of belief. He declares that "one should be wary about attributing too much significance to a person's set of political beliefs, since these are neither consistent nor are they all equally developed and strongly held" (68). Kertzer's conception does not conform to beliefs about Richard Nixon, which may have been ambivalent but never ambiguous or casual. This is what makes eulogists' praise as important politically as critics' condemnations. Each interpreter—whether eulogist or critic—claims to be disclosing the true meaning of Nixon's life, but he or she is really altering what he or she finds unacceptable in it. For critics, Nixon's accomplishments were, in Freud's phrase, manifest contents concealing a latent realm of unworthy motives; for supporters, Nixon's manifest offenses concealed his latent beneficence. The facts remain unchanged, but each side, seeking to make them manageable in its own way, sees a part of the man that is invisible to the other.

Understanding Richard Nixon's relation to America's historical narrative requires not only our moving beyond the ritual and sentiment that it evokes but also our distinguishing between eulogy and biographical commentary. Critically formulated in nonritual contexts, biography disenchants its object; eulogy, the ritually certified distilling of the noble and virtuous from the imperfect life, elevates its object. The contrast between biography and eulogy is not entirely clear-cut. Richard Nixon's biography reflects the ideals his eulogies express while his eulogies are rooted in biographical reality. This is necessarily the case. Whether a person's death promotes sorrow because we respect him or whether we attribute our (ritually induced) sorrow to his personal qualities (Bem 1972), funeral rites help reconcile the nation to the person who offended it because they make relevant the values whose existence the life history of that person ostensibly embodies.

Affirmative state ritual exaggerates national virtue, but, in some contexts, it is intellectually liberating. Thus, if critical journalists, as Zelizer (1992) might suggest, typically legitimate their own authority as they tell their stories, they must compete against other storytellers, including official eulogists. The journalists do not always prevail. The weekend after President Nixon's funeral, radio and television talk shows logged thousands of calls, the vast majority of which referred favorably to both the dignity of the ceremony and the ultimate decency of the man. Local newspaper editors received letters from readers shocked by the vileness of anti-Nixon commentary. The issue, however, is not whether Nixon's funeral rites elevated his reputation. Our data do not bear on this question, although Michael Schudson (1992) may have been right when he asserted that history resists attempts to be made over and that the stigma of Watergate would permanently mark this man. The issue is whether state funeral rites affirm the merit of Richard Nixon, as a president and a man, solely by manipulating emotion or by also revealing facts or by making positive accomplishments more relevant than faults (Iyengar and Kinder 1987). The merits and faults of individual leaders do not vanish when they are transformed into collective symbols.

References

Aitken, Jonathan. 1993. *Nixon: A Life*. London: Weidenfeld & Nicolson.

Alexander, Jeffrey C. 1988. Culture and Political Crisis: "Watergate" and Durkheimian Sociology. In *Durkheimian Sociology: Cultural Studies*, ed. Jeffrey C. Alexander. New York: Cambridge University Press.

Apple, Richard W. 1994. In the End, the Words Were Those He Sought. *New York Times*, 19 June.

Barone, Michael. 1990. *Our Country: The Shaping of America from Roosevelt to Reagan*. New York: Free Press.

Bem, Daryl J. 1972. Self Perception Theory. In *Advances in Experimental Social Psychology: Learning, Memory, and Cognition*, ed. Leonard Berkowitz. Vol. 13. New York: Academic Press.

Broder, David. 1994. A Farewell Not Only to a Man but Also to an Era. *Washington Post*, 28 Apr.

Burke, Vincent and Vee Burke. 1974. *Nixon's Good Deed: Welfare Reform*. New York: Columbia University Press.

Carey, James W. [1975] 1989. A Cultural Approach to Communication. In *Communication as Culture: Essays on Media and Society*, ed. James W. Carey. Boston: Unwin Hyman.

Chapman, David. 1994. Nixon Tributes Kept a Safe Distance from the Truth. *Chicago Tribune*, 1 May.

Cheakalos, Christina. 1997. Law Student Wants Nixon Portrait Rehung. *Atlanta Constitution*, 22 Nov.

Counter-Obituaries for Richard Milhous Nixon. 1994. *Radical History Review* (Fall):132-202.

Dayan, Daniel and Elihu Katz. 1988. Articulating Consensus: The Ritual and Rhetoric of Media Events. In *Durkheimian Sociology: Cultural Studies*, ed. Jeffrey C. Alexander. New York: Cambridge University Press.

———. 1992. *Media Events: The Live Broadcasting of History*. Cambridge, MA: Harvard University Press.

Ducharme, Lori J. and Gary Fine. 1995. The Construction of Nonpersonhood and Demonization: Commemorating the Traitorous Reputation of Benedict Arnold. *Social Forces* 73:1309-31.

Durkheim, Emile. [1915] 1965. *The Elementary Forms of Religious Life*, trans. Joseph Ward Swain. New York: Free Press.

Edelman, Murray. 1988. *Constructing the Political Spectacle*. Chicago: University of Chicago Press.

Elliott, Philip. 1982. Media Performances as Political Rituals. *Communications* 7:115-30.

Emery, Fred. 1994. Watergate—Worse Than You Thought. *New York Times*, 12 June.

English, Bellah. 1994. The Last Rap on Nixon. *Boston Globe*, 27 Apr.

Erikson, Kai T. 1966. *Wayward Puritans: A Study in the Sociology of Deviance*. New York: John Wiley.

Fine, Gary Alan. 1996. Reputational Entrepreneurs and the Memory of Incompetence: Melting Supporters, Partisan Warriors, and Images of President Harding. *American Journal of Sociology* 101:1159-93.

Friedrich, Otto. 1994. I Have Never Been a Quitter. *Time*, 2 May.

Garfinkel, Harold. 1956. The Conditions of Successful Degradation Ceremonies. *American Journal of Sociology* 61:420-24.

Geertz, Clifford. 1973. Ideology as a Cultural System. In *The Interpretation of Cultures*. New York: Basic Books.

Gilmore, Michael. 1978. Eulogy as Symbolic Biography: The Iconography of Revolutionary Leadership, 1776-1826. In *Harvard English Studies*, ed. Daniel Aaron. Vol. 8. Cambridge, MA: Harvard University Press.

Goodman, Walter. 1994. Private-Public Moment Beamed into History. *New York Times*, 28 Apr.

Greenberg, Bradley S. and Edwin B. Parker, eds. 1965. *The Kennedy Assassination and the American Public*. Stanford, CA: Stanford University Press.

Gusfield, Joseph R. and Jerzy Michalowicz. 1984. Secular Symbolism: Studies of Ritual, Ceremony, and the Symbolic Order in Modern Life. In *Annual Review of Sociology*, ed. Ralph H. Turner and James F. Short, Jr. Vol. 10. Palo Alto, CA: Annual Reviews.

Hertz, Robert. 1960. *Death and the Right Hand*, trans. Rodney Needham and Claudia Needham. Aberdeen: Cohen & West.

Hobsbawm, Eric and Terence Ranger, eds. 1983. *The Invention of Tradition*. Cambridge: Cambridge University Press.

Hoff, Joan. 1994. *Nixon Reconsidered*. New York: Basic Books.

Iyengar, Shanto and Donald Kinder. 1987. *News That Matters*. Chicago: University of Chicago Press.

Kertzer, David. 1988. *Ritual, Power, and Politics*. New Haven, CT: Yale University Press.

Margolick, David. 1994. Beneath Heavy Moon, Chilly Wait for Last Farewell. *New York Times*, 28 Apr.

McManamon, John M. 1989. *Funeral Oratory and the Cultural Ideals of Italian Humanism*. Chapel Hill: University of North Carolina Press.

Metcalf, Peter and Richard Huntington. 1991. *Celebrations of Death: The Anthropology of Mourning Ritual*. New York: Cambridge University Press.

Morris, Kenneth E. 1996. *Jimmy Carter: American Moralist*. Athens: University of Georgia Press.

Queenan, Joe. 1994. Gag Me with a Eulogy. *Washington Post*, 29 May.

Roper Center for Public Opinion Research. 1997. Surveys of post-Watergate assessments of Nixon. Storrs, CT.

Sapir, Edward. 1930. Symbols. In *Encyclopedia of the Social Sciences*. Vol. 14. New York: McGraw-Hill.

Schudson, Michael. 1992. *Watergate in American Memory*. New York: Basic Books.

Schuman, Howard, Charlotte Steeh, Lawrence Bobo, and Maria Krysaw. 1997. *American Racial Attitudes*. Cambridge, MA: Harvard University Press.

Schwartz, Barry. 1979. Vengeance and Forgiveness: The Uses of Beneficence in Social Control. *School Review* 86:655-68.

———. 1986. The Character of Washington: A Study in Republican Culture. *American Quarterly* 38(2):202-22.

———. 1991. Mourning and the Making of a Sacred Symbol: Durkheim and the Lincoln Assassination. *Social Forces* 70(2):342-64.

Semple, Robert, Jr. 1994. Notes from a Funeral. *New York Times*, 1 May.

Silverstone, Roger. 1988. Television Myth and Culture. In *Media, Myths, and Narratives: Television and the Press*, ed. James W. Carey. Newbury Park, CA: Sage.

Spillman, Lyn. 1997. *Nation and Commemoration: Creating National Identities in the United States and Australia*. New York: Cambridge University Press.

Swidler, Ann. 1997. From the Chair. *Newsletter of the Sociology of Culture Section of the American Sociological Association* 10:1-2.

Theroux, Phyllis. 1997. *The Book of Eulogies*. New York: Scribner's.

Thompson, Hunter S. 1994. Redbaiter Liar Warmonger Crook. *Rolling Stone*, 16 June, 39-44.

Thrall, William F., Addison Hibbard, and C. Hugh Holman. 1960. *A Handbook to Literature*. New York: Odyssey Press.

Von Drehle, David. 1994. Men of Steel Are Melting with Age. *Washington Post*, 28 Apr.

Warner, William Lloyd. 1959. *The Living and the Dead: A Study in the Symbolic Life of Americans*. New Haven, CT: Yale University Press.

Whitaker, John C. 1976. *Striking a Balance: Environment and Natural Resources Policy in the Nixon-Ford Years*. Washington, DC: American Enterprise Institute.

———. 1997. Nixon's Domestic Policy: Both Liberal and Bold in Retrospect. *Presidential Studies Quarterly* 27(1):131-50.

White, Theodore H. 1982. *America in Search of Itself: The Making of a President, 1956-1980*. New York: Harper & Row.

Wicker, Tom. 1991. *One of Us: Richard Nixon and the American Dream*. New York: Random House.

Yardley, Jonathan. 1994. National Day of What? *Washington Post*, 2 May.

Zelizer, Barbie. 1992. *Covering the Body: The Kennedy Assassination, the Media, and the Shaping of Collective Memory*. Chicago: University of Chicago Press.

The Rule of Product Substitution in Presidential Campaign News

By JOHN ZALLER

ABSTRACT: This article develops a model of the relationship between candidates, journalists, and citizens in the game of media politics. For politicians, the goal is to gain public support by using reporters to get their story out, while, for reporters, the goal is to do stories that increase market share while emphasizing the independent and significant voice of journalists. These goals conflict with one another, leading the two groups into a turf war for control of political communication. The article proposes the rule of product substitution to explain how this struggle plays out in the context of presidential election campaigns. The rule asserts that reporters react to candidates' attempts at news management by creating alternative forms of news—most of it negative—that they can market to the public in place of candidate-supplied information, thereby vindicating journalistic voice. The article shows that, consistent with this rule, candidates who try to control their media images through aggressive news management suffer more frequent press criticism, even after controlling for the media negativity that may initially cause aggressive news management.

John Zaller is coauthor (with Herbert McClosky) of The American Ethos *(1984) and author of* Nature and Origins of Mass Opinion *(1992). He is currently completing work on* A Theory of Media Politics: How the Interests of Politicians, Journalists, and Citizens Shape the News. *He received his Ph.D. in political science from the University of California, Berkeley, in 1984.*

NOTE: I am grateful to Michael Alvarez, Bill Bianco, Lara Brown, Jim DeNardo, John Geer, Shanto Iyengar, Elihu Katz, Taeku Lee, Dan Lowenstein, Warren Miller, Jonathan Nagel, John Petrocik, Tom Schwartz, Jim Sidanius, Michael Traugott, and especially to Larry Bartels, Barbara Geddes, and George Tsebelis for helpful comments on earlier drafts. The research for this article, along with the larger project of which it is a part, has been generously supported by several institutions, including the Center for Advanced Study in the Behavioral Sciences, the National Science Foundation, the Guggenheim Foundation, and the Academic Senate Research Fund at the University of California at Los Angeles.

F LAG sales are doing well and America is doing well and we should understand that and we should appreciate that." So declared presidential candidate George Bush in 1988 from a flag-festooned podium at a New Jersey flag factory. Although Bush gave another address that day, it mostly repeated ideas from earlier speeches. As a result, the rally at the flag factory became the centerpiece of television news reports on that day's Republican campaign.

This, of course, is what the Bush campaign intended. In serving up a visually attractive backdrop, a sound bite to fit it, and an otherwise light schedule, campaign strategists sought to compel the media to present Bush in a patriotic vein.

Bush's rally at the New Jersey flag factory was one of the signature events of the 1988 presidential campaign. But what I have related so far is only half the story. Professional reporters loathe running politicians' press releases, and events like the Bush rally at the flag factory are, in effect, visual press releases. Reporters therefore rewrote the script. On NBC, Tom Brokaw announced that "the vice president wrapped himself in the flag again." Dan Rather said on CBS that "George Bush gives his 'my patriotism is better than yours' the hard sell." ABC's Brit Hume reminded viewers of an event a week earlier in which the vice president had used the word "America" 31 times in 15 minutes, for an average of twice a minute (Grove 1988). NBC's Lisa Myers added that Bush's use of national symbols "lead some to quote Samuel Johnson that patriot-ism is the last refuge of scoundrels" (quoted in Siegel 1988).

Thus, although all three networks carried Bush's rally at the flag factory, the coverage may not have won many votes for Bush. "That," as campaign manager Lee Atwater said afterward, "was one flag factory too many" (quoted in Germond and Witcover 1989, 408).

If attempts by campaign strategists to influence what journalists report are a staple of modern election campaigns, so are attempts by reporters to resist. Hence the central argument of this article: that the harder presidential campaigns try to control what journalists report about their candidate, the harder journalists try to report something else instead. I call this the rule of product substitution.

The first part of this article proposes a theory of media politics to explain why this sort of product substitution occurs. The second part reports an empirical test of the rule.

A THEORY OF MEDIA POLITICS

With the weakening of traditional parties, candidates must reach and persuade voters on their own. Political advertising is one way of doing this. Getting out on the campaign trail and creating events that a non-partisan media will see fit to report as news is another. The goal of such campaigning is to use journalists to get the candidate's story out.

The techniques by which politicians try to create favorable news are well known. On one hand, they take actions and stage events that promote their campaign agenda and that are so compelling that reporters will feel obliged to report them as news. On the other hand, they attempt to avoid situations, such as news conferences, that make it difficult for them to control the kind of news that gets made.

Both elements were present in the flag factory rally discussed earlier. The Bush campaign calculated that journalists would be unable to resist the visual appeal of the patriotic setting, even if what the vice president said was somewhat vacuous. Also, campaign managers kept Bush physically separated from reporters on that day, so as to prevent journalists from asking Bush to address questions that would distract from his primary message of patriotism.

All this smacks of manipulation, but when politics is conducted by means of mass communication, politicians must approach communication strategically. Candidates who fail to be strategic will be beaten by— that is, judged by voters to be less attractive than—candidates who do handle communication strategically.

But if candidates are constrained to approach communication strategically, journalists are not constrained to like it, and most do not. Yet it is not immediately obvious why they do not. Why could journalists not sell as many newspapers, or get as many audience rating points, by providing straight reports of campaign events? Why do journalists so often feel compelled to make sarcastic or other negative comments when, as in the case of the flag factory rally, the candidates do such a good job of appeal-

ing to the production values of journalists? Why not just cooperate with politicians rather than treat them as adversaries?

In the space available for this essay, I can only sketch answers to these questions (see Zaller, forthcoming, for a fuller argument). I also limit discussion to elite journalists, that is, those who work for television network news or prestigious national publications.

Let me begin with a commonly given argument that I consider unsatisfactory: that the reason reporters take an adversarial stance toward politicians is that they distrust and dislike them. An alternative argument, essentially the same, is that reporters' values lead them to distrust politicians.

I consider such arguments unsatisfactory for two reasons. First, there are numerous cases in which journalists cooperate closely with politicians, including, most notably, foreign policy coverage (Zaller with Chiu 1996). According to Kernell (1997), even the relationship between the presidential press corps and the president was once very cooperative. Second, and more fundamentally, the argument that reporters adopt an adversarial stance toward politicians because their values lead them to do so is like arguing that they do it because they want to do it. It is hardly an explanation at all.

The explanation I shall propose is that reporters adopt an adversarial posture toward their sources because it is in their self-interest to do so. I reach this conclusion through the following logic. Like other professional groups—lawyers, doctors, architects, and university professors—journalists value autonomy both as an end in itself and as a means to creating the kind of product they wish to create. The kind of product they wish to create is one that requires as much personal skill and expertise as possible. The exercise of skill and expertise is not only inherently satisfying; it also leads to higher pay and higher status.

Consider, as a parallel, the case of architecture. If an architect had a choice between designing a no-frills box of a building according to someone else's instructions and, instead, an irregularly shaped and elaborately styled structure of her own design, which would she choose? The latter, of course, since architects get higher fees, more intellectual satisfaction, and greater peer recognition for producing the latter type of building. The major constraint on this preference is the consumer, who might want just a box, or at least something that costs what a box costs.

It is much the same for journalists. Journalists have an occupational interest in a relatively activist and autonomous conception of journalism, one that offers more than stenographic transcription of what others have said and that has appeal beyond the lowest common denominator of the mass market. Journalists want to be members of a profession that adds something to the news—a profession that not only reports, but also digs, selects, frames, investigates, interprets, and regulates the flow of political communication.

If journalists allowed themselves to become a mere transmission belt for the communication of politicians— if, that is, they ceded politicians control over the content of the news by simply reporting the information that politicians give them to report— their professional standing would erode. They would gradually lose status, the opportunity for interesting work, and perhaps even pay. They would gradually come to resemble the glittering personalities of happy-talk television news—widely seen but not widely admired.

What journalists want, then, is to be in charge of political communication—to control their turf in the same way that elite architects, doctors, lawyers, and professors control their turf—and to use this control to create and sell a product that shows off their special knowledge and skill.[1] Summarizing this general argument in a form specific to journalism, I propose that, acting from occupational interest, journalists seek to control the content of the news and to use this control to maximize their independent and distinctive voice in the news.

This occupational interest brings journalists into regular conflict with politicians, who, as noted earlier, also have a clear occupational interest in controlling the content of the news. In the first half of the twentieth century, journalists fought for and largely won the autonomy to report the news as they saw it rather than as their publishers saw it (Halberstam 1978); in the second half of the twentieth century, they are fighting to keep politicians from dominating the news product. This basic conflict of interest, rather than the values or personal dislikes of journalists, explains the conflictual relationship that exists between politicians and journalists.

One might suppose that, inasmuch as journalists make final decisions about what counts as news, they would be able to control news content without any special effort. But it is not so simple. For one thing, politicians, with their armies of media consultants, determine most of the day-to-day content of campaigns, which are the raw material of news. If, as campaign managers try to ensure, journalists can find nothing more interesting to report, they are constrained to report what the candidates give them.

The other factor is the constraining influence of the mass audience, which critically affects the power balance between politicians and journalists. Citizen consumers of news have no rational interest in permitting either politicians or journalists to dominate the flow of political communication. Their interest, rather, is in having the two groups share control, as actually occurs in practice most of the time.

Since this latter point is a key proposition for which there is no direct evidence, I shall develop an a priori argument from first principles. To begin with, each individual voter is more likely to be mugged on the way to the polls than to affect an election outcome through voting.[2] Thus an individual citizen could devote his entire lifetime studying how to cast wise votes in elections and be no better off than if he had spent no time studying politics at all—and

quite possibly worse off for having wasted time on politics. As Anthony Downs (1957) argued, it is therefore individually rational for most citizens to be largely ignorant of politics.

Most citizens behave as if they had been raised from infancy on the book of Downs. Americans sometimes say they are interested in politics, but, in practice, few are. As Doris Graber (1984) found in her study of news consumption habits:

[Citizens] grumbled frequently about the oversimplified treatment of all news, including elections news, on television. Yet when the debates and other special news programs and newspaper features presented a small opportunity for more extensive exposure to issues, they were unwilling to seize it. For the most part, the [study subjects] would not read and study carefully the more extensive versions of election and other news in newspapers and news magazines. Masses of specific facts and statistics were uniformly characterized as dull, confusing, and unduly detailed. (105)

Over the years, journalists have tried schemes to increase the attention that citizens pay to news, mostly without success. As Lance Bennett (1996) reports, editors and marketers have concluded that efforts "to improve election issue coverage and offer more in-depth political reporting are up against a basic obstacle: People really do not want more serious news, even when they say they do" (22-23).

Yet citizens consume some political news. What do they want from the small amount of political news they consume?

To whatever (modest) extent that rational voters seek information whose purpose is to help them form informed opinions or cast wise votes, they will look for time-saving heuristics to minimize their effort. Party attachment and peer group opinion are, as Downs pointed out, two such heuristics. Another obvious time-saving device is to focus on points of political controversy. When elites achieve a consensus on a policy, there is no reason for each voter to trouble to figure out which side is best and how the parties line up. If, on the other hand, elites disagree, citizens may wish to prepare themselves to express an opinion on it. By this reasoning I reach the conclusion that the rational voter is engaged by news of political conflict and bored by news of political consensus. Consistent with the argument that citizens want news about conflict, Cook (1998) remarks that "conflict may be one of the few cross-cultural characteristics of news" (101).[3]

When elites engage in public disagreement, each side works hard to advance the best arguments for its position and to expose the weaknesses of the other side. By monitoring such disagreements, citizens can often get incisive information for little effort. Of course, even a little bit of effort may be more than many citizens want to make. But, even so, rational citizens want the option of paying attention in case a really important issue comes up. Also, they know that some of their fellow citizens are paying attention, and they want this minority of politics junkies to be able to see what is going on. For these reasons, rational citizens do not want major conflict swept under the carpet, away from public view; nor do they want any group—politicians or journalists or corporate owners—to monopolize public discourse with its own point of view. Rather, when political elites disagree, rational citizens want exposure to both sides of the argument, and under no circumstances do they want to see one side monopolize public discussion.

I do not claim that citizens are consciously aware of any of these principles. In the same way, however, that many citizens vote their class interest without thinking consciously of either class or interest, I propose that citizens tend to make habitual news choices that reflect their actual interests.

Returning to my main line of argument, I claim that conflict between politicians and journalists is played out within this set of audience constraints. Citizens want some original exposure to what politicians are saying, and they would be indignant if journalists were, for any reason, to refuse to provide it routinely. Even though a witty exchange between Sam Donaldson and Cokie Roberts would be at least as interesting as any politician's speech, the public wants to hear the speech anyway, or thinks it does. This attitude strengthens the hand of politicians in their turf war with journalists. Yet the public also remains both easily bored by politicians and suspicious of them and so is willing to cede journalists wide leeway to criticize and dig up dirt on politicians. This strengthens the hand of journalists against politicians.

This three-cornered contest—politicians and journalists struggling to control news content within constraints set by the mass audience—is, as I claim, at the heart of media politics. In the next section, I show how this general conflict works out in the context of presidential campaigning.

THE RULE OF
PRODUCT SUBSTITUTION

All presidential candidates behave in ways designed to attract good news coverage, but their approaches vary. Two idealized approaches may be identified. The first is to engage in aggressive news management, the essential feature of which is, in the context of presidential campaigns, to control what journalists can report by serving up a limited number of carefully crafted and controlled events. Politicians who follow this strategy tend, for example, to campaign in friendly territory, where chances of unplanned occurrences are minimal, and to hold events in closed settings, such as indoor arenas, where attendance can be limited to loyalists. In addition, since the candidate's utterances are most important of all, they avoid any unscripted exchanges, either with journalists or ordinary citizens. Even simple visual access of journalists to the candidate is routinely controlled, as illustrated by an incident from Nixon's 1968 campaign in which reporters were denied permission to come into a television studio to watch the candidate respond to questions from a panel of local denizens. Instead, the national press was forced to watch on television monitors in an adjacent room. Why not let us watch firsthand, the reporters demanded. Because, a campaign official

told them, "if that happens you're going to write about the lights, the cameras and that sort of thing and you're not going to understand what happens in the living rooms across America" (quoted in Jamieson 1996, 260).

The second of the two idealized approaches is an open-news style: candidates mount relatively freewheeling campaigns in which there are multiple, somewhat loosely scripted events each day, including regular opportunity for citizens and reporters to quiz the candidate. Such campaigns can create a sense of energy and spontaneity that makes for naturally good news coverage.

The famous Truman "give 'em hell" whistle-stop campaign of 1948 adhered to the open-news strategy, as did the Kennedy and Nixon campaigns of 1960. Among recent campaigns, Michael Dukakis's 1988 campaign was relatively open. Ronald Reagan's 1984 campaign, by contrast, nearly matched the idealized account of aggressive news management.

The closed-news strategy of aggressive news management attempts to force journalists into a role they detest, that of mechanically conveying politicians' words and actions to the public. Campaign strategists are well aware that journalists detest this role, but many calculate that any journalistic retribution over loss of voice will be more than offset by the candidate's ability to control his message most of the time. The open-news strategy gives journalists a wide choice of material from which to select the ingredients of their stories. The hope of this strategy is that, if journalists have ample scope to exercise voice, they will lack the motivation to dig up unflattering information or make negative remarks.

Media negativity toward candidates is, in this view, determined in significant part by the candidate's strategy of news management. When aggressive news management limits journalistic opportunities to express voice, journalists create their own outlets in the form of investigations, critical analyses, and, to the extent they think the public will tolerate it, blunt expressions of sarcasm. Journalists, in effect, substitute their own news, most of which is negative, for that which the campaign has provided.

What journalists substitute must, however, meet two constraints. First, it must permit politicians some opportunity to speak directly to the mass audience. This is because, as just explained, the public dislikes having any one group dominate communication. Thus journalists cannot offer general commentaries on the election in place of stories that show what the candidates are doing. Second, like a detergent company that wants to get consumers to buy liquid gel instead of soap bars, journalists must offer something that is the functional equivalent of the product they replace, that is, something that provides information about the campaign. Much horse-race coverage—in which, for example, journalists let the candidate deliver his sound bite of the day but then explain how everything he has said is really just an appeal for votes—meets both of these constraints. Clever editing of sound bites to show how the candidate has contradicted himself also does so. More generally, I propose the rule of product substitution as the central hypothesis of this article: the more strenuously politicians challenge journalists for control of a news jurisdiction, the more journalists will seek to develop substitute information that the mass audience is willing to accept as news and that gives expression to journalistic voice.

As suggested previously, most of the information that journalists substitute for candidate-supplied information is negative. My expectation, then, is that candidates' efforts at news management will correlate with the amount of media-initiated negativity directed toward them. To test this expectation, it is necessary to make reliable measurements of both news management and media-initiated negativity. I turn now to this task.

EMPIRICAL TESTS

In this section, I reduce the complexity and drama of 16 major-party presidential campaigns to numerical scores on a handful of variables, the most important of which are media-initiated negativity and news management style. Having thus measured the key concepts in my theoretical analysis, I test the extent to which they are statistically correlated with one another.

Measuring media negativity

In this study, I define media negativity as negative information or opinion that reporters themselves insert into the news. Negativity from other sources, such as the attack of one candidate on another, is outside my definition, which stresses media initiation of the negativity. Like most other scholars, I also exclude horse-race evaluations, that is, statements by reporters about how well or badly a candidate is faring in the competitive struggle. Horse-race statements from ordinary citizens—"soccer moms," "angry white males," and so forth—that include negative comments about one of the candidates are likewise omitted from my conception of media-initiated negativity. In determining the overall amount of media negativity, I calculate media negativity as a fraction of all campaign coverage.

Working with this conception of negativity, I find many instances of media negativity in coverage that contains no explicit negative evaluation. For example, after Gennifer Flowers's allegation of an extramarital affair with Clinton surfaced in a tabloid in 1992, many news outlets reported it as news. Yet few reports offered any explicit criticism of Clinton's alleged behavior. They simply recounted Flowers's allegation and Clinton's response. Thus, without saying anything directly negative, reporters gave Clinton a heavy dose of what I count as media-initiated negativity. Most of what I have classified as media negativity consists, as in this example, of ostensibly straight news about topics that candidates would prefer not to have reported or discussed.

This conception of media negativity differs in important ways from that used in other research. Most scholars, for example, count negative evaluative statements as media ne-

gativity but not media-initiated negative information, such as the information in the Flowers story. They also count negative evaluations that derive from non-press sources, especially the attacks of candidates on one another. Space limitations preclude discussion of these conceptual issues, except to acknowledge them (see, however, Zaller, forthcoming).

I have collected data on media negativity in four media: the *New York Times*; *Time* and *Newsweek* magazines; and network television news. Coding of the *New York Times* was based on abstracts of campaign coverage, as reported in the *Index to the New York Times*, and coding of the network news was based on the Vanderbilt abstracts. For the newsmagazines, the original texts of campaign and campaign-related stories were coded. Coding was done at the level of individual sentences or, when sentences contained multiple and especially conflicting bits of information, at the level of major phrases.

Following is a randomly selected sample of the *New York Times* abstracts from three different elections that were coded as instances of media-initiated negativity:

1. "Gov Clinton, stung by recurring questions about his credibility, gives television interview from his mansion in Little Rock, Ark, in effort to control campaign coverage."
2. "Clinton and Bush campaigns have started using paid-for airtime to fling mud, ushering in season of negative advertising."
3. "Gov Bill Clinton and his running mate, Sen Al Gore, have campaigned together on 20 of 52 days

since their nomination in July. . . . subtext is to draw comparisons between Democratic package and Republican one, since Pres Bush almost never shares stage with Vice Pres Quayle." (This was coded also as positive for Clinton.)

4. "Newsmen from at least 6 natl pubs and Dem Natl Com agents have been at work for wks searching through data . . . for material on Agnew. . . . probes focus on old charges of conflicts of interest."

5. "Nixon lr to securities indus leaders pledging to ease Govt regulatory policies disclosed; aide A Greenspan says it was not made pub because it covers 'narrow policy area.' "

6. "Sen Brooke flies to Cleveland to rejoin Nixon campaign; says he is bewildered about Nixon's remarks on school desegregation but stresses he is not leaving the campaign."[4]

7. "Pres Reagan, during televised briefing, says he will meet on September 28 at White House with Soviet Foreign Min Andrei Gromyko . . . denies he has been motivated by election campaign and by criticism that Soviet-American relations have worsened under his Administration and that he has not met with any Soviet leader."

8. "Pres Reagan assails suggestions from some Democrats and news commentators that he showed signs of age in debate with Walter Mondale."

9. "Mayor A Starke Taylor of Dallas insists that Republican National Convention is still the 'free enterprise' convention city leaders said it would be, even though city's taxpayers will end up paying from $1 million to $1.5 million for convention-related expenses."

All coding was done by Mark Hunt, who began work for me as an undergraduate at the University of California at Los Angeles and now works on a professional basis. As a partial check on his coding, I used his codes to replicate the measure of media negativity in Figure 2.1 of Patterson's *Out of Order* (1993). The correlation between Hunt's and Patterson's measure was .96.

Measuring news management

As explained earlier, the essence of news management in the context of political campaigns is to control what reporters can report by serving up a limited number of carefully controlled events. All presidential campaigns now engage in such management, but there is significant variation in the extent to which they do so, and it is this variation that I seek to measure.

To do so, I developed a set of 48 codes, each denoting either high (positive) or low (negative) concern for news management. For example, excluding reporters from a fund-raising event is coded as a positive indicator of news management, while taking reporters' questions at an informal press availability is coded as a negative indicator. Similarly, screening attendance at rallies is counted as a positive instance of news management, while taking unrehearsed questions from crowd members is counted as a negative instance. A sample of positive and negative

TABLE 1

SAMPLE CODES FOR NEWS MANAGEMENT SCALE

Message control
1. Candidate cancels major rally or event to avoid demonstrators. (Positive)
2. Candidate responds to specific opponent attacks, excluding debates. (Negative)
3. Candidate takes questions from group or individual, where questioners have been screened or selected by the candidate himself. (Includes friendly talk show.) (Positive)
4. Candidate engages in exchange—that is, back-and-forth discussion—with demonstrators or hecklers in crowd. (Negative)

Crowd exposure
5. Rally or speech takes place in unfriendly territory, for example, Clinton addresses a Veterans of Foreign Wars convention during draft controversy. (Negative)
6. Rally takes place in controlled setting; audience has been screened or selected by the campaign. (Positive)

Willingness to debate
7. Candidate refuses to debate with major-party opponent. (Positive)

Interview access
8. Press conference for national press takes place. (Negative)
9. There is press availability; that is, candidate meets informally with group of reporters. (Negative)
10. On his own initiative, candidate engages in light, nonsubstantive banter with reporters. (Negative)

Interview restrictions
11. No one in the campaign, including press secretary, will respond to queries about sensitive issue. (Positive)
12. In response to queries from reporters about a sensitive issue, the candidate or press secretary issues a statement, but no one will verbally respond to questions. (Positive)
13. Candidate has interview with selected print journalists, with restrictions on content. (Positive)
14. Candidate refuses request from traveling journalists for press conference. (Positive)

Media exclusion
15. A public or quasi-public event, such as a fund-raiser, is held from which reporters are excluded. (Positive)
16. Campaign creates impediments to reporting of news; for example, party workers hold up signs to block picture taking. (Positive)

codes, grouped into six subscales, is shown in Table 1.

Information on candidate behavior was gleaned from campaign stories covering the period 10-30 September in the *New York Times*, the *Washington Post*, the *Los Angeles Times*, Vanderbilt television news abstracts, and, for elections since 1980, the Associated Press wire. Coding was again done by Hunt.[5] As part of the coding task, Hunt copied the text that he relied upon in assigning codes into electronic files, and these files have been put on my Web page. Thus each of the roughly 1100 behaviors coded for the news management scale has a publicly available justification.[6] Further information on the coding and scaling of candidate behavior is available upon request.

Converting 48 codes and 1100 candidate behaviors into a usable measure of news management is not a straightforward task. To do it, I grouped the 48 codes into six subsets,

TABLE 2

CORRELATIONS BETWEEN NEWS MANAGEMENT SUBSCALES AND MEDIA NEGATIVITY

	Correlations with Media Negativity					Subscale Loading on General News Management Factor
	Newsweek Magazine	Time Magazine	New York Times	Network Television News	Row Average	
(Limited) interview access	.18	.25	.41	.44	.32	.56
(Un)willingness to debate	.23	.29	.54	.28	.34	.57
Interview restrictions	.39	.39	.47	.44	.42	.39
Media exclusion from events	.41	.29	.57	.50	.45	.66
(Limited) crowd exposure	.18	.22	.37	.67	.36	.54
Message control	.23	.30	.49	.39	.35	.46
Column average	.27	.29	.48	.45		

NOTE: Cell entries are correlation coefficients based on scores of 16 major-party candidates from 1968 to 1996. Italicized entries are averages of correlations in the indicated row or column.

as outlined in Table 1, and gave each candidate a score on each subset of items by adding up positive and negative points. Note from Table 1 that three of the subscales refer to behavior of candidates toward reporters and three refer to the management of campaign events independent of reporters. As Table 2 shows, scores on these subscales are correlated with negative coverage within each of the four media. When I performed a principal components analysis on the six subscales, all loaded reasonably well on a common factor, as shown in the last column of Table 2.

These preliminary results contain two notable pieces of information. Candidates who score high on one facet of news management (such as reluctance to debate) tend to score high on others as well (such as lim-

ited reporter access to events, low exposure to potentially unfriendly crowds). Further, each facet of news management correlates with press negativity (albeit somewhat unevenly).

An obvious concern in measuring candidate behavior from media reports, as I have done, is that the reports may be biased in some way. This concern, however, is greater for some subscales than others. For example, one can be confident that when candidates give on-the-record interviews or press conferences, some reference to them will appear in print (for example, "Speaking with reporters on Air Force One, the President said . . ."). Similarly, one can be confident that when candidates exclude reporters from events, reporters will usually note it (often in the form of a complaint). On the other hand, one cannot be confident that every case in which a campaign screens access to its rallies will be noted; the most one can hope is that there will be more frequent references to such screening for candidates who screen more. In light of this concern, it is reassuring that all six subscales of the news management scale have a zero-order relationship with media negativity, as shown in Table 2.

One might also be concerned that, because reporters have focused more on horse-race matters in recent years (Patterson 1993), they would point out more instances of news management now than in the past, even if nothing had changed. However, one might also entertain the opposite worry: that many forms of news management attracted more attention in campaigns during the 1960s and 1970s, when they were newer. One might also be concerned that a liberal media would attribute more instances of news management to Republican candidates, out of prejudice against them. To control for these possibilities, I repeated my main analysis, as described in Table 3, after purging the news management scale of the effects of year and party of candidate. The results left the effect of news management entirely unchanged.

Findings

As shown earlier, higher levels of news management, as measured in September, are correlated with higher levels of media negativity, as measured in October. Yet, to demon-

strate that these correlations represent a causal relationship, it is necessary to control for potentially confounding variables, as follows:

1. Inspection of the data indicate that, beginning with Nixon in 1968, Republican candidates tended to make more aggressive efforts at news management than Democrats did. This makes it necessary to control for the party of the candidate. Absent such a control, any effect of news management could be a spurious indicator of media bias against Republicans.

2. As Patterson (1993), in particular, has shown, media negativity has increased in recent decades. To control for this general trend, it is necessary to control for the year of the election.

3. In a separate analysis, I have shown that reporters are more inclined to dig up negative information about candidates who are politically strong. I call this the rule of anticipated importance. The idea is that journalists, in serving a news audience that is only minimally interested in politics, concentrate their attention on candidates and causes that have anticipated future importance—that is, they focus on winners rather than losers. Thus, in 1996, reporters investigated Bill Clinton's fund-raising practices but not Bob Dole's. Reporters also ignored Bob Dole's marital indiscretions, despite the fact that *Washington Post* reporter Bob Woodward gathered the information necessary to write such a story. To control for a candidate's anticipated importance, I use the average of his share

TABLE 3

EFFECTS OF NEWS MANAGEMENT ON MEDIA NEGATIVITY, 1968 TO 1996

	(1)	(2)	(3)	(4)
News management (mean = 0, SD = 1)				
β	.51	—	—	—
b	.53			
one-tailed p value	.03			
Reporter management (mean = 0, SD = 1)				
β	—	.55	—	—
b		.57		
p value		.05		
Event management (mean = 0, SD = 1)				
β	—	.04	.26	.34
b		.04	.27	.36
p value		.44	.15	.03
September media criticism* (mean = 0, SD = .87)				
β	.18	.17	.20	—
b	.22	.20	.12	
p value	.30	.28	.29	
Political strength† (range 36 to 62)				
β	.38	.39	.37	.44
b	.06	.06	.05	.06
p-value	.03	.03	.05	.01
Year (0 to 7)				
β	.34	.38	.26	.28
b	.15	.17	.11	.06
p value	.02	.01	.07	.04
Democratic candidate‡ (0 or 1)				
β	.14	.18	−.02	—
b	.29	.35	−.04	
p value	.28	.34	.47	
Incumbent (0, .50, 1)				
β	.15	.12	.24	.32
b	.32	.25	.52	.68
p value	.25	.30	.17	.04
Intercept	−3.47	−3.63	−3.16	−3.79
R^2	.84	.86	.79	.78
Adjusted R^2	.73	.73	.65	.69

NOTE: Estimation is by means of ordinary least squares. Number of cases is 16. All p values are one-tailed. The dependent variable is a weighted average of the October media negativity scores of *Newsweek, Time,* the *New York Times,* and television network news. To create this variable, I standardized all four variables; averaged them so as to give equal weight to each type of media, that is, one-sixth weights to each news magazine, one-third weight to the newspaper, and one-third weight to television news (which was already an average across the three major networks); and restandardized the final variable to a mean of zero and a standard deviation (SD) of 1.

*September criticism scores from the *New York Times* and television news were standardized and combined. (September scores for *Time* and *Newsweek are unavailable.)*

†An average of a candidate's support in the early October Gallup poll and in the final vote.

‡The nonincumbent nominee of the incumbent party receives a score of .50.

of the two-party vote in the early October Gallup poll and the final election results.

4. Candidates may resort to aggressive management as a response to media negativity toward them. To control for this possibility, I control for the September level of media criticism. Since September criticism is correlated with October criticism at the level of $r = .77$, this is a strong control.

5. The data indicate that reporters are more critical of incumbents. Hence I add an incumbency control.

Using five control variables in a regression having only 16 observations makes it difficult to show the effect of the variable of interest, news management. Compounding this difficulty is the fact that three of the five controls are correlated with news management at the level of $r = .50$ or greater. Nonetheless, Table 3 shows that news management has a significant effect.

The dependent variable in Table 3 is media-initiated negativity, which has been formed by combining negativity scores from all four media (*Time*, *Newsweek*, the *New York Times*, and television network news). The key independent variable is news management, which is a linear combination of the six subscales in Table 2, as weighted by the factor scores from a principal components analysis.[7] Look first at column 1 of Table 3, where the effect of news management on criticism is both statistically significant ($p = .03$, one-tailed) and substantively large. (The standardized coefficient of .51 means that a change of 1 standard deviation

[SD] on the news management scale is associated with a change of .51 SDs in press-initiated criticism.) Column 2 of Table 3 breaks the news management scale into two subscales—a three-item subscale that I shall call event management (crowd exposure, message control, plus willingness to debate) and a three-item subscale that I shall call reporter management (media exclusion, interview restriction, plus lack of interview access). In the regression in column 2, reporter management has a very large and significant effect, while event management has almost none. Column 3 shows that, when reporter management is taken out of the model, event management has a moderate but statistically marginal effect on media negativity.

The latter results suggest that how a candidate treats reporters has a big effect but that little else matters. Yet it would be a mistake to accept this conclusion. The two subscales of news management are, to begin with, correlated at .80. In light of the measurement error that no doubt exists in both subscales, this is a high correlation—one strongly suggesting that event management and reporter management tap a common syndrome. It is quite possible that the vagaries of measurement error, in combination with multicollinearity in a small data set, have made it artificially easier to show effects for one part of the syndrome than for the other, even though the overall syndrome, rather than either part alone, is what matters.

A partial test of this supposition is possible. Note that the coefficient for Democratic candidate is small and statistically insignificant in columns 1, 2, and 3 and, further, that it has the "wrong" sign in two of the tests. (The positive sign indicates that, contrary to expectation, the media appear to be slightly more critical of Democrats than Republicans.) These results suggest that party is a superfluous control variable with no real effect at all. Note also that September media criticism was included only to control for the possibility of a reciprocal relationship between media negativity and candidate behavior toward the reporters and that there is little reason to worry about such reciprocity if we are testing the effect of event management by itself. Given this, it is reasonable to omit party and September media criticism as control variables when testing the effect of event management separately from the effect of media control. The results of such a test, as reported in column 4 of Table 3, show that event management is both statistically and substantively significant when freed of the need to compete with a set of highly collinear and arguably superfluous rivals.

The conclusion I draw from these results is that attempts by candidates to manage journalists and campaign events are part of a common syndrome and have common effects on media negativity. It may be, as the evidence in column 2 suggests, that reporters are more reactive to attempts to manage them than to attempts to manage campaign events. But it is quite likely, in my opinion, that attempts to measure the former seem more important simply because they are easier to measure accurately.

A final point to notice in Table 3 is that both political strength and year have reliable effects on media negativity. The former effect is consistent with my rule of anticipated importance, as described earlier. The latter has no definite theoretical interpretation and could capture any number of temporal developments, such as changes in journalistic norms or the effects of increased competition between media outlets, among other possibilities. As I will explain, however, I regard the effect of the year variable as an indication of the escalating struggle between politicians and journalists to control the content of political communication.

DISCUSSION

An interesting question is why, if this analysis is correct, candidates persist in news management techniques that offend the media and result in media criticism. Why not simply ease up and get better coverage in return?

Much of the reason seems to be the belief of campaign consultants, especially on the Republican side, that candidates gain more from the controlled images they get, especially on television, than they lose from the criticism, much of it petty and strained, that journalists visit upon them in return. This belief is on open display in an oft-told tale from Ronald Reagan's 1984 campaign. Frustrated that the Reagan campaign consisted of vacuous hoopla, CBS News reporter Leslie Stahl assembled a repetitive montage of campaign scenes that seemed especially vacuous—cheering crowds, colorful balloons rising into the sky, Reagan smiling and waving—and used it as visual backdrop for an acid commentary about Reagan's supposedly empty campaign. But, as related by Michael Schudson (1995):

A White House official called [Stahl] soon after the piece aired and said he'd loved it. "How could you?" she responded. He said, "Haven't you figured it out yet? The public doesn't pay any attention to what you say. They just look at the pictures." Stahl, on reflection . . . came to believe that the White House was probably right: all she had done was to assemble, free of charge, a Republican campaign film, a wonderful montage of Reagan appearing in upbeat scenes. (115)

It is hard to believe that media stories about Watergate and Clinton fund-raising were quite as harmless as Stahl's attack on Reagan's campaign style. But I have been able to find no systematic evidence that media criticism during the final phase of the election campaign has any negative effect—and a slight suggestion that it might sometimes help. Consistent with this possibility, I spoke to a Republican adviser who said that the Bush campaign knew in 1988 that it might be criticized by journalists for visiting flag factories but felt that this sort of criticism from none-too-popular journalists could perhaps be helpful with swing voters. No doubt this kind of thinking is why campaigns are as willing to anger the media as some obviously are.

Another question is why media negativity has accelerated in recent decades. Although, as indicated, I have no strong answer to this question, I regard media-initiated negativity as a defensive response to the increasingly aggressive attempts at news management on the part of politicians. As Ansolabehere, Behr, and Iyengar (1993) observe,

In a sense, the relationship between reporters and government officials or candidates is akin to a chess game in which each side vies for control. As conditions change, both sides must adapt. Politicians must learn to "game" the system for their own benefit, while reporters must respond in ways that prevent the officials and campaigns from dominating the process.

The relationship between political figures and the media has changed dramatically since the advent of television. Politicians have been much quicker to adjust to these changes than the media. Elected officials, candidates and their consultants have developed intricate strategies for using the media to their advantage. The media, on the other hand, have only just begun to develop counter-strategies for protecting their independence. (234)

What I have called media-initiated negativity—much of it carping complaints about overuse of balloons and patriotic symbols—seems the best counterstrategy that journalism has so far come up with.

CONCLUSION

This article has sketched a theory of interactions between politicians, journalists, and citizens and has examined a single testable implication of that theory, the rule of product substitution. The theory has numerous other implications for media politics in both electoral and nonelectoral settings, as I show in the full-length version of this monograph (Zaller, forthcoming). The most important of these implications is one that bears a strong relation to the theme of this volume, the future of fact: that the content of political communication is heavily determined by the disparate self-interests of politicians, journalists, and citizens as each group jostles to get what it wants out of politics and the political communication that makes politics possible.

Notes

1. Professors at research universities, who are the primary audience for the present article, do not differ much from journalists or other professionals in these matters. Certainly, we are as jealous of our autonomy as any professional group, and more effective in maintaining it than almost any. We use our autonomy to create and market the most sophisticated product we can—research. We generally consider that the best research is research that does not mechanically report the facts but interprets, analyzes, and theorizes them. Those who are most successful at this derive higher status, higher pay, and perhaps greater intellectual satisfaction than other researchers and colleagues at nonresearch institutions.

2. My colleague Tom Schwartz coined this witty aphorism.

3. Notwithstanding the claim that citizens are attracted to conflict, they often say they dislike it. However, I am more inclined to believe that journalists, who fill their news reports with conflict, know what sells their product than that citizens know their opinions.

4. Reporters were pressing Brooke, a black Republican, to respond to a speech in which Nixon had seemed critical of the Supreme Court's *Brown* decision.

5. It is a weakness of this research that one person, Hunt, coded both media negativity and candidate behavior. The two concepts, however, are quite different, and the two projects were separated by about a year.

6. These files may be found at www.sscnet.ucla.edu/polisci/faculty/zaller/ data.files/campaign.conduct.files/. There is a separate file for each election year. The files are in Word format.

7. The alpha reliability of the composite measure is about .90.

References

Ansolabehere, Stephen, Roy Behr, and Shanto Iyengar. 1993. *The Media Game*. New York: Macmillan.

Bennett, W. Lance. 1996. *News: The Politics of Illusion*. White Plains, NY: Longman.

Cook, Timothy E. 1998. *Governing with the News*. Chicago: University of Chicago Press.

Downs, Anthony. 1957. *An Economic Theory of Democracy*. New York: Harper.

Germond, Jack and Jules Witcover. 1989. *Whose Broad Stripes and Bright Stars*. New York: Warner Books.

Graber, Doris. 1984. *Processing the News*. White Plains, NY: Longman.

Grove, Lloyd. 1988. Goldwater Quip About Bush Reflects Changing Dynamics of Campaign on TV. *Washington Post*, 23 Sept.

Halberstam, David. 1978. *The Powers That Be*. New York: Dell.

Jamieson, Kathleen Hall. 1996. *Packaging the Presidency*. 3d ed. New York: Oxford University Press.

Kernell, Sam. 1997. *Going Public*. Washington, DC: CQ Press.

Patterson, Thomas. 1993. *Out of Order*. New York: Knopf.

Schudson, Michael. 1995. *The Power of News*. Cambridge, MA: Harvard University Press.

Siegel, Ed. 1988. A Campaign Dominated by Images, Not Issues. *Boston Globe*, 24 Sept.

Zaller, John. Forthcoming. *A Theory of Media Politics*. Chicago: University of Chicago Press.

Zaller, John with Dennis Chiu. 1996. Government's Little Helper: Press Coverage of Foreign Policy Crises, 1945-1991. *Political Communication* 13(4):385-406.

ANNALS, *AAPSS*, **560**, November 1998

Manipulating Public Opinion with Moral Justification

By KATHLEEN M. McGRAW

ABSTRACT: Justifications that invoke moral claims are highly effective in shaping public opinion. But moral justifications ("I am obeying the dictates of my conscience"; "This policy is in the community's best interests") are difficult to verify as to their truthfulness, raising the possibility that they can be used deceptively. In this article, the psychological and political literatures are reviewed to illustrate why it is so difficult to detect deceptive moral justifications. The difficulty arises because (1) people are not very good at detecting deception in general; (2) the mediated nature of political communication eliminates the nonverbal cues that are most predictive of deception; (3) social judgment biases lead people to focus on the individual and inhibit suspicion; (4) the norms of political culture constrain politicians from accusing each other of lying, so that the public is not prompted by other sources to regard moral claims with suspicion.

Kathleen M. McGraw is professor of political science at the Ohio State University. She previously was professor of political science at the State University of New York–Stony Brook. Her research interests are concerned with political accountability and public support, for both individual public officials and political institutions.

NOTE: The author thanks Tali Mendelberg and Jeffrey J. Strange for their thoughtful comments on this article, and John Sullivan for his gentle nudging to think seriously about these issues.

The polls in the state clearly favored him. . . . From a political standpoint, I badly wanted to vote for Clarence Thomas. However, my conscience wouldn't let me do it. I thought she was telling the truth.

Senator Harry Reid (D, NV),
16 October 1991, after the
Senate confirmation vote
for Clarence Thomas's
nomination to the
Supreme Court

[My conservative principles] are not in the agenda of the House Democratic leadership. My decision was based on conscience, principle, honor, and good sense.

Representative Greg Laughlin
(R, TX), 26 June 1995,
on his decision to switch
from the Democratic to
the Republican Party

I won't let you raise taxes on working families $48 billion. That is not the right way to balance the budget. It isn't fair. These bills undermine our values: our values of supporting both work and family; our values of being responsible and creating opportunity.

President Clinton,
19 October 1995,
signaling his intention
to veto the House
Medicare bill

This procedure is a violation of the Fifth Commandment, "Thou shalt not kill."

Representative Cliff Stearns
(R, FL), 19 September 1996,
explaining his vote for HR1833,
overriding Clinton's veto
of a bill banning certain
late-term abortions

The fact is, [homosexuality] is morally wrong. [The bill] is discrimination toward the act, not the individual.

Representative Tom Coburn
(R, OK), 12 July 1996,
explaining his vote for
HR3393, barring recognition
of same-sex marriages

The check was to buy stones for a backyard shrine to the Virgin Mary.

Representative Robert Dornan
(R, CA), March 1992,
explaining his House
bank overdraft

The foregoing statements illustrate the obvious point that public officials are not passive bystanders in the electoral process. Rather, they engage in strategic behaviors, including attempting to influence their constituents' perceptions of controversial events through explanatory rhetoric, or accounts. Strategic behavior by definition serves to further personal goals (such as job security), but the use of account rhetoric is also consistent with the obligations politicians accept when entering the public arena, because accountability is a critical feature of a representative democracy: "a representative is someone who is to be held to account, who will have to answer to another for what he does" (Pitkin 1967, 55).

The second point illustrated by these quotations, and the main focus of this article, is that accounts often invoke moral values or normative claims. This is neither surprising nor disturbing. Politics and moral values are intrinsically linked, so accounts invoking moral claims would be expected to be prominent and, in many instances, highly desirable. The purposes of this article are threefold: (1) to demonstrate that accounts that invoke normative claims can have a powerful impact on public opinion, (2) to consider the possibility that moral accounts can be employed by politicians deceptively, and (3) to outline a variety of reasons that make it difficult for citizens to detect such deception.[1]

TYPES OF ACCOUNTS AND JUSTIFICATIONS

The term "account" is typically defined as "a statement made by a social actor to explain unanticipated or untoward behavior" (Scott and Lyman 1968, 46). There is widespread agreement that four types of accounts are fundamental. The first, concessions, involve an acknowledgment that a negative event occurred and an implicit or explicit admission of responsibility for the consequences. Excuses, like concessions, acknowledge that the offense occurred but are characterized by a denial of full responsibility. The third type, justification, is the opposite of an excuse; it is an attempt to deny or minimize the undesirable nature of the event while accepting (usually implicitly) responsibility for the outcome. Finally, denials are statements in which the actor does not really explain but, rather, denies his or her involvement in an event.

It is through justifications that moral claims most easily make their appearance in account rhetoric. The aim of any justification is to minimize or deny the apparent negative aspects of some event; when justifications work, they lead the audience to reevaluate the predicament and judge it to be either less negative than originally thought or even to be desirable. Schlenker (1980) discusses three ways that undesirable events can be justified, which can be illustrated through examples from the investigation of Newt Gingrich's ethics violations in the latter part of 1996. The first type involves a direct minimization of the negativity of the outcome (for example, some Republicans' claims that Speaker Gingrich's transgressions were comparable to "jaywalking," the slightest infraction of the criminal code). The second type invokes social-comparison processes (for instance, the classic "everybody does it" justification, such as Representative Mike Parker's (R, MS) defense of Gingrich—"There isn't a person in the House who isn't guilty of a technical violation"—the implication being that what is consensual is acceptable). The third type of justification embeds the incident in the context of higher, more desirable goals (for example, one of Gingrich's lawyers stated that Gingrich's "purpose was good in that he was trying to advance a political philosophy").

It is through this final type of justification that moral claims and appeals are most likely to occur. Four variants of moral-claim justifications occur in politics (although the boundaries of these are admittedly fuzzy):

1. The first involves an invocation of personal ethical standards, such as moral conscience, or any claim along the lines of "I believe this is the right/morally correct thing to do."

Senator Reid's justification of his Clarence Thomas vote and Representative Laughlin's account for party switching are good examples.

2. The second variant invokes shared political values. Clinton's appeal to the values of "work and family, responsibility and opportunity," is an example of this second type.

3. The third type differs from the second in the invocation of moral claims that are not consensually shared. These can involve appeals to religion-specific principles or icons (for example, Representative Dornan and the Virgin Mary; Representative Stearns and the Fifth Commandment) or contestable values (for example, Representative Coburn's statement that homosexuality is "morally wrong"). This type of moral justification is obviously riskier, because the speaker risks offending those who reject the value claim or confusing those who might not understand a particular allusion.

4. The final type involves a claim of collective benefits (that is, any claim that the decision is in the best interests of the nation or local community), appealing to the utilitarian value of "the greatest good for the greatest number."

All of these moral justifications can be thought of as framing devices. Although clear, consistent definitions of the construct are elusive, Gamson and Modigliani's is perhaps best known: a frame is "a central organizing idea or story line that provides meaning to an unfolding strip of events" (1987, 143). In other words, framing occurs when some authoritative source defines and constructs the meaning of a political issue or controversy. Moral justifications can be considered a type of frame because the politician is attempting to redefine the parameters along which the controversy is evaluated: "If you apply this moral principle, you will see that I made a good [or positive or desirable] decision."

THE POWER OF MORAL JUSTIFICATION

Our empirical work on the effectiveness of various accounts that public officials often provide for controversial decisions[2] has consistently found that justifications appealing to moral principles—particularly personal ethical standards like fairness and moral conscience, as well as collective social benefits—are the most accepted and satisfactory of all accounts (McGraw 1991, forthcoming; McGraw, Best, and Timpone 1995; McGraw, Timpone, and Bruck 1993; Chanley et al. 1994 also reach this conclusion). Many accounts fail miserably—are evaluated quite negatively—but moral justifications consistently elicit high levels of satisfaction. Moreover, moral justifications have important positive public opinion consequences. First, moral justifications produce more positive evaluations of the controversial decision (McGraw, Best, and Timpone 1995). Second, moral justifications influence judgments about character. Accounts claiming "I did what my conscience dictates" imply independence of judgment and integrity and accordingly result in enhanced attributions of leadership and integrity; accounts claiming "this is in the best interest of the community" imply a social concern and accordingly result in heightened attributions of empathy (McGraw, forthcoming; McGraw, Timpone, and Bruck 1993).

Finally, because of these reactions—satisfaction with the account, positive reevaluations of policy decisions, and positive judgments of character—moral justifications result in more positive global opinions of the politician involved in the predicament. If the ultimate purpose of an account is to maintain the approval of valued constituent groups, there is little doubt from the extant research that justifications invoking moral principles are the most effective.

WHAT IF THEY ARE LYING?

The potency of moral justifications in shaping public opinion poses no problems if we assume that moral principles are indeed the real reasons for the decision. But if we believe that public officials sometimes lie, then we have reason to question the veracity of moral justifications and to consider the unique problems associated with detecting deception when moral claims are involved. I will take as a given that politicians lie occasionally (or not so occasionally—the frequency is irrelevant; see Jamieson 1992; Page 1996; Page and Shapiro 1992 for political discussions; see Bok 1989 for an extended essay on lying). Bok defines a lie as "any intentionally deceptive message which is *stated*" (1989, 13, italics in original). Similarly, Page and Shapiro discuss "manipulation" as an "intentional, human action" designed to "mislead the

public consciously and deliberately" (1992, 356). Accordingly, I designate a moral justification as a lie if the official intentionally misstates his or her real reason(s) for the decision or behavior. I make the further assumption that lies can be objectively defined—there are real differences between true and false statements. As Robinson (1993) argues, "*false statements* contrast with *true statements* and the test question about any claim is whether it corresponds to reality more closely than its denial does. If it does, it is true. If it does not, it is false" (393, italics in original). Not all versions of an event can be true—this is logically impossible. This does not deny that subjectively defined realities exist, that value-laden political problems are contestable, and that it is difficult, even impossible at times, for outside observers to determine whether a statement is true or false. But if a public official intentionally makes a deceptive statement about these contestable political realities, then he or she has told a lie.

One final assumption, regarding moral neutrality: following Bok (who follows Aristotle), I assume that "truthful statements are preferable to lies in the absence of special consideration" (1989, 30). All things equal, the truth is morally superior to a lie, and so citizens have the right to expect the truth from public officials.

Although I have no evidence to suggest that moral justifications are more likely to be lies than other types of political rhetoric, focusing on moral justifications as a particular type of political falsehood is instructive for two reasons. The first, as we have just seen, is that they are particularly potent shapers of public opinion: the deft use of a moral justification can have the double-barreled benefit of persuading the public to accept an initially disliked decision as well as to shore up support for the official linked to the decision.

Moreover, there is reason to believe that finding out a moral-justification lie is particularly difficult because of the unique characteristics involved in invoking a moral motive. Bennett (1980) has provided the most thoughtful analysis of this particular problem, and I want to be clear as to where I agree and part company with Bennett's argument. Bennett argues, "As long as information control is possible, a purely normative account is the least risky strategy for defining a political situation" (807). Accounts that are built around moral motives ("I am obeying the dictates of my conscience") and that do not point to "factual propositions and detailed descriptions of behavior" (800) are rarely successfully challenged—after all, who can convincingly raise the counterargument, "Your conscience does not dictate that!"? Graber (1976) similarly notes that, when a politician "proclaims that a policy that benefits his constituency was designed primarily to benefit the entire community, verification of his claim to altruism is well nigh impossible" (219).

It is undeniably the case that, when accounts are based upon moral motives, outside verification is usually "well nigh impossible." Bennett's analysis falters when, in acknowl-edging the difficulty in verifying the credibility of normative accounts, he proposes that "truth and credibility is virtually irrelevant as a criterion for interpreting (and responding to) political accounts ... most accounts can be judged independently of their credibility and most accounts provide grounds for sensible political responses (including challenge, acceptance, and acquiescence) whether or not they are regarded as true" (1980, 798-99). Bennett argues that "the criterion of judgment" on which political accounts can and therefore should be evaluated is "suitability," defined as an account's "internal consistency and its relevance to the developing situation" (810).

I have no doubt that "suitability" is one criterion on which political accounts are evaluated. Bennett's mistake is in ruling out the criteria of credibility and truthfulness. First, from a purely normative perspective, citizens have the right to expect the truth from their officials and should not be content to settle for the "ritualized, banal" rhetoric implied by the "suitability" criterion. Second, as an empirical matter, given the heightened cynicism about politics that exists in this country, it is reasonable to propose that some citizens under some circumstances will be suspicious about political rhetoric. That suspicion may lead them to ruminate about the truthfulness of a given statement, which in turn will influence their acceptance of it. The problem, to which I now turn, is that reaching confident conclusions about the truth or falsity of moral justifications is enormously difficult.

At this juncture, I turn to the empirical literature on detecting deception. I then discuss other psychological mechanisms that play a role in the failure to detect deceptive claims. The third section discusses political factors that pose unique problems for detecting moral-justification lies.

Detecting deception

In a recent review, Friedman and Tucker (1990) conclude that "detection accuracy in research typically falls in the modest range of 45% to 60%, with 50% accuracy being expected by chance. Most people can detect deception but only at slightly above-chance levels" (258). A large part of the problem is that there is a discrepancy between the cues that are perceived to be indicative of deception and those cues that actually predict deception. Naive theories about deception emphasize speech (such as hesitations and high pitch) and facial (such as averted gaze, increased smiling) cues, but these are the cues that are most easily controlled by liars (Ekman and Friesen 1974). Deception tends to leak through other indicators, such as restless hand and foot movements. In fact, when the motivation to deceive is high, nonverbal cues are associated with deception to a greater extent than speech cues (DePaolo, Lanier, and Davis 1983). However, citizens often do not have direct access to the nonverbal cues emitted by politicians when they make speeches or answer questions. To the extent that account rhetoric is mediated through other communication sources (for example, staff members, the media), the very cues that are most useful for detecting deception are stripped away.

Friedman and Tucker emphasize that the abilities to deceive and to detect deception are skills that are developed and refined through ongoing social interaction. From this perspective, deceivers have the advantage because they receive feedback that allows them to refine their ability to deceive—the success or failure of each deceptive attempt is known. But detectors do not receive such clear feedback—their successful detection efforts may be effectively challenged ("But I really am telling the truth") while their failure to detect deception goes unnoted.

Professionals (for example, police officers, investigative reporters, attorneys, and college professors) who work with potential deceivers have strategies that they believe to be effective in detecting deception. Kalfbleisch (1994) summarized 38 of these "pragmatic" detection tactics, all of which rely on direct interaction between detector and deceiver. The actual effectiveness of these professional strategies is largely unknown, but, to the extent that any of them work, the dynamic interaction requirement has two implications for the public's ability to detect political deceit: citizens must be both willing and able to confront the official and challenge the veracity of his or her comments. "Ability" need not and, pragmatically, cannot be limited to direct access but may also occur through surrogate routes—news reporters, other politicians, and citizen activists. Willingness to confront is a different matter; I will return to this point shortly.

In sum, the deception literature suggests that (1) people are simply not very good at detecting deception; (2) the mediated nature of political communication can eliminate many of the most predictive nonverbal cues; (3) the feedback associated with the skills of deceiving and detecting deceit favors the deceivers; and (4) potentially effective detection tactics require a willingness and an ability to confront speakers about the veracity of their claims.

Biases in social judgment

Detecting deception presupposes a willingness to consider the possibility that a statement is not truthful. The "most commonly documented bias in social perception" (Fiske and Taylor 1991, 67)—the fundamental attribution error (FAE)—may operate to minimize the likelihood of being suspicious of the veracity of political accounts. The FAE refers to the tendency to (over)attribute another person's behavior to his or her internal, dispositional qualities, rather than external, situational forces. There are compelling cognitive reasons to expect the FAE to be prominent in political reasoning. To avoid the FAE, individuals must be aware of situational constraints before they can be incorporated in the judgment process. If citizens are unaware of the activities of special interest groups, the cajoling of party leaders, vote trading with those on the other side of the aisle, and the public official's own personal agenda, they cannot consider the role these factors play in policy decisions and so cannot consider them in evaluating an account that claims moral motives. Moreover, internal attributions are spontaneous and cognitively simple, whereas incorporating external situational information requires mental effort (Gilbert, Pelham, and Krull 1988). Given the truism that most citizens are unwilling to expend much cognitive capital in thinking about the world of politics, even if they have some awareness of external constraints, they will be unlikely to make use of that information when reacting to account rhetoric.

The failure to consider situational constraints does not by itself predict acceptance of the stated laudatory motives—an attribution to stable *moral* qualities ("She is an honest person") or stable *immoral* qualities ("You can never believe a word he says") can both result from the FAE. Consideration of the individual's mental anchor, or reference point, is necessary to differentiate between the two. The well-documented declining levels of trust in government (Hibbing and Theiss-Morse 1995) that have become a staple of op-ed pages and scholarly discourse suggest the initial hypothesis that for many, if not most, citizens, the anchor will be negative. However, there is good reason to refute this assertion, because opinions about individual politicians and reactions to moral justifications are both typically positive.

Paradoxically, while trust in government and political institutions has declined in recent decades, impressions about individual political leaders still tend to be positive. In part, this is attributable to the "person positivity bias" (Sears 1983): judgments about individuals, including politicians, tend to be favorable rather than unfavorable. This contributes to what is known as Fenno's paradox (Fenno 1978): Americans hold negative views about Congress as an institution while at the same time expressing positive opinions about their own representative. Existing opinions about the politician are relevant because initial impressions shape our subsequent interpretation of new evidence (Asch 1946). Simply, if I have a positive impression of a politician, I am likely to interpret ambiguous situations—like the proffering of a moral justification for a misdeed—positively and accept the moral redefinition of the situation. As a result, politicians can provide moral justifications to their supporters in a deceptive manner with a minimal risk of negative repercussions precisely because supporters are predisposed to accept the sincerity of the claim.

Suspicion can be aroused by making salient the possibility of strategic behavior, such as the appearance of ingratiating oneself to please an audience (Hilton, Fein, and Miller 1993). However, our empirical exploration of the dynamics of suspicion found that agreement with a political statement—that is, having a positive reaction to what a politician has to say—inhibits suspicion (McGraw, Lodge, and Jones 1997). Consequently, even if nascent levels of suspicion toward a politician exist, they are unlikely to be made manifest given the positive reactions that moral justifications elicit.

In sum, a number of psychological principles minimize the likelihood of suspicions about deceptive intent being spontaneously entertained. Perhaps, then, suspicion must be prompted by other people, which leads to a consideration of the role of political norms of conduct.

Political culture:
Norms of conduct

If citizens are disinclined to be suspicious of the account rhetoric if left to their own psychological devices, suspicion may be prompted by the responses of other politicians. In the simplest case, another politician (undoubtedly of a different partisan stripe) might charge after a moral justification that the justification given is not the real reason that the first politician voted for the policy, made the decision, or engaged in the action in question. If made public, this kind of charge could very well raise public suspicion about the veracity of the account. However, there are several reasons to believe that this kind of countercharge does not happen very frequently.

First, it is recognized (by scholars, politicians, and the public) that political rhetoric is "heavily ritualized and that the expected must be said" (Graber 1976, 12). In campaigns, public assemblies, and other political contexts, we accept the fact that exaggerated and false claims are part of the political spectacle. Edelman (1977) and Bennett (1980) have argued forcefully that political accounts are among the most ritualized and "banal" of political discourse. Respect for the ritual is a key reason why moral justifications are so rarely challenged by other politicians, because they participate in the same ritual themselves.

Second, legislative bodies develop and sustain norms of conduct (Hedlund 1985). Among the rules of the game are respect and courtesy. Fenno argued a few decades ago that political debate is couched in language that is temperate and unlikely to anger the opposition; representatives develop "accepted ways of disagreeing which minimize, rather than exacerbate, interpersonal friction" (1962, 322; cited in Graber 1976, 222). Many observers have noted that the power of the "courtesy norm" in Congress declined markedly in the 1980s and 1990s (for example, Uslaner 1994). It is an open question as to how much the norms of civility in Congress have actually declined (Patterson 1995) and, more pertinent here, which norms have seen the greatest change. If accounts, especially moral justifications, are firmly rooted in ritual, then the reluctance to attack their validity may be less affected by changing congressional norms that permit partisan sniping and attacks in other contexts.

Third, as in law, the burden of proof is likely to be on the politician charging liar. Even if an official has sound political motivations for wanting to reveal another's deception, in the absence of supportive evidence, such a charge is likely to fail. It is precisely because normative accounts are not testable that declaring one to be a lie is a no-win situation for the accuser. Robinson (1993) has ar-

gued that, because lying is so pervasive in everyday life, "to call someone a liar is potentially dramatic, and even if true, can rebound on the challenger. Conventionally, it appears that it is the challenger and not the alleged liar who has broken the stronger rule" (364). Robinson's insight is that labeling someone a liar can be perceived as a worse transgression than actually telling a lie. Gingrich's formal reprimand in 1997 and the surrounding debate is telling on this point. Speaker Gingrich was formally charged with "disregard and a lack of respect for the standards of conduct" that a member of Congress should follow. This is not the place for a litany of Gingrich's misdeeds. What is striking in reading through the Ethics Committee report and the accompanying debate is that although it is clear the committee believed that Gingrich "deliberately misled" them, a direct accusation of lying is nowhere to be found. Indeed the word "liar" is noticeably missing from the report, floor debate, and other spin, with the clearest accusation coming from Representative Nancy Pelosi (D, CA) of the Ethics Committee that "Mr. Gingrich, in his dealings with the committee, is not to be believed."[3]

Robinson's thoughtful analysis (1993) raises one final, sobering thought: "Being seen as a winner commands more popular support than being seen as a truth teller" (365). In the world of politics, where success is paramount, the assertion that "truth is the first casualty of war" is particularly apt. Robinson's analysis is aimed at understanding why public figures lie, but the point is also useful for understanding why politicians let others get away with lies. Too often in politics, the truth is irrelevant. As a result, only when the stakes (winning) and the likelihood of success are high is a politician likely to question the veracity of another's comments.

In summary, the professional political culture and its attendant norms of conduct—including the seemingly benign respect accorded to ritual, norms of civility, pragmatic concerns about accusations backfiring, and the jaded view that the truth is irrelevant—explain the reluctance of politicians to accuse their colleagues of lying. Because moral-justification claims are so rarely verifiable, these norms take on even more force. The result is that the public receives a one-sided version of reality ("My conscience tells me this is the right thing to do") and no external prompts that might lead them to view the statement with suspicion.

CONCLUSION

Both political and psychological forces work to minimize suspicion of deceptive account rhetoric, pointing to a pessimistic conclusion: politicians can deceptively use moral justifications to shape public opinion about controversial policies and to bolster their own reputations with little fear of negative repercussions. Moral justifications are, as Bennett (1980) noted, "the least risky strategy" (807). Although my focus has been on moral justifications, it should be obvious that because political rhetoric routinely invokes moral values, the potential for abuse is also broader than the context of personal blame management. For example, in framing policy debate, moral values and themes are common (Gamson 1992; Kinder and Sanders 1990; Nelson, Clawson, and Oxley 1997). Relatedly, the rhetoric and ethic of just war (Walzer 1977) is by definition a matter of moral suasion. To the extent that "campaign strategies generally ally the favored candidate with things uncritically accepted, such as flag and freedom, and tie the opponent to such viscerally noxious things as the murder of innocent men, women, and children" (Jamieson 1992, 44), contemporary advertising campaigns are also implicated.

The linking of moral and political rhetoric is inevitable and often laudable. Social scientists have a long tradition rightfully valuing principled reasoning (Converse 1964; Kohlberg 1969; Piaget 1932), and encouraging the public to think about the political world in an ethical and principled manner is commendable (Gutmann and Thompson 1996). But we need to recognize that the linking of moral and political rhetoric can be a double-edged sword. Recognizing the potential for abuse and understanding the powerful mechanisms that facilitate successful deception do not mean we should accept Bennett's conclusion (1980) that the truth is irrelevant in evaluating account rhetoric. If we value a "fully informed public opinion," then the public and scholars need to be vigilant about instances of "elite domination" where "elites induce citizens to hold opinions that they would not hold if aware of the best available information and analysis" (Zaller 1992, 313). As

Robinson (1993) noted, the social sciences "have not paid much attention to the operation of either successful or unsuccessful lies in the public domain" (359), and careful empirical attention to when and why the public is susceptible to deception and, more optimistically, able to resist deceptive claims is warranted.

The goal—as scientists and informed members of a democracy—is to recognize that elite framing of public opinion can be rooted in both laudatory and unscrupulous motives and to be willing to try to tell the difference. Philosophers and scientists caution against committing what Moore (1903) labeled the "naturalistic fallacy": drawing prescriptive, moral conclusions from factual, empirical descriptions of reality. As Hume noted long ago, one cannot derive an "ought" from an "is." We must recognize that the reversal of the naturalistic fallacy is also problematic, if misleading claims invoking moral principles are used to manipulate factual beliefs about the political world.

Notes

1. By way of clarification and disclaimer: the introductory quotations were taken from the *Congressional Quarterly Weekly Report* as well as my files. Although I believe that moral justification is fairly common in politics, I have not gathered systematic frequency data. Moreover, I do not mean to imply that all of these examples are lies. In line with the theme of this article, I am suspicious of some but ultimately cannot say with confidence whether any of them are true or false.

2. The research referred to in this section has been concerned with controversial policy decisions, not acts of personal misconduct.

3. The final draft of the present article was written in early 1998, amid widespread published skepticism about the veracity of President Clinton's denials of sexual involvement with Paula Jones and Monica Lewinsky. Accordingly, I want to be clear that my claim that charges of lying violate political norms of conduct is limited to accusations between politicians. It is my impression—absent systematic analysis—that the direct charges of lying against President Clinton are being raised by journalists and prominent members of ideologically driven interest groups. In contrast, politicians have tempered their public statements, couching them in hypotheticals—"If the president is lying, then . . ."—consistent with the argument that politicians are reluctant to raise direct charges of lying against each other. Of course, systematic empirical work on the propensity to make accusations of lying, with careful consideration of changing trends over time and differences across political institutions, would be desirable to further our understanding of these processes.

References

Asch, Solomon. 1946. Forming Impressions of Personality. *Journal of Abnormal and Social Psychology* 41:1230-40.

Bennett, W. Lance. 1980. The Paradox of Public Discourse: A Framework for the Analysis of Political Accounts. *Journal of Politics* 42:792-817.

Bok, Sissela. 1989. *Lying: Moral Choice in Public and Private Life*. New York: Vintage Books.

Chanley, Virginia, John L. Sullivan, Marti Hope Gonzales, and Margaret Bull Kovera. 1994. Lust and Avarice in Politics: Damage Control by Four Politicians Accused of Wrongdoing (or, Politics as Usual). *American Politics Quarterly* 22:297-333.

Converse, Philip E. 1964. The Nature of Belief Systems in Mass Publics. In *Ideology and Discontent*, ed. D. E. Apter. New York: Free Press.

DePaolo, Bella M., K. Lanier, and T. Davis. 1983. Detecting the Deceit of the Motivated Liar. *Journal of Personality and Social Psychology* 45: 1096-1103.

Edelman, Murray. 1977. *Political Language: Words That Succeed and Policies That Fail.* New York: Academic Press.

Ekman, Paul and W. V. Friesen. 1974. Detecting Deception from the Body or Face. *Journal of Personality and Social Psychology* 29:288-98.

Fenno, Richard F. 1962. The Appropriations Committee as a Political System. *American Political Science Review* 56:310-24.

———. 1978. *Home Style: House Members in their Districts.* Boston: Little, Brown.

Fiske, Susan T. and Shelley E. Taylor. 1991. *Social Cognition.* New York: McGraw-Hill.

Friedman, Howard S. and Joan S. Tucker. 1990. Language and Deception. In *Handbook of Language and Social Psychology*, ed. Howard Giles and W. Peter Robinson. New York: John Wiley.

Gamson, William A. 1992. *Talking Politics.* New York: Cambridge University Press.

Gamson, William A. and Andre Modigliani. 1987. The Changing Culture of Affirmative Action. In *Research in Political Sociology*, ed. Richard D. Braungart. Greenwich, CT: JAI Press.

Gilbert, Daniel T., Brett W. Pelham, and D. S. Krull. 1988. On Cognitive Busyness: When Person Perceivers Meet Persons Perceived. *Journal of Personality and Social Psychology* 54:733-39.

Graber, Doris A. 1976. *Verbal Behavior and Politics.* Urbana: University of Illinois Press.

Gutmann, Amy and Dennis Thompson. 1996. *Democracy and Disagreement.* Cambridge, MA: Harvard University Press.

Hedlund, Ronald R. 1985. Organizational Attributes of Legislative Institutions: Structure, Rules, Norms, and Resources. In *Handbook of Legislative Research*, ed. Gerhard Loewenberg, Samuel C. Patterson, and Malcolm E. Jewell. Cambridge, MA: Harvard University Press.

Hibbing, John R. and Elizabeth Theiss-Morse. 1995. *Congress as Public Enemy: Public Attitudes Toward American Political Institutions.* New York: Cambridge University Press.

Hilton, James L., Steven Fein, and Dale T. Miller. 1993. Suspicion and Dispositional Inference. *Personality and Social Psychology Bulletin* 19:501-12.

Jamieson, Kathleen Hall. 1992. *Dirty Politics: Deception, Distraction, and Democracy.* New York: Oxford University Press.

Kalfbleisch, Pamela J. 1994. The Language of Detecting Deceit. *Journal of Language and Social Psychology* 13:469-96.

Kinder, Donald R. and Lynn M. Sanders. 1990. Mimicking Political Debate with Survey Questions: The Case of White Opinion on Affirmative Action for Blacks. *Social Cognition* 8:73-103.

Kohlberg, Lawrence. 1969. Stage and Sequence: The Cognitive-Development Approach to Socialization. In *Handbook of Socialization Theory and Research*, ed. D. A. Goslin. Chicago: Rand-McNally.

McGraw, Kathleen M. 1991. Managing Blame: An Experimental Investigation into the Effectiveness of Political Accounts. *American Political Science Review* 85:1133-58.

———. Forthcoming. Political Accounts and Attribution Processes. In *Political Psychology*, ed. James Kuklinski. New York: Cambridge University Press.

McGraw, Kathleen M., Samuel Best, and Richard Timpone. 1995. "What They Say or What They Do?" The Impact of Elite Explanation and Policy Outcomes on Public Opinion. *American Journal of Political Science* 39:53-75.

McGraw, Kathleen M., Milton Lodge, and Jeffrey Jones. 1997. The Pandering Politicians of Suspicious Minds. Manuscript.

McGraw, Kathleen M., Richard Timpone, and Gabor Bruck. 1993. Justifying Controversial Political Decisions: *Home Style* in the Laboratory. *Political Behavior* 15:289-308.

Moore, G. E. 1903. *Principia Ethica*. Cambridge: Cambridge University Press.

Nelson, Thomas E., Rosalee A. Clawson, and Zoe M. Oxley. 1997. Media Framing of a Civil Liberties Conflict and Its Effect on Tolerance. *American Political Science Review* 91:567-84.

Page, Benjamin I. 1996. *Who Deliberates? Mass Media in Modern Democracy*. Chicago: University of Chicago Press.

Page, Benjamin I. and Robert Y. Shapiro. 1992. *The Rational Public*. Chicago: University of Chicago Press.

Patterson, Samuel C. 1995. Review of *The Decline of Comity in Congress*, by Eric Uslaner. *American Political Science Review* 89:215-16.

Piaget, Jean. 1932. *The Moral Judgment of the Child*. New York: Free Press.

Pitkin, Hanna F. 1967. *The Concept of Representation*. Berkeley: University of California Press.

Robinson, W. Peter. 1993. Lying in the Public Domain. *American Behavioral Scientist* 36:359-82.

Schlenker, Barry R. 1980. *Impression Management*. Belmont, CA: Brooks/ Cole.

Scott, Marvin B. and Stanford M. Lyman. 1968. Accounts. *American Sociological Review* 33:46-62.

Sears, David O. 1983. The Person-Positivity Bias. *Journal of Personality and Social Psychology* 44:233-40.

Uslaner, Eric. 1994. *The Decline of Comity in Congress*. Ann Arbor: University of Michigan Press.

Walzer, Michael. 1977. *Just and Unjust Wars: A Moral Argument with Historical Illustrations*. New York: Basic Books.

Zaller, John R. 1992. *The Nature and Origins of Mass Opinion*. New York: Cambridge University Press.

ANNALS, *AAPSS*, **560**, November 1998

"Just the Facts, Ma'am": Political Facts and Public Opinion

By JAMES H. KUKLINSKI, PAUL J. QUIRK, DAVID W. SCHWIEDER, and ROBERT F. RICH

ABSTRACT: An important dimension of the future of fact is the status of political facts in research on public opinion. Analyzing the public's factual knowledge about public policy is central to addressing citizen competence yet more problematic than scholars have acknowledged. To show this, the authors first summarize a study of theirs that uses typical measures of citizens' information. In a survey of Illinois citizens, they measured factual perceptions about welfare policy. They found that citizens are not only uninformed about welfare but often misinformed—confident in erroneous perceptions. Such misinformation apparently has significant effects on attitudes toward welfare. The authors then consider some conceptual difficulties in research on citizens' information about policy. If the purpose is to ascertain how much information citizens possess, then the researcher must stipulate the relevant facts about an area of policy. But political facts are in large part politically determined, and the researcher often cannot identify precisely what the true and relevant facts are. Finally, the authors suggest a research approach in which citizens, in effect, choose the relevant facts themselves.

James H. Kuklinski and Paul J. Quirk are professors in the Department of Political Science and the Institute of Government and Public Affairs (IGPA); David W. Schwieder is a doctoral candidate in political science; and Robert F. Rich is a professor in the College of Law and IGPA—all at the University of Illinois at Urbana–Champaign.

I N the final chapter of *Voting* (1954), Berelson and his colleagues wrote two sentences that are among the most influential and widely quoted in scholarly works on American politics. The familiar words read as follows: "The democratic citizen is expected to be well informed about political affairs. He is supposed to know what the issues are, . . . what the relevant facts are, what alternatives are proposed, [and] what the likely consequences are" (308). Berelson himself rejected this standard as unrealistic. Indeed, he argued that a vast amount of citizen ignorance is consistent with, and even required for, a well-functioning political system. If most citizens were well informed and highly involved in politics, the resulting conflict could cause serious instability.

However, Berelson's legacy has been his statement of the expectation, not his rejection of it. From the publication of Converse's classic essay on mass opinion (1964) to the present, the normative thrust in public opinion research has been unwavering: a factually informed citizenry is preferable to an uninformed one. Delli Carpini and Keeter (1996) eloquently summarize this view in their recent book on citizen knowledge about politics. "Political information," they assert, "is to democratic politics what money is to economics; it is the currency of citizenship" (8). More precisely,

facts prevent . . . the trivialization of public discourse. Such facts as the percentage of the American public living below the poverty line, how the line is determined, and how the percentage has changed over time provide a foundation for delibera-

tion about larger issues. They prevent debates from becoming disconnected from the material conditions they attempt to address. (11)

The seemingly self-evident premise that more political information is better than less has led political scientists to pursue two lines of inquiry. Most fundamentally, they have tried to identify what people do and do not know about politics, typically by measuring citizens' knowledge of processes (for example, by requesting a definition of the line-item veto), institutional structures (by asking how many Supreme Court justices there are), and current politicians (by asking who the Speaker of the House is). The data consistently support the conclusion that many people are ill informed and unsophisticated about politics (Luskin 1987). Closely related, and a logical follow-up to the first task, is the second line of inquiry: scholars have tried to ascertain whether the amount of factual information that people possess shapes their judgments or the reasoning processes underlying them (Bartels 1996; Sniderman, Brody, and Kuklinski 1984). Delli Carpini and Keeter (1996), for example, conduct a simulation, based on parameters obtained from survey data, to estimate how often uninformed people would make different political judgments if they were well informed. Apparently they would do so quite often.[1]

Two premises underlie the preceding and related research: first, political facts, pieces of objective data, exist; and, second, it is just a matter of researchers' identifying the relevant facts and ascertaining whether people know them. The facts, according to this widely accepted view, are realities that are out there, for citizens to acquire and for researchers to study. In the first part of this article, we draw on our own research to illustrate how natural it is to adopt this Sgt. Joe Friday "just the facts, ma'am" perspective. Indeed, taking facts for granted has greatly facilitated the study of information and public opinion. However, in the second, more speculative part of the article, we confront the underlying, often implicit assumption that political facts are objective pieces of information. We argue that relevant facts about policy are, in crucial respects, not external to and independent of the political process but defined and determined by it. We reach this conclusion, moreover, without relying on any philosophically controversial cultural relativism or epistemological skepticism. However reached, this conclusion makes it unclear how researchers committed to nonpartisan scholarship can presume to specify what facts citizens should know. Moreover, we must face up to a serious question: Can we examine citizens' political knowledge without becoming mere partisans in political debate?

In our view, to dismiss such inquiry would prevent any serious assessment of the competence of the citizenry, the effectiveness of political communication, or the performance of democracy. It would lead to the view, which we find not only implausible but potentially disastrous, that all political beliefs and discourse have equal merit. We argue that we can indeed study citizen knowledge

and information, without imposing an arbitrary specification of the relevant facts. For illustration, we briefly outline some possible procedures that in effect allow citizens to choose the most relevant and useful facts. This kind of research strategy admittedly complicates the researcher's task, but it has the potential to overcome some of the inherent difficulties associated with the empirical study of information and public opinion.

AN ILLUSTRATIVE STUDY OF CITIZEN MISINFORMATION

The news about how informed American citizens are has not been good. Bartels's blunt statement (1996, 184) that "the political ignorance of the American voter is one of the best documented data in political science" captures the thrust of three decades of research. Many citizens, scholars have shown over and over, are profoundly uninformed.

In research reported elsewhere (Kuklinski et al. 1997), we contend that the problem of citizen information, at least with respect to knowledge about public policy, goes even deeper than researchers have portrayed. The problem is not merely that people are uninformed. There are constructive ways to deal with that problem, such as deferring judgment or relying upon elected representatives. Rather, the problem, in our view, is that many people are misinformed. They have the facts wrong, often in systematic ways, and confidently believe they have them right. Such misinformation distorts people's policy preferences. Moreover, their misplaced confidence leads them to resist accepting and using the correct facts even if these are made available.

In the study, we randomly divided a survey sample of Illinois residents into three different experimental groups, each consisting of more than 200 respondents. One group received a short factual briefing, with accurate information deemed relevant to evaluating welfare policy. Interviewers presented a series of six facts in the guise of asking people whether they had heard about them ("Have you heard that ... ?") A second group was given a multiple-choice quiz on the same items of information. Each item had five options from which respondents could choose.

After each of the quiz items, respondents were asked how confident they were of their answer, with the four options ranging from "very confident" to "not at all confident." In both groups, the items were presented in random order across individuals. Respondents in the third, no-treatment, group were neither briefed nor questioned about welfare-related facts. Respondents in all groups were then questioned in the same manner about their policy attitudes. Specifically, respondents were asked their preferences about cutting welfare and imposing a two-year limit on welfare payments.[2]

The resulting data enabled us to address some important issues about information, misinformation, and policy preferences. Within the fact-quiz group, we found that many people had systematically inaccurate factual beliefs (for example, they grossly overestimated the payments received by a typical family). Although the misperceptions were polarized, we found a substantial overall bias toward beliefs that one would expect to be associated with negative views about welfare. We also found that people held their beliefs confidently. By statistical analysis we showed that these beliefs are strongly linked to policy preferences in the expected ways. We infer that to the extent that factual beliefs shape policy preferences, misinformation biases aggregate preferences against welfare.

So far, then, not so good. But are misinformation and its effects incorrigible? To find out what happens when people are given correct facts, we compared the fact-briefing group to the no-treatment group. In view of the random assignment, both groups were assumed to have had prior factual beliefs similar to those of the fact-quiz group and to each other's—that is, to have had beliefs with the same overall bias against welfare. If people absorb and use correct facts when they are made available, the fact-briefing group should have learned from the briefing and thus been less supportive of welfare cuts and the two-year limit than the no-treatment group. In fact, however, there was no difference between the two groups on the policy items. At least in this rather mild treatment, then, misinformation resists change. (In a separate experiment, we have found that correct information can make a difference when it is presented in an extremely obtrusive manner that virtually compels recognition of its significance.)

Our primary interest in this discussion is not our substantive conclusions but the measures we used to reach them. In selecting the specific factual items to include in the survey, we consulted with academics and welfare policy analysts. They agreed on six contextual facts that an informed individual should know. These are the percentage of families in the United States who are on welfare (Aid to Families with Dependent Children [AFDC]); the proportion of the federal budget that goes to welfare; the average annual benefit a typical welfare family (a mother with two children) receives; the percentage of welfare mothers who are on welfare for more than eight years; the percentage of welfare families who are African American;[3] and the percentage of welfare mothers who have less than a high school education.

Other researchers working from the Joe Friday perspective could squabble with our choices. Would 10 other experts also have identified these particular items? Are these really the kinds of facts that we can expect to engage average citizens? Of course, we could counter by noting that the factual items we chose are precisely the kinds of facts that Delli Carpini and Keeter (1996) say are essential to effective citizen deliberation. Alternatively, we could counter by pointing out that some of these facts actually became part of congressional argument. What is crucial to note here is that, squabbles aside, our measures do not greatly violate scholarly expectations about how to study information and public opinion empirically. As we will now argue, however, they do not adequately take into account the very politics they were designed to help us understand.

To make this argument requires stepping outside the Joe Friday framework.

POLITICAL FACTS AS POLITICALLY DETERMINED

Like other researchers concerned with citizens' information, we conducted the preceding investigation without probing the main character: the political fact. We treated the facts about welfare as objective and unproblematic states of the world. The facts are just there, so to speak, and the citizen's task is to pay them heed. Of course, it is not actually that simple. In this section, we show that political facts are less straightforwardly factual in the Joe Friday sense than we often recognize. They are problematic in various respects. To a great extent, the criteria for and relevance of political facts are determined within, not outside, politics. They are politically controversial, and thus so are the criteria for identifying an informative debate or an informed citizen. In this section, we offer some preliminary and rather casual reflections on these points, and on their significance for our concerns. We will continue to focus on facts relevant to public policy.[4]

Facts, generic and political

Because facts subsume political facts, we must briefly visit the generic category. We define a fact in the simplest, most orthodox way: as an item of correct information, one that accurately represents the real world.[5] (We do not entirely dismiss postmodern doubts about objective knowledge, especially in social and political matters. In our view, however, the most serious difficulties in identifying political facts arise within ordinary empiricism.) The crucial term in our definition is "correct." Some purported facts are more indisputably correct than others. If so, where do we draw the line between facts and nonfacts, if we draw one at all? More directly, should we construe facts in categorical terms—something either is a fact or is not—or recognize a continuum from definitely a fact to definitely not one?

That we currently hold teaching positions (in one case, as a graduate assistant) at a university is a fact. Legal contracts say so, and anyone who reads them would agree. But is it a fact that we teach there? Most of our students would confirm it (we hope), but some might say that what we do is not teaching. Finally, is it a fact that we are competent teachers? Probably not, for some students might think so while others place us on their "worst ever" lists.

How does this discussion help us to construe a fact? It underlines what seems to us a fundamental point: because facts are, by definition, correct, their truth is not open to interpretation. We know what they mean, and know they are true. It is thus a fact that we have contracts with a university, but it is not a fact that we are good teachers.

We distinguish a fact, as correct information, from a matter of consensus. Suppose, for example, that everyone who ever took our courses rated them mediocre. Is it thus a fact that the courses are mediocre? Not necessarily (we would hasten to point out), for course evaluations are open to interpretation; that everyone renders the same judgment does not make the judgment correct. It is a fact that everyone who has taken the courses finds them mediocre, but not that they really are. Once we recognize that consensus is not the criterion for a fact, we can see more readily that facts either do exist or they do not. They cannot exist more or less, falling along a continuum of "factness." Consensus can vary, but, in principle, facts are categorical.[6]

Unfortunately, what is true in principle often has little relevance when the discussion turns to what are represented as facts pertinent to public policy. Very often such factual representations are not prior to or independent of the political process but arise within it. Consequently, very few factual claims are beyond challenge; if a fact is worth thinking about in making a policy choice, it is probably worth disputing. Rival advocates compete to define the facts, control their presentation, and determine their relevance.

Construing purported political facts as politically determined, and controversial with respect to truth and relevance, forces us to recognize complications that political scientists have typically overlooked in their efforts to identify certifiably correct and relevant political facts. Four complications are especially noteworthy.

Facts and uncertainty

Because information comes in all shades of certainty and uncertainty, the boundaries that distinguish facts, debatable claims, and outright lies are contested. Nowhere is this more true than in the area of cause and effect. As any social scientist can attest, proving the existence of a causal relationship is difficult under the best of circumstances; the complexity of modern society can render the task almost intractable. Yet it is this kind of fact—cause and effect—that citizens most often would like to know.

Is it a fact that cigarette smoking causes lung cancer? Is it a fact that increasing the minimum wage causes unemployment? In both instances, there is substantial evidence in the affirmative. Most specialists accept the evidence about the minimum wage, and nearly everyone the evidence on smoking. Yet some cigarette companies reject the first claim and most liberals and some economists reject the second, offering arguments for dissenting positions. Which of the claims, if either, crosses the threshold to fact—and could be used to identify informed citizens?

There are other kinds of facts that seem more readily identifiable as such. Descriptive facts associated with legislative proposals—the kind we used in our study of misinformation—fall into this category: How many teenagers smoke? How much does the federal government spend on welfare? How many people are unemployed? Even here, however, the facts often are not beyond dispute. For example, what are the proper criteria by which to measure unemployment? Do the unemployed include discouraged workers who are no longer looking for jobs? Skilled workers who will not accept low wages? Democrats and Republicans probably will agree up to a point; it is their disagreement at the margins that provokes heated policy debate. Recently, Congress debated a change in the consumer price index to help the government save on inflation-indexed entitlements such as Medicare and Medicaid. What, then, is the true level of inflation? Advocates for the elderly have one answer; advocates of budget cutting, another.

Factual relevance

Even when a fact is clear and certain, politicians and others often disagree on its relevance to policy. Is it relevant that the rate of welfare dependency has risen dramatically since the early 1960s? Or that it did not rise from the 1970s to the 1990s? What about the fact that, proportionately many more blacks than whites receive welfare benefits? A liberal may attribute concern about this racial difference simply to racism, but a conservative might contend that it demonstrates how welfare dependency has undermined African Americans' family structure. Values and theories determine relevance.

That politicians evaluate factual relevance on the basis of their values does not imply that knowing the facts serves no purpose. The person who knows the facts and then decides their relevance is more competent than a person who has only values to go on. Our point is more limited: in the political domain, disputing facts (often by ignoring them) on grounds of relevance is a major feature of strategic rhetoric. Because there is no objective way to determine relevance, the analyst cannot resolve the resulting differences.

Framing and factual forms

In their highly acclaimed research, Kahneman and Tversky (see Kahneman, Slovic, and Tversky 1982 for a summary) have demonstrated convincingly that different forms of the same fact lead to different evaluations. In one study, for example, some subjects were asked to choose between two government programs: one that would produce 12 percent inflation and 10 percent unemployment and one that would produce 17 percent inflation and 5 percent unemployment. A sizable majority chose the second program. Other subjects also chose between two programs: one that would produce 12 percent inflation and 90 percent employment and one that would produce 17 percent inflation and 95 percent employment. In this instance, a majority chose the first program. The two descriptions of the programs are identical, except that one gives rates of employment and the other gives the equivalent rates of unemployment. In short, factual framing has substantial consequences.

We are conducting similar research on welfare. It is factually true that about 1 percent of the federal budget went to AFDC payments (prior to the 1996 welfare reform). It is equally and equivalently true that the federal government has spent about $10 billion annually on AFDC benefits. We expect to find that people given the absolute dollar amount will express less support for the AFDC program than those given the percentage of the budget. We presume further that people given an exact dollar figure—say, $10,297,346,981—would express even less support. And imagine the effect of giving people yet another version of this fact (roughly correct, by our calculations): that the amount is equivalent to a stack of thousand-dollar bills three times as high as the Empire State Building. Not surprisingly, proponents of welfare emphasize the percentage form while opponents use forms that convey large magnitudes of money. What makes factual framing effects so crucial to politics, of course, is that once again there is no objective way to choose one frame over another. As long as the choice of factual form is open to discretion, it is impossible to speak of the facts as a determinate body of information.

Useful facts

We care about political facts because we believe that people's knowing them will improve their judgments. This belief implicitly assumes, in turn, that acquiring additional facts has automatic benefits for decision making: people might choose not to overlook certain facts, but if they do use them, it will improve their judgments. Facts are useful.

This is not necessarily the case, however. Suppose 10 American soldiers are killed as part of the peacekeeping effort in Bosnia, that a citizen learns about it, and that he or she wants to judge the wisdom and likely success of the mission. What does the death of 10 U.S. soldiers mean? That the mission has failed? That the mission is very successful, on the whole, despite the unfortunate incident? That the United States should redefine the role of American soldiers? The decision the individual reaches will depend on an interpretation of the fact: the death of 10 soldiers is a big loss; a relatively minor loss, given the overall mission; a harbinger of things to come; an unfortunate accident that probably will not happen again. For the most part, it will be politicians who seek to provide the interpretations. Not only facts in themselves, therefore, but also their interpretations are politically determined.

The informed-citizen perspective also assumes that the more facts a person knows, the better. But perhaps a citizen can be deluged with too much information, such that additional facts merely confuse. Psychologists have measured the limits of working memory. People can remember only a few bits of information at a time. They have difficulty integrating large amounts of it. If we somehow opened up the spigots that controlled the flow of information to citizens, they might become so overwhelmed with facts that confusion, not well-integrated judgments, would result.

BEYOND SKEPTICISM: LETTING
CITIZENS CHOOSE FACTS

None of the difficulties we have discussed about what political facts are valid, relevant, or useful appeal to any advanced or unorthodox thinking about epistemology, culture, or the social construction of reality. They do not depend on deep differences in values, theories, or conceptual schemes, nor do they call into question our ability to observe the world, in crucial respects, objectively. Clearly, values and ideology come into play in selecting political facts and judging their relevance. Liberals seize upon some facts; conservatives, others. But any of the constructions of facts we have described would be understood by almost any citizen. For the most part, the difficulties about political facts seem to reflect the complexity of politics, the diversity of our concerns, and the vast flexibility of language.

Even so, the ambiguities about political facts pose a problem for scholars who study citizens' political knowledge, media performance, and the quality of political discourse. If the facts are inherently controversial or politically determined, one might suppose that all factual claims in political life are equal. The implications of that view would be profound. Provided that people have any beliefs at all that they consider relevant to a political judgment, they are informed. Provided that politicians and the media supply some information and portray it as relevant, they are informative. To allow a form of evaluation, analysts might apply a criterion of volume: how many facts do people receive, regardless of what kind? Alternatively, they might possibly apply a criterion of satisfaction: did the audience find the debate informative?

Implicitly, the criteria of volume and subjective satisfaction underlie the strategy of so-called deliberative polls, sponsored by James Fishkin (1995) at the University of Texas. Both in several days of briefings and discussion and through written materials provided in advance, Fishkin (along with his collaborator, Robert Luskin) exposes a representative sample of citizens to a massive amount of competing advocacy. At the end, he asks them whether the presentations and discussions were informative and fair, and obtains consistently favorable responses. There is evidence that deliberative polls improve people's judgments. At least, they often alter people's opinions. From a practical standpoint, however, the utility of deliberative polls is limited by their reliance on the volume, rather than the quality, of information; they are far too costly in both money and participants' time to extend to a significant fraction of the citizenry, much less to all of it.

In any case, we reject the view that all facts are equal, largely because we are unwilling to go where it leads. Suppose that one citizen's factual information on welfare is, "People on welfare buy steak with food stamps." A second citizen's information is, "A welfare family gets about $6000 per year, plus food stamps and Medicaid." Should one regard the two citizens as equally informed? We would not.[7]

We are committed, then, to saying that some facts are more valid and pertinent than others. If some standards are to be applied, however, what are they? Who sets them? How can researchers choose which facts to use in testing citizen knowledge, or which facts to count as relevant in evaluating the information content of

media coverage or political debate? In particular, how can researchers make such choices without becoming self-appointed arbiters of right political thinking?

We have only preliminary suggestions to make. We believe that relevant facts can be conceived much as some theorists have conceived genuine interests (Mansbridge 1980) or moral convictions in reflective equilibrium (Rawls 1971). That is, we can infer relevance from what people think is relevant, or what information they use, when they have had opportunity to reflect carefully and reach settled judgments about what information is most useful. To make that possible, of course, they would need help to discover what potentially relevant information is available.

We can see two general approaches to such an exercise. First, one could directly ask an appropriate sample of citizens to select from a menu, constructed by appropriate experts, the factual questions to which they would most want to receive answers in order to make up their minds on an issue. To decide about cutting welfare, for example, what would they want to know: the costs of the welfare program expressed in dollars; those costs expressed as a percentage of the budget; the costs per taxpayer; a typical welfare family's expenditures for rent, food, and entertainment; or the costs of the program expressed in the height of a stack of thousand-dollar bills? For causal and other disputed facts, such as whether welfare encourages dependency, they could be given a parallel set of options: summaries of advocates' arguments on both sides, the results of a survey of experts, findings of the most widely cited studies, and so on. We believe that people would choose evidence that looked sensible to well-informed observers and would avoid obscurantist or manipulative presentations. In these circumstances, we think they would not want to waste their time on food-stamp purchases of steak or huge stacks of thousand-dollar bills.[8]

Second, more indirectly, researchers could do experiments to determine which sets of facts provide citizens the most assistance in arriving at stable opinions. In the simplest terms, the idea is this: tell one randomly selected group of citizens the cost of welfare as a percentage of the budget, and another such group the cost per taxpayer. Induce both groups to reflect, and measure the resulting opinions about cuts in welfare. Then expose both groups to one-sided presentations of facts, arguments, and even emotional rhetoric about those costs. Finally, measure opinion a second time. The group that received the most useful facts in the initial briefing should respond least to the subsequent treatment. The group whose facts were least relevant or most misleading should be most susceptible to subsequent persuasion. Again, we would expect this approach to pick out a fairly edifying selection of facts.

Under either of these approaches, then, citizen experimental subjects would make the final selection of the facts. Using such facts in studies of political information would put research on solid, nonpartisan ground. An accumulation of similar efforts could produce general findings on the kinds of facts that are most useful in citizen judgment. In the long run, such findings could be used not only for research but also to evaluate media performance and political discourse.

To be sure, the facts identified would still depend on values and theories (those held by the samples of citizens) and thus would be culturally determined in the usual ways. But that kind of relativism is not very bothersome for our purposes. We assume that a political system operates within a given culture. In seeking to assess political discourse or citizens' knowledge in the United States, we are concerned about the use of information relevant in our political culture. We do not urge that political deliberation should aspire to a culture-free universality. We would be satisfied if both leaders and citizens would apply their basic values and beliefs to concrete choices of public policy with more seriousness and intelligence—judging more intelligently, in other words, within their culture. Research on political facts and deliberation can be culture-bound as well.

Notes

1. Another stream of literature begins with the assumption that many people are not politically informed and asks whether they can still make reasonable decisions by using heuristics, or simple rules of thumb. The leading proponents of the heuristics perspective include Lupia (1994), Popkin (1991), and Sniderman, Brody, and Tetlock (1991).

2. Response options were on a five-point scale ranging from strong support to strong opposition.

3. Our experts proposed including this fact not because it should be relevant to judging

policy but because people very possibly do deem it relevant.

4. Our critique does not apply to textbook facts such as the number of Supreme Court justices. Scholars have used such items to measure general political sophistication, in our view, correctly so.

5. As Jeffrey Strange pointed out after reading an earlier draft of this article, there is also information about fictional and imaginary worlds—for example, "Captain Queeg likes to roll two metal balls in the palm of his hand." We would call such information, if correct, fictional or imaginary fact.

6. If we want to be strict enough, of course, we never have complete certainty about any fact. We believe that Bill Clinton is now the president of the United States. But maybe there is just a vast media conspiracy to mislead us: Bob Dole really won the election and is serving as president behind closed doors. An interesting parlor game is to invent the most plausible scenario that would render any given accepted fact erroneous. But the parlor game is mainly that and not a constructive activity for people who want to find their way in the world.

7. For a contrary argument, see Sanders (1997).

8. A potential problem is that people will seek out the information they believe will reinforce their already existing preferences.

References

Bartels, Larry M. 1996. Uninformed Votes: Informational Effects in Presidential Elections. *American Journal of Political Science* 40:194-230.

Berelson, Bernard, Paul Lazarsfeld, and William McPhee. 1954. *Voting*. Chicago: University of Chicago Press.

Converse, Philip E. 1964. The Nature of Belief Systems in Mass Publics. In *Ideology and Discontent*, ed. David Apter. New York: Free Press.

Delli Carpini, Michael and Scott Keeter. 1996. *What Americans Know About Politics and Why It Matters*. New Haven, CT: Yale University Press.

Fishkin, James S. 1995. *The Voice of the People: Public Opinion and American Democracy*. New Haven, CT: Yale University Press.

Kahneman, Daniel, Paul Slovic, and Amos Tversky, eds. 1982. *Judgment and Uncertainty: Heuristics and Biases*. New York: Cambridge University Press.

Kuklinski, James H., Paul J. Quirk, David Schwieder, and Robert F. Rich. 1997. Misinformation and the Currency of Citizenship. Paper.

Lupia, Arthur. 1994. Shortcuts versus Encyclopedias: Information and Voting Behavior in California Insurance Reform Elections. *American Political Science Review* 88:63-76.

Luskin, Robert C. 1987. Measuring Political Sophistication. *American Journal of Political Science* 31:856-99.

Mansbridge, Jane. 1980. *Beyond Adversary Democracy*. Chicago: University of Chicago Press.

Popkin, Samuel L. 1991. *The Reasoning Voter*. Chicago: University of Chicago Press.

Rawls, John. 1971. *A Theory of Justice*. Cambridge, MA: Harvard University Press.

Sanders, Lynn. 1997. Against Deliberation. *Political Theory* 25:347-76.

Sniderman, Paul M., Richard A. Brody, and James H. Kuklinski. 1984. Political Reasoning and Political Values: The Problem of Racial Equality. *American Journal of Political Science* 28:75-94.

Sniderman, Paul M., Richard A. Brody, and Philip E. Tetlock. 1991. *Reasoning and Choice*. New York: Cambridge University Press.

ANNALS, *AAPSS*, **560**, November 1998

The Legal and Ethical
Limitations of Factual Misrepresentation

By GEOFFREY COWAN

ABSTRACT: Using examples from journalism, nonfiction books, theater, television, and film, this article examines the ways in which truth has been distorted in the name of storytelling. It briefly reviews the law (and the limits of the law) that governs such distortions and then offers some possible ethical guidelines. There is, in the author's view, an unwritten contract between the writer (as well as the editor, publisher, producer, and distributor) and the audience. Although some aspects of that contract are spelled out in the law, the First Amendment dictates that most of its provisions rely on the ethical sensibilities of the participants. A reasonable approach, it is argued, would be based on a continuum, calling for more accuracy and balance for the daily news media; somewhat less for columnists, journals of opinion, and docudramas that deal with contemporary events; and less still for historical dramas and novels based on fact.

Geoffrey Cowan is dean of the University of Southern California's Annenberg School for Communication, where he is professor of journalism and law. An award-winning producer and playwright, he is author of See No Evil: The Backstage Battle over Sex and Violence on Television *and* The People v. Clarence Darrow: The Bribery Trial of America's Greatest Lawyer. *Prior to becoming dean, Cowan served as director of the Voice of America.*

ALL storytellers know the difficulty of telling a story truthfully.
Each detail skews the description—
and can, if desired, skewer the subject. There are, of course, some facts
that are verifiable. For example, this
article is based on a speech given at
the Annenberg School for Communication at the University of Pennsylvania in Philadelphia on 28 February
1997. I was wearing a blue jacket and
a tie with a red pattern. But no doubt
each listener would have described
the speech, and the speaker, differently. The speech quoted from a *New
York Times* column the day before, in
which Maureen Dowd roasted the
Disney shareholders' meeting by describing Disney chairman Michael
Eisner's hosiery and the appearance
of his legs. She observed what she
called "his hairy shins showing above
his short black socks." Not every account of the meeting featured those
details, but Ms. Dowd had a point to
make, and she was able to illustrate
it with a less than elegant detail.

Just as all writers know the elu-
siveness of truth, so, too, do they
know the ease with which a story can
be twisted, or facts highlighted or
omitted, to prove a point, embarrass
a subject, or support an ideological
thesis. The law of selective detail applies equally to journalists, historians, filmmakers, and academics. It
would be both folly and impossible to
penalize those who make their points
through the use of selective detail.
Indeed, great writing depends on the
choice of detail. The best corrective
for selective fact is more fact, a point
that lies at the heart of the First
Amendment. Nevertheless, it would
also be folly to ignore the lesson of

societies that have made the selective
use of fact the basis for fomenting
ethnic and racial hatred or for promoting nationalistic pride. Every nation, every ethnic and racial group,
every religion, every profession has
produced scoundrels to be accused,
accurately but unfairly, of enough vil-
lainy to create the appearance of a
pattern of evil behavior. On a lesser
scale, the same could be said of individuals; we all have our failings and
our weaknesses.

The principal ethical guideline, it
can be argued, is the implicit contract
between writers and their audiences.
Janet Malcolm, who was herself the
target of a celebrated libel verdict,
makes a similar point in "Reflections:
The Journalist and the Murderer,"
her long essay on the relationship
between Jeffrey MacDonald, the con-
victed murderer, and the author Joe
McGuinniss. In discussing the difference between nonfiction and fictional
works such as *Ragtime*, works that
mix history and fiction, she argues
that "what is at stake for the reader
is the issue of whether or not a writer
has violated the rules of his genre."
The rules, she contends, are based on
an unstated contract between the
writer and his audience. "The writer
of non-fiction," she says, "is under
contract to the reader to limit himself
to facts that actually occurred and to
characters who have counterparts in
real life, and he may not embellish
the truth about these events or these
characters" (Malcolm 1989, 38).

The contract between writer and
audience is not spelled out in the law,
nor should it be. In a nation that
celebrates the First Amendment, the
law neither can nor should be seen as

a substitute for individual ethics or for personal conscience; nevertheless, it does offer some guidance. The U.S. Supreme Court has correctly stated that "erroneous statement is inevitable in free debate and . . . must be protected if the freedoms of expression are to have the 'breathing space' that they 'need . . . to survive' " (*New York Times* v. *Sullivan*, 376 U.S. 254, 271-72 [1964]). If the press had to worry about being sued each time it made a mistake, publishers and editors would engage in too much self-censorship and would have been forced to avoid crucial stories—from the civil rights movement, to the war in Vietnam, to Watergate, to Whitewater.

However, the Court has also noted that "the individual's right to the protection of his own good name reflects no more than our basic concept of the essential dignity and worth of every human being—a concept at the root of any decent system of ordered liberty"[1] (*Gertz* v. *Robert Welch, Inc.*, 418 U.S. 323, 341 [1973], quoting Mr. Justice Stevens in *Rosenblatt* v. *Baer*, 383 U.S. 75, 92 [1966] [concurring opinion]). Some of the normative goals of the law, as well as the law's limitations, are spelled out in scores of cases involving libel.

A libel is defined as a false, reputation-damaging statement that is of and concerning a person (Restatement [Second] of Torts 1977, § 558). In principle, the law exhorts writers to avoid engaging in libel. But while the law disapproves of such statements, it makes it very difficult for those who are libeled to recover, particularly if they are public figures. To win a libel case, a "public figure" must show that the defendant acted with "actual malice," or with the knowledge that the information was probably false (*New York Times* v. *Sullivan*). For "private figures" the standard is somewhat easier, but they, too, must show that the defendant acted negligently (*Gertz* v. *Robert Welch, Inc.*). What is more, libel cases are very expensive to finance. Though many people may be described in a way that is false and reputation-damaging, very few are able to recover.

Nevertheless, the contract implied by libel law is that the writers will attempt to avoid making false statements of fact. The First Amendment protects virtually all speech from legal attack in order to ensure an informed citizenry. But a functioning democracy also presumes that the public will not be deliberately misinformed. As the Supreme Court has underlined, "there is no constitutional value in false statements of fact. Neither the intentional nor the careless error materially advances society's interest in 'uninhibited, robust, and wide-open' debate on public issues" (*Gertz* v. *Robert Welch, Inc.*, 340). Writers, in short, have an ethical duty of care to their audience. Readers and viewers have a real but unenforceable right to rely on the accuracy of what they learn through those media that they expect or believe to be accurate. For the news media, there is no more vital commodity than credibility. For that reason, some news organizations have codes that celebrate accuracy over speed. Good editors know that it takes years to gain credibility but only seconds to lose it.

The Code of Ethics of the Society of Professional Journalists provides an exemplary standard for the profession. Its preamble notes that "public enlightenment is the forerunner of justice and the foundation of democracy" and that "professional integrity is the cornerstone of a journalist's credibility" (Society of Professional Journalists 1997-98, Preamble).

In the past few years, it seems that there have been an increasing number of inaccurate stories in the mainstream press. Some involved Richard Jewell, the Atlanta security guard who was falsely accused of setting off a bomb during the Atlanta Olympics in 1996. That same summer, the *New York Times* ran a totally inaccurate front-page story claiming that the government had concluded that the destruction of TWA flight 800 was the work of terrorists. During the effort to examine President Clinton's relationship with Monica Lewinsky, the mainstream media reported several stories that later proved to be false. Such stories do not only damage the reputation of those involved. They undermine the public's ability to rely on the press for information; unintentionally, they violate the contract between the press and the public; and, in the end, if the public ceases to find the press credible, such errors damage a fundamental pillar of democracy.

One might wonder if this is a new phenomenon. Perhaps it is not. But a survey by the Pew Research Center for the People and the Press in February 1998 found that "today, 63 percent of the public complain that press accounts are 'often inaccurate,' a 7 percent jump since 1997 and by far the worst rating the press has received on this in a decade" (Pew Research Center for the People and the Press 1998).

But the mainstream press is by no means the worst violator. For all of its failings, the mainstream press tries exceptionally hard to be accurate and to avoid intentionally misleading its readers. The same cannot be said of all news outlets. People used to worry about the *National Enquirer* and the *Globe*. Then they worried about such television shows as *Inside Edition* and *Hard Copy*. Now they worry about Internet outlets such as *The Drudge Report* and more marginal online sources of information—or misinformation. Digitalization has made it easy to alter images, making it exceptionally hard to distinguish fantasy from reality. Even the Department of Justice's Web site is not safe, as hackers demonstrated when they turned the site into a Nazi cell as part of a protest against the Communications Decency Act. We are now living in an era when seeing is no longer believing. One can only speculate on the impact of the nonmainstream press on the public's perception of the rest of the media.

In addition to the daily press, our view of the world and history is formed by a variety of media, including books, theater, and theatrical as well as made-for-television movies. How accurate are they? How accurate should they be?

Just as all of us have selective memories, and tend to shade a good story to make ourselves look better or wiser or funnier,[2] so, too, have memoirs always been suspect.[3] Nevertheless, it seems reasonable to trust personal accounts somewhat more when they are based on diaries and are written contemporaneously. When Robert Reich's delightful memoir *Locked in the Cabinet* (Knopf) appeared in the spring of 1997, only a few months after Reich left his job as secretary of labor, it seemed to offer wonderful insights into the inner workings of the administration and Capitol. Many of those who were serving or had served in the administration were impressed and surprised that he had managed to keep a daily journal, but in an introductory "Note to the Reader," Reich said that the book was based on "my notes." By using dates as section headings, as in a diary, Reich added to the apparent authenticity of his story. It was, therefore, particularly troubling when journalists were later able to show that many of the stories in the book were verifiably inaccurate.[4] If readers cannot trust the memoirs of Bob Reich, whose memoirs can they trust?

Audiences probably expect somewhat less accuracy from theatrical productions and movies. Certainly, Shakespeare is not held to the strictest standards of veracity, and yet generations of theatergoers have been influenced by his portrait of subjects ranging from English history to Julius Caesar. Like it or not, much of what Americans now know of history is learned from film. Are dramatists to be held to the same standard of truth as journalists or historians or memoirists? In a useful new book called *Past Imperfect: History Accord-*

ing to the Movies (Carnes 1995), that subject is probed by a list of major journalists and historians, each examining the accuracy of a famous film.

There has, of late, been a torrid debate about the accuracy of the book, play, and movie based on the life of Anne Frank. In a caustic essay in the *New Yorker*, Cynthia Ozick (1997) attacked virtually everyone who had been associated with the work. "The story of Anne Frank in the fifty years since 'The Diary of a Young Girl' was first published," she wrote,

has been bowdlerized, distorted, transmuted, traduced, reduced; it has been infantilized, Americanized, homogenized, sentimentalized, falsified, kitschified, and, in fact, blatantly and arrogantly denied. Among the falsifiers have been dramatists and directors, translators and litigators, Anne Frank's own father, and even—or especially—the public, both readers and theatergoers, all over the world. A deeply truth-telling work has been turned into an instrument of partial truth, surrogate truth, or anti-truth. (78)

Along with other commentators (see Melnick 1997), Ozick argued that Anne Frank had been robbed of her Jewishness and recast as a surrogate for all races. In the play, which was written by the authors of *It's a Wonderful Life*, "comedy overwhelmed darkness," Ozick wrote. "Anne became an all-American girl" (85). Even the Nazis were sanitized.

To some extent, the public expects and accepts some alteration of fact in the fascinating and somewhat controversial art form called the docudrama, or drama based on fact.

In *Masson* v. *New Yorker Magazine* (501 U.S. 496 [1991]), which involved a story by Janet Malcolm that took liberties with quotations by Freud scholar Jeffrey Masson, the U.S. Supreme Court held that docudramas are entitled to greater latitude with the facts than are newspapers or magazines. The Court said, "An acknowledgment that the work is so-called docudrama or historical fiction, or that it recreates conversations from memory, not from recordings, might indicate that quotations should not be interpreted as the actual statements of the speaker to whom they are attributed" (*Masson* v. *New Yorker Magazine* 512-13).

The Court seems to believe that the public, in effect, takes docudramas with a grain of salt, that docudramas are less likely to violate the contract between the writer and the audience. At the very least, the public seems to understand that dramatists need to consolidate characters and invent some dialogue to tell an important story. They may also be familiar with classic docudramas, from Homer through Shakespeare, where artists have taken more than a little poetic license, in the interest of drama and perhaps, too, in the interest of making a larger moral or historical point.

The dangers inherent in the docudrama, however, were highlighted recently by *Hoodlum*, a film starring Laurence Fishburne as Ellsworth "Bumpy" Johnson, a black gangster who fought with Dutch Schultz for control of the numbers racket in Harlem in the 1930s. The film is based on fact, and it is filled with historical figures including Lucky Luciano and Meyer Lansky. But what makes the film particularly troubling is its portrayal of Thomas E. Dewey, the racket-busting district attorney, New York governor, and two-time Republican Party presidential candidate. Throughout the film, Dewey is portrayed as a corrupt prosecutor; he is shown taking suitcases full of cash from Luciano and, later, from Johnson. No such thing ever happened, nor do the filmmakers claim that it did. Dewey was known as an incorruptible public servant. His heirs were furious and took their case to the press (Dewey 1997). They had no legal recourse, however, nor did members of the public who may now falsely think that an incorruptible prosecutor who twice ran for president was, in fact, a crook.

Had he been alive, Dewey could have sued for libel, claiming damage to his reputation. All states, however, observe the centuries-old rule against liability for defamation of dead people (Brown 1989, 1525). It is possible that a state could extend defamation laws to protect the dead, allowing their heirs to recover for a period after their death, and that such a law would be held constitutional (Brown 1989, 1525). In the late 1980s, New York Governor Mario Cuomo supported such a proposal in response to statements of a black teenager named Tawana Brawley, who falsely accused several white men, including a recently deceased police officer, of gang rape. Such a law, however, would present countless problems. For how long after a person has died, for example, should such a right of action survive? A better solution would be a code of personal, corporate, or professional responsibility.

It is also difficult to apply the law of defamation to novels, though novels are increasingly commingling factual and fictional depictions of real persons, some of whom are alive. Dominick Dunne's recent account of the O. J. Simpson trial is a case in point. On the dust jacket of *Another City, Not My Own*, Dunne, who covered the case for *Vanity Fair*, calls the book "a novel in the form of a memoir," a category that, as the *New Yorker* observed, was "unanticipated by the Dewey decimal system, and one that allows Dunne to make up a name for the character based on himself, while using the real names of all of his sources" (Mead 1997, 38). Yet Dunne then goes on to put real people in fictionalized and highly questionable situations. For example, he laces the serial killer Andrew Cunanan into the book, bringing him into questionable contact with several people whom he never met, including the biographer A. Scott Berg and the producer Ray Stark. (Dunne told the *New Yorker*, "Ray Stark was very unhappy with me for putting Andrew Cunanan in his house.")

After struggling with the problem of defamation in fiction, many courts have come up with a standard that essentially reflects the terms of the contract between the writer and subject. The test used in some cases asks whether "a reader of ordinary intelligence" reading the entire book or article would understand that the situation and statements were purely imaginary. The court then looks at a variety of external factors, including the way the book was promoted and advertised—whether it was treated as fact or fiction—and the inherent plausibility of the story (Anderson 1985, 383). Interestingly, the authors of a significant number of recent best-selling nonfiction books, such as *Midnight in the Garden of Good and Evil*, have admitted that portions of their narrative were invented.

The audience also has a right to expect that facts set forth by journalists and historians will not be presented in a biased or selective fashion that totally or substantially distorts the truth. A story can be accurate—yet fundamentally false. If a story only described a man as a world leader in the 1930s and 1940s who built his nation's economy, the description could fit either FDR or Hitler. Details are crucial. The work of reporters and editors is to choose the salient facts. But one can distort the picture terribly by omitting context, by emphasizing the positive facts, or by listing only the negative ones. In this respect, perspective and balance are as important as factual accuracy, but the ground rules of the contract are somewhat different. Citizens have a right to expect history textbooks and daily news accounts to be balanced, for example, but they should be prepared for selectivity when reading an editorial or a columnist or a magazine that represents a political or ideological point of view, or when listening to some forms of talk radio. The key, in each instance, is disclosure, whether implicit or explicit.

CONCLUSION

A nation that has been blessed by the freedoms ensured by the First Amendment should be slow to adopt any legal remedy for the problems presented in this article. Instead, writers and others should adopt codes of ethics to deal with problems posed by the misrepresentation of fact. Such codes can be personal, corporate, or industrywide. The essential challenge in each case is to come to terms with the implicit agreement between the reader, listener, or viewer, on one hand, and the writer, editor, producer, or distributor, on the other.

If a news organization holds itself out as an accurate and balanced source of news, then it should scrupulously seek to be accurate and balanced. If a news organization or writer wishes to be seen as aggressive and at least occasionally reckless or sensational, or as ideological and one-sided, and if its audience understands that perspective, then it is arguable that its contract with its audience allows it greater leeway. Readers may expect more accuracy from the *New York Times* than from the *National Enquirer*. There is a somewhat analogous distinction between a news story and a political advertisement. The facts in both should be accurate. But the audience is nevertheless wary of political advertisements and, in any case, does not expect the facts in a political advertisement to be balanced.

It is possible to construct a hypothetical continuum of accuracy and balance. At one end are entities that hold themselves out as reliable sources of information on the day's events. Such outlets have the highest degree of responsibility to be balanced and accurate. Magazine pieces and works of nonfiction and history would reside at that same place on the continuum, so long as they hold themselves out as authoritative.

Next on the continuum, it could be argued, are opinion pieces, ideological magazines, or books written with a clear point of view. Readers expect the facts in such publications to be accurate, but they also know that they will be chosen selectively.

Finally, one could cut the greatest slack for docudramas or movies and plays based on fact. Here, as the Supreme Court has suggested, audiences expect some degree of dramatization. Even so, the essence of the characters, the dialogue, and the story should remain faithful to the truth. A writer can, understandably, create a scene that might have happened and that is consistent with what is known about the events and characters. But writers should not invent scenes that did not happen if they distort the essence of the characters or of the story.

Even in a docudrama, there is a moral if not legal responsibility to insert some kind of language that is truly designed to inform viewers of the nature of the distortions. The degree of permissible distortion naturally depends on several variables. Writers, for example, might feel freer to change the facts of a story with no great historic significance and where the real people are no longer alive. Moreover, writers might understandably take more liberties as events recede into the past.

In each of these instances, the contract can also be satisfied by a statement, inserted in a place where it is likely to be seen by the average member of the audience. But one of the cornerstones of our democracy will be badly eroded if the contract is regularly ignored and if the public is seriously misinformed or if it learns, over time, that it cannot trust the media.

Notes

1. The opinion continues: "The protection of private personality, like the protection of life itself, is left primarily to the individual States under the Ninth and Tenth Amendments. But this does not mean that the right is entitled to any less recognition by this Court as a basic of our constitutional system."

2. Several remarkable examples of this phenomenon involving public figures came to light in late 1997 and early 1998. One involved Larry Lawrence, who died while serving as ambassador to Switzerland. Mr. Lawrence had long boasted of his service in the Merchant Marines during World War II and claimed to have been wounded in 1945 when his ship was torpedoed by the Germans. When the story, accepted by all who knew him, proved to be false, his body was removed from Arlington Cemetery. Similarly, U.S. District Judge James Ware, who was in line to be nominated to the U.S. Court of Appeals for the Ninth Circuit, withdrew his name from consideration when forced to admit that for years he had been lying about an incident in his youth in which, he claimed, he had seen two white teenagers kill his brother in the streets of Birmingham, Alabama. Also, according to her biographer, Christopher Ogden, Pamela Harriman changed the facts of her biography as printed in *Who's Who* at the time of her confirmation hearings as ambassador to France. Apparently she was not, as the entry said, a college graduate, nor had she done graduate work at the Sorbonne. The *Los Angeles Times* reported in 1997 (Kelleher 1997) that statistics suggest that 25 percent of all applicants lie about some part of their résumé.

3. Lillian Hellman was not only a great playwright but also one of the finest memoirists of her era. Yet some of the stories that she described appeared later to be false or to have involved others and not Ms. Hellman. In "Pentimento," the story that served as the basis for the movie *Julia*, Ms. Hellman heroically rescued a Jewish woman from Germany. Later accounts revealed that the true heroine of the story was another woman.

4. *Slate* magazine carried a long-running, highly entertaining, yet also serious dissection and discussion of *Locked in the Cabinet*. The exchange started with "Robert Reich, Quote Doctor," by Jonathan Rauch, first posted on 29 May 1997. Touching on some of the issues raised by this article, Rauch wrote: "The book reads like good fiction. Unfortunately, some of it is. Call me old-fashioned, but I've always believed that there is something special about quotation marks. Whatever is between them, in nonfiction, is supposed to reflect accurately words that some real person actually said. Now 'accurately' leaves room for quibbling, and a memoir will be understood by most readers to be offered on an 'as remembered' basis. Reich says, in his prefatory note, that he jotted notes to himself, 'usually late at night,' and then consolidated them to make a book." Responding to some of the examples offered by Rauch and others, Reich made some changes in the paperback version of his book. For a full discussion, see the archives collected at www.slate.com.

References

Anderson, David A. 1985. Defamation in Fiction. *Brooklyn Law Review* 51(Winter):383-99.

Brown, Lisa. 1989. Dead but Not Forgotten: Proposals for Imposing Liability for Defamation of the Dead. *Texas Law Review* 67(June):1525-67.

Carnes, Mark C., ed. 1995. *Past Imperfect: History According to the Movies*. New York: Henry Holt.

Dewey, Thomas E. L. 1997. *Washington Post*, 30 Sept.

Kelleher, Kathleen. 1997. The Strangest Species/Behavior: Lies, Damned Lies and Good Stories. *Los Angeles Times*, 2 Dec.

Malcolm, Janet. 1989. Reflections: The Journalist and the Murderer. *New Yorker*, 13 Mar.

Mead, Rebecca. 1997. Ink. *New Yorker*, 8 Dec.

Melnick, Ralph. 1997. *The Stolen Legacy of Anne Frank*. New Haven, CT: Yale University Press.

Ozick, Cynthia. 1997. Who Owns Anne Frank? *New Yorker*, 6 Oct.

Pew Research Center for the People and the Press. 1998. Scandal Reporting Faulted for Bias and Inaccuracy; Popular Policies and Unpopular Press Lift Clinton Ratings. Survey, 6 Feb.

Reich, Robert. 1997. *Locked in the Cabinet*. New York: Alfred Knopf.

Restatement (Second) of Torts. 1977.

Society of Professional Journalists, Code of Ethics. 1997-98. Preamble.

ANNALS, *AAPSS*, **560**, November 1998

The Impact of Factual Versus Fictional Media Portrayals on Cultural Stereotypes

By SHEILA T. MURPHY

ABSTRACT: The present article explores how factual and fictional media portrayals may activate culturally shared racial and gender stereotypes and influence subsequent judgments involving members of stereotyped groups. In line with previous research (Power, Murphy, and Coover 1996), new data are presented that demonstrate that exposure to a stereotypic or counterstereotypic portrayal primes consistent interpretations of unrelated events (such as the Anita Hill–Clarence Thomas hearings, the William Kennedy Smith–Patricia Bowman rape accusations, and spousal abuse). Both cognitive and motivational factors such as ingroup-outgroup bias appear to influence the relative weight given factual as opposed to fictional portrayals. For instance, men were equally harsh in the wake of a stereotypic female portrayal regardless of whether they believed it to be factual or fictitious. Moreover, men tended to discount a fictitious counterstereotypic portrayal of a female, whereas women were more likely to dismiss a fictitious stereotypic portrayal. Recommendations are offered suggesting how media portrayals might successfully reduce prejudice.

Sheila T. Murphy is an associate professor at the Annenberg School for Communication at the University of Southern California as well as a consultant for the Centers for Disease Control and Prevention in Atlanta. Her research revolves around the influence of cognition, emotion, and culture on judgments and decision making.

DURING the O. J. Simpson criminal trial, there was tremendous concern regarding the media's ability to influence the jurors and their subsequent deliberations. In an attempt to shield jurors from an onslaught of information, speculation, and innuendo, they were sequestered and their exposure to the mass media was censored. Each day, newspaper articles that made reference to either the trial itself or to any of its cast of characters were meticulously excised.

This editing, it was argued, effectively eliminated any potential influence of the mass media on the jurors' judgments. But while this exercise may have removed the most obvious and direct sorts of influences, it may have left unchecked myriad more subtle and indirect influences. After all, jurors still had access to the sports section in which athletes like the defendant were glorified, if not deified, for aggressive behavior. Would exposure to the sports section in which individuals are lauded for pummeling, slashing, trouncing, and engaging in any number of other aggressive acts, somehow make the same behavior outside the sports arena more acceptable? Conversely, would seeing images of African American gang members lead jurors to interpret "evidentiary matters of fact" in a very different light? What about the incessant images of blonde beauties, many of whom seemed to bear an uncanny resemblance to the victim, Nicole Simpson, smiling back at the reader from virtually every page? In short, is it possible that what was left in the newspaper after the censoring could sway the jurors just as much as what was cut out? The present article first explores how the activation of culturally shared racial and gender stereotypes through both factual and fictional media representations might influence attributions of responsibility and credibility and then offers recommendations to reduce prejudice.

Psychologists have long recognized that we do not enter the perceptual arena empty-handed but, rather, with what is sometimes referred to as perceptual baggage. Perceptual baggage includes our unique idiosyncratic collection of experiences, needs, and desires as well as more common, culturally shared beliefs. As Jerome Bruner has been pointing out for the past 50 years, the way in which we perceive the world around us is not merely a neutral registration of some external reality. Instead, perception involves an active construction that incorporates our past memories and expectations as well as the current context (see Bruner 1992 for a review). In an early illustration of this point, Bruner and Goodman (1947) had children from different ends of the socioeconomic spectrum estimate the physical size of coins. The less well-to-do children made a greater number of errors in their size estimates. Interestingly, neither the direction nor the magnitude of the errors was random, as one might have expected given differential levels of experience handling money. Among the less well-to-do children, as the value of the coin increased, so, too, did its perceived physical size. This suggests that an individual's internal needs and desires can influence perceptions even of something as objective and incontrovertible as physical size. In demonstrating this, Bruner opened the door for the study of the extent to which our preconceptions and desires shape the far more subjective social reality.

Thus, according to Bruner and other cognitive constructivists, there is no pure percept. Rather, we tend to draw on our past experiences and present desires to "go beyond the information given" in a particular context (Bruner 1957, 41). If social reality arises out of the interaction of the individual mind and the external world as this constructivist framework posits, then by extension one could argue that there is likewise no pure fact. While a case could be made for this position, we cannot dismiss the overwhelming consensus in the way in which we perceive the world. Like the less well-to-do children in Bruner and Goodman's study, even our errors in judgment are not random but show a marked similarity. Where do we learn that the Irish are alcoholics, Californians are flaky, and Asians are good at math? While some of these stereotypes may be transmitted interpersonally, the consistency and pervasiveness of these and other cultural stereotypes suggest another route of transmission, namely, the mass media (see Durkin 1985a, 1985b, 1985c for a review).

THE MASS MEDIA AND THE PERPETUATION AND ATTENUATION OF CULTURAL STEREOTYPES

In 1922, Lippmann described stereotypes as "a very partial and inadequate way of viewing the world" (72). Perhaps nowhere is the view of minorities and women more partial and inadequate than in the mass media. Content analyses reveal that men continue to be overrepresented on prime-time television by a ratio of 3 to 1 (Basow 1992). Moreover, the women who do appear are typically portrayed as passive, overemotional, dependent on men, and inordinately concerned with "getting rings out of collars and commodes" (Wood 1994, 232). A parallel problem exists with respect to depictions of African Americans, who, when they do appear, are frequently portrayed as drug-traffickers or criminals (Lichter et al. 1987).

More recently, however, there has been a shift away from purely stereotypic representations of women, ethnic minorities, senior citizens, and other stigmatized groups (Berry 1980; Lichter et al. 1987; Montgomery 1989; Seiter 1986). In fact, there has been a concerted effort in certain quarters to include counterstereotypic images, or images that run counter to the cultural stereotype. These counterstereotypes contain what Hewstone (1989) refers to as "disconfirming information" that directly contradicts the prevailing stereotype. For example, in *The Cosby Show*, audiences were presented with a nuclear African American family in which the father is a doctor and the mother is a lawyer. The rationale driving the proliferation of this and other counterstereotypic portrayals is that, through exposure to counterstereotypic examples, cultural stereotypes will be disconfirmed and rendered obsolete and, consequently, the prejudice that often accompanies them will be diminished.

Thus far, however, the bulk of research on media images has primarily monitored the prevalence of various depictions without directly assessing their impact (Friedman 1977; Signorielli 1985). Consequently, there exists scant evidence as to whether the presentation of such counterstereotypic images actually accomplishes the goal of reducing prejudice against members of a stereotyped group. In one such study, however, my colleagues J. Gerard Power and Gail Coover and I explored the extent to which a stereotypic or counterstereotypic media portrayal could prime social perception, making it more likely that subsequent incidents involving members of the stereotyped group would be interpreted along similar lines (Power, Murphy, and Coover 1996). More specifically, we tested the notion that media portrayals might operate intertextually (Gray 1989) and that even seemingly unrelated portrayals of African Americans or women could, in fact, influence later judgments of the guilt, innocence, or credibility of other members of these stereotyped groups.

Pilot surveys of undergraduates at a large West Coast university revealed that the four most frequent negative stereotypic attributes for African Americans were "lazy," "unintelligent," "aggressive," and "criminal." These elements of the cultural stereotype were integrated into an ostensibly autobiographical article written by a freshman named Chris Miller. A second version of the same article was also constructed that presented an African American Chris Miller in a counterstereotypic manner, namely, hardworking, intelligent, gentle, and law abiding. It is important to note that the counterstereotype is not merely the positive elements of the cultural stereotype, for example, the suggestion that African Americans are musically gifted. Rather, counterstereotypic portrayals stress attributes that directly contradict or run counter to any element, negative or positive, of the prevailing stereotype. A third version of the article was designed to be equal in length and touched on many of the same topics but did not depict Chris Miller in either a stereotypic or counterstereotypic way.

Four hundred undergraduates were subsequently asked to fill out two ostensibly unrelated surveys. The first survey dealt with an evaluation of a proposed campus newsletter, titled *People and Places*. This newsletter was introduced as the pilot version of a newsletter that would feature a different first-person profile of a student and a different place on campus each month. In fact, it featured one of the three versions of our Chris Miller text. Having read the newsletter, participants were asked a series of questions regarding how effective and attractive they found the format and how interesting they considered the articles. Participants were then asked by another experimenter to complete a second, ostensibly unrelated survey dealing with opinions and attributions of responsibility with regard to various media events, including Magic Johnson's contracting the human immunodeficiency virus (HIV) and Rodney King's beating at the hands of the Los Angeles Police Department.

Our results indicate that being exposed to stereotypic and counter-stereotypic portrayals did cue consistent interpretations of unrelated media events. Individuals who read a stereotypic portrayal of an African American Chris Miller were much more likely to make internal or personal attributions of blame with regard to Rodney King and Magic Johnson, suggesting that they somehow "brought it on themselves." Conversely, being exposed to a counter-stereotypic portrayal led to more external or situational attributions of blame.

A parallel effect was found for stereotypic and counterstereotypic portrayals of women. Pilot surveys had previously determined the four strongest attributes for women to be "weak," "unintelligent," "over-emotional," and "self-centered/shrewlike." After being exposed to a stereotypic, counterstereotypic, or neutral, control version of an autobiographical sketch by a blond, female Chris Miller, participants were asked the following:

The Clarence Thomas/Anita Hill hearings raised some serious questions regarding sexual harassment in the workplace. Some believed Hill's testimony while others believed Thomas' testimony. On a scale from 1 to 10, where 1 implies believing Hill and 10 implies believing Thomas, please indicate whose testimony you believe.

William Kennedy Smith was recently acquitted of raping Patricia Bowman. Some people believe Bowman's testimony while others believe Kennedy Smith's testimony. On a scale from 1 to 10, where 1 implies believing Bowman and 10 implies believing Kennedy Smith, please indicate whose testimony you believe.

Some people believe that spousal abuse is exclusively the fault of the husband whereas others believe that the wife can act to instigate the violence and therefore bring it on herself. On a scale from 1 to 10, where 1 implies that the wife is completely innocent and 10 implies that she brings it on herself, please indicate your position.

Being exposed to a stereotypic portrayal of a female led individuals to doubt the credibility of Anita Hill (the woman who accused then Supreme Court nominee Clarence Thomas of sexual harassment) and Patricia Bowman (the woman who accused William Kennedy Smith of rape), whereas exposure to a counterstereotypic portrayal increased the perceived credibility of these women. Similarly, the stereotypic version of the article resulted in more blame being directed at the wife in spousal-abuse situations, whereas the counterstereotypic version resulted in a tendency to direct greater blame at the husband.

In honor of the Annenberg conference on the "future of fact," I extended the gender stereotyping study by analyzing additional data that had been collected simultaneously with that just described. In this previously unreported data, 84 participants from the same subject pool (approximately half male and half female) were informed that Chris Miller, the woman featured in the newsletter, was fictitious. In other words, while the texts themselves were identical to the stereotypic and counterstereotypic conditions described previously, participants in this condition were explicitly told that the student editors had fabricated Chris Miller to give readers a sense of the possible format of the proposed newsletter. These conditions will subsequently be referred to as the fictitious conditions, and the previous conditions where individuals thought that Chris Miller actually existed and had authored the article will be referred to as the factual conditions.

Comparison of factual versus fictitious media portrayals

The common wisdom is that individuals are quite capable of distinguishing reality from fantasy, or fact from fiction. Moreover, it is widely assumed that our ability to discriminate between the two immunizes us from any potential effects of fiction. In other words, because fictitious information is categorized as such, it should not enter into our calibrations of reality. Several recent lines of work, however, suggest that this assumption may not hold. Gilbert (1991), for example, found that people tend to first give credence to anything they comprehend and only later evaluate and reject information they believe to be false. He suggests that acceptance of information may, in fact, be the cognitive default. Similarly, Prentice, Gerrig, and Bailis (1997) propose that "fiction, like fact, necessitates a *willing construction* of disbelief: Readers will initially accept the assertions in a fictional work as true and will subsequently reject those assertions only if they are mo-

tivated to and able to evaluate their veracity" (417).

Comparisons between the data described earlier from Power, Murphy, and Coover (1996) and the additional conditions in which participants were informed that the blonde female Chris Miller was fictitious may shed further light on the extent to which individuals discount fictional portrayals. Participants' reactions following exposure to the stereotypic (unintelligent, overemotional, weak, and self-centered or shrewlike), counterstereotypic (intelligent, levelheaded, strong, and compassionate), and neutral, control versions of the female Chris Miller are quantified in Figures 1, 2, and 3.[1] The credibility of Anita Hill (Figure 1), Patricia Bowman (Figure 2), and women who have been sexually abused more generally (Figure 3) was clearly affected by the stereotypic, counterstereotypic, or neutral content of the newsletter article. Individuals who were exposed to the stereotypic Chris Miller were significantly less likely to believe Anita Hill and Patricia Bowman and were more likely than those in the counterstereotypic condition to believe that women who were abused by their husbands "brought it on themselves."

But it is also obvious that acceptance or rejection of the cultural stereotype of women depends at least in part on the gender of the reader. An analysis of the control conditions of the three dependent measures reveals that, even without any media portrayal intervention, men and women start out with very different opinions on these matters, with

FIGURE 1

RELATIVE CREDIBILITY OF CLARENCE THOMAS AND ANITA HILL

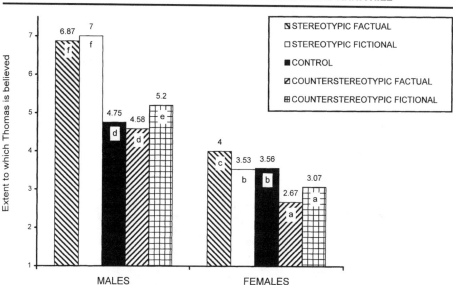

NOTE: Columns sharing a letter are not significantly different from one another at $p < .05$ level.

women being far more sympathetic to members of their own ingroup (Tajfel 1982). The media portrayals seem to further exacerbate this initial gender-based disparity. Men who were exposed to the stereotypic Chris Miller were significantly less likely to believe Anita Hill and Patricia Bowman and were significantly more likely to hold women accountable for spousal abuse. Interestingly, for male readers, it did not matter whether they believed the text to be autobiographical or fictional, as both resulted in increased attributions of blame and decreased perceptions of credibility. For female readers, however, the stereotypic article resulted in a significant shift in judgment only when it was thought to be factual in nature.

The counterstereotypic portrayal likewise yielded a very different pattern of results for men and women. Reading an article about an intelligent, strong, level-headed Chris Miller tended to have a far greater impact on female readers. For females, the counterstereotypic Chris Miller resulted in significantly higher judgments of credibility with respect to Anita Hill and Patricia Bowman and lower attributions of blame with regard to spousal abuse regardless of whether they believe the article to be factual or fictitious. In contrast, while men appear to make some adjustments to their opinions in the appropriate direction when confronted with a "factual" counterstereotypic Chris Miller, they appear particularly prone to discount

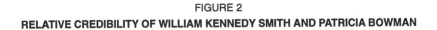

FIGURE 2
RELATIVE CREDIBILITY OF WILLIAM KENNEDY SMITH AND PATRICIA BOWMAN

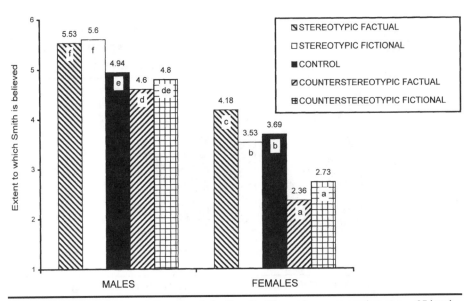

NOTE: Columns sharing a letter are not significantly different from one another at $p < .05$ level.

such a positive portrayal when it is presented as fictional.

CONCLUSION

In line with previous research (Power, Murphy, and Coover 1996), the current data demonstrate that being exposed to stereotypic and counterstereotypic portrayals can influence judgments of unrelated individuals and events. The present data also bolster the contention that the impact of media portrayals is heavily contingent on the reader's relation to or "position" (Hall 1982; Power, Murphy, and Coover 1996) with respect to the text. For instance, women were considerably more swayed by the counter-

stereotypic portrayal than were men. Conversely, men appear to be more susceptible to the negative stereotypic portrayal than their female counterparts.

Gender also played a key role in determining the relative weight given factual as opposed to fictional portrayals. For instance, men's judgments of the unrelated individuals and events were significantly swayed by a stereotypic portrayal of Chris Miller, regardless of whether they believed it to be factual or fictitious. Women, on the other hand, tended to discount the stereotypic fictitious portrayal but continued to be influenced by the fictitious counterstereotypic portrayal. In sum, it appears that fictitious portrayals are particu-

FIGURE 3
ATTRIBUTIONS OF BLAME IN SPOUSAL ABUSE

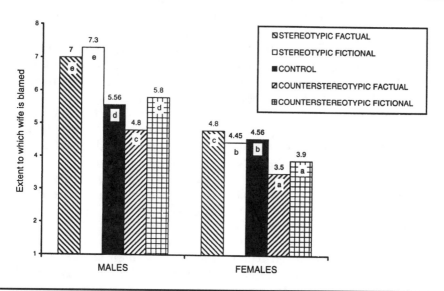

NOTE: Columns sharing a letter are not significantly different from one another at $p < .05$ level.

larly likely to be embraced or rejected based on the readers' underlying motivations and their position with respect to the protagonist. This serves to underscore Bruner's observation (1957, 1992; Bruner and Goodman 1947) that we are not merely passive observers but, rather, active architects of our own reality.

To return to the questions posed at the beginning of this article: were seemingly innocuous images of star athletes or blond beauties capable of influencing the O. J. Simpson jurors? The present data suggest that unrelated media images may indeed produce such unintended and insidious effects. The extent of the influence may be a function both of individuals' preexisting cognitive schemata and their motivation to maintain a particular worldview. Indeed, the idea

that media content may be understood in similar ways based on group membership or "interpretive communities" (see Power, Murphy, and Coover 1996 for a review) may account for the widespread gap in perceptions of O. J. Simpson's guilt between Anglos and African Americans.

Recommendations

Admittedly, the effects observed, based on responses by undergraduates to a survey, are at least one step removed from actual judgments such as whether to convict, hire, or even walk on the same side of the street as another human being. At the same time, however, it is important to note that the demonstrated shifts in judgment were evoked by a single exposure to a portrayal that is far more pallid than those readily available in the mainstream media. Operating under the assumption that repeated exposure to even more vivid stereotypic and counterstereotypic portrayals would have an even greater impact on individuals' judgments and beliefs, I draw from the extant research to offer the following policy recommendations.

1. Inform both mass media producers and consumers of the potential impact of stereotypic representations. Consider for a moment the longstanding use of stock characters in which cultural stereotypes are employed as a heuristic to cue the audience to the identity of a particular character. A young African American male dressed in baggy pants and a cap telegraphs a wealth of information to an audience by evoking our collective gang-member schema. While those responsible for producing newspapers, movies, and television programs are obviously aware of the power and efficiency of such images, we should not presume that they are equally cognizant of the long-term detrimental effects of such portrayals. It is egocentric to assume that those involved in production have the time or energy to devote to searching out relevant research published in fairly obscure academic journals.

As academics and as individuals who care about curtailing prejudice, we must strive to make our findings more accessible not only to industry professionals but to the general public as well. Research has shown that when the potential influence of a prime is brought to an individual's attention, its power is virtually eliminated. For example, Schwartz and Clore (1983) have shown that the weather has a very systematic influence on judgments. For instance, when the weather is pleasant, people are much more positive in their overall assessments. However, when it is pointed out to them that the weather may be influencing their judgments, they self-correct and the effect disappears. Perhaps highlighting the effect of stereotypic portrayals would result in a similar diminution of effect.

2. Avoid the temptation to focus on the so-called positive elements of racial and gender stereotypes. As children, many of us were taught some version of "If you can't say something nice about someone, then you shouldn't say anything at all." Well-meaning individuals sometimes attempt to combat racism and sexism by drawing attention to the so-called positive elements of cultural stereotypes. It is important to realize that these elements comfortably coexist with their more negative counterparts. For instance, suggesting that women are nurturing is not incompatible with women also being overemotional. Likewise for African Americans, having athletic ability is not incompatible with being capable of physical aggression. Consequently, attempting to cast a particular group in a more favorable light by focusing on the so-called positive elements of a cultural stereotype may do more harm than good by making accessible (Tversky and Kahneman 1973) and lending credence to the overall stereotype.

However, it may also be possible to dampen boomerang effects that might be associated with the positive elements of stereotypes. Work in psychology on cross-categorization (Marcus-Newhall et al. 1993) suggests that individuals who simultaneously belong to categories that do not typically co-occur—for example, people who are both Republican and African American—make us reexamine our preconceptions. Thus, when profiling an individual who exemplifies some positive stereotypic trait (such as an African American athlete), we might avoid activating the negative elements of the stereotype by also mentioning some dimension on which the same individual seems counterstereotypic (such as this athlete's enjoyment in doing the *New York Times* crossword puzzle).

3. Encourage studios, networks, and newspapers to include more representations that challenge the cultural stereotype. A single counterexample may be dismissed as an aberration or "subtyped" (Mauer, Park, and Rothbart 1995) as being an exception to the rule. Thus, numerous counterstereotypic examples spread over time would be necessary to slowly chip away at cultural stereotypes (Johnston and Hewstone 1992; Weber and Crocker 1983).

4. Avoid counterstereotypic exemplars that are too atypical. As Gray (1989) has noted, the representation of minorities in the mass media often depicts either deficient or highly gifted individuals. Yet research clearly demonstrates that the atypicality of counterstereotypic examples is often cited as grounds for dismissing them (Kunda and Oleson 1997). For instance, a study by Murphy and Power (1997) evaluated the impact of a television series titled *Discovering Women* that profiled successful women scientists. They found that the more impressive the achievements of the woman featured, the less likely audience members were to consider her a typical woman. This perceived atypicality had a dramatic impact on the extent to which audience members felt that the female scientist's accomplishments could be replicated by another woman. In short, extremely atypical or deviant examples may be excluded from the relevant category and have no impact on the cultural stereotype or, worse yet, provoke boomerang effects that bolster the very stereotype they violate.

5. Include factual as well as fictitious counterstereotypic exemplars. A study by Hansen and Hansen (1988) demonstrates that even clearly fictional media representations can affect judgments of reality. In this particular study, participants who viewed sex-role stereotypic portrayals in rock music videos were more likely to interpret subsequent interactions between men and women in a consistent manner. As Hansen and Hansen note,

The impact of mass media fantasy depictions of sex role stereotypic persons and behaviors (even if they are recognized to be stereotypic caricatures or fantasy) can be extended to the domain of the real by their capacity to prime biased appraisals of subsequently encountered real persons and behaviors. (212)

However, as the present article and other work demonstrate, the impact of a fictional representation on beliefs clearly depends on the relation of the reader to the text (Prentice, Gerrig, and Bailis 1997, 417). Individuals who are motivated to maintain the cultural stereotype need only point to the fictional nature of the counterstereotypic information as a basis for dismissal. Consequently, it is imperative that at least some counterstereotypic media representations be factual in nature.

6. *Do not ignore societal constraints by focusing exclusively on the individual.* Gray (1989) has argued that prevailing media representations of the successes and failures of individual African Americans shift attention away from the societal and structural underpinnings of racism. Along similar lines, Iyengar (1990, 1991) contends that episodic stories—stories that focus on specific individuals rather than societal themes such as racism or poverty—will draw attention to the individual actors. As a result, he argues, episodic stories will prompt audiences to seek individual determinants of social problems (for example, that poverty among African Americans is caused by their inherent laziness) and to ignore societal constraints. In other words, the subtext of such personalized portrayals may be that success or failure ultimately resides in the individual.

If Iyengar is correct, the outlook for using fictional media representations to combat racism and sexism appears bleak. Nearly all fictional accounts focus on individual protagonists rather than broad social themes. However, research by Strange and Leung (in press) suggests that stories about individual actors can emphasize either dispositional or situational causes of a protagonist's own success or failure. For instance, a story may portray a student who fails to complete high school either because he or she is lazy or because the school environment is not conducive to learning. These researchers showed that stories that focus on the situational underpinnings of problems faced by specific characters can prime situational or societal attributions of responsibility. This finding provides hope that, if social context is placed prominently in the foreground of the narrative, fictitious portrayals can promote consideration of systemic causes of success and failure. Strange and Leung further demonstrated that personalized accounts which foreground the social context of individual behavior are more likely to result in systemic, as opposed to individual-level, attributions of responsibility when they evoke "remindings of related experiences in a reader's personal or mediated past" (2). This suggests that the ability to empathize with the individual portrayed may play a key role in attributions of responsibility and blame. Indeed, media depictions that draw on more overarching or universal themes, such as birth, death, and family, which resonate across cul-

tures, may ultimately prove a power-
ful weapon against prejudice (Katz,
Liebes, and Iwao 1991; Larsen and
Seilman 1988).

Note

1. The slight discrepancies in the means for
the factual stereotype, factual counterstereotype, and control conditions reported here and
those reported in Power, Murphy, and Coover
(1996) are due to the inclusion of additional
participants in those conditions.

References

Basow, Susan. 1992. *Gender: Stereotypes
and Roles*. 3d ed. Pacific Grove, CA:
Brooks/Cole.

Berry, G. 1980. Television and African
Americans, Past Legacy and Present
Portrayals. In *Television and Social
Behavior, Beyond Violence and Chil-
dren*, ed. S. B. Withey and D. Zillman.
Hillsdale, NJ: Lawrence Erlbaum As-
sociates.

Bruner, Jerome. 1957. Going Beyond the
Information Given. In *Contemporary
Approaches to Cognition*, ed. Howard
Gruber. Cambridge, MA: Harvard
University Press.

———. 1992. Another Look at the New
Look 1. *American Psychologist* 47
(6):780-83.

Bruner, Jerome and Charles Goodman.
1947. Value and Need as Organizing
Factors in Perception. *Journal of Abnormal Social Psychology* 42:33-44.

Durkin, Kevin. 1985a. Television and
Sex-Role Acquisition: I. Content. *British Journal of Social Psychology*
24(2):101-13.

———. 1985b. Television and Sex-Role
Acquisition: II. Effects. *British Journal
of Social Psychology* 24(3):191-210.

———. 1985c. Television and Sex-Role
Acquisition: III. Counter-Stereotyp-

ing. *British Journal of Social Psychology* 24(3):211-22.

Friedman, Leslie. 1977. *Sex Role Stereotyping in the Mass Media*. New York:
Garland.

Gilbert, Daniel. 1991. How Mental Systems Believe. *American Psychologist*
46(2):107-19.

Gray, Herman. 1989. Television, Black
Americans and the American Dream.
*Critical Studies in Mass Communica-
tion* 6:376-86.

Hall, Stewart. 1982. The Rediscovery of
Ideology: Return of the Repressed in
Media Studies. In *Culture, Society and
the Media*, ed. M. Gurevitch, T. Bennett,
J. Curran, and J. Woolacott. London:
Methuen.

Hansen, Christine and Ronald Hansen.
1988. How Rock Music Can Change
What Is Seen When a Boy Meets a
Girl: Priming Stereotypic Appraisal of
Social Interactions. *Sex Roles* 19(5-
6):287-316.

Hewstone, Miles. 1989. Changing Stereotypes with Disconfirming Information. In *Stereotyping and Prejudice:
Changing Conceptions*, ed. Daniel
Bar-Tal, Carl Grauman, Arie Kruglan-
ski, and Wolfgang Stroebe. New York:
Springer-Verlag.

Iyengar, Shanto. 1990. Framing Responsibility for Political Issues: The Case
of Poverty. *Political Behavior* 12:19-40.

———. 1991. *Is Anyone Responsible?
How Television Frames Political Is-
sues*. Chicago: University of Chicago
Press.

Johnston, Lucy and Miles Hewstone.
1992. Cognitive Models of Stereotypic
Change: III. Subtyping and the Perceived Typicality of Disconfirming
Group Members. *Journal of Experimental Social Psychology* 28(4):360-86.

Katz, Elihu, Tamar Liebes, and Sumiko
Iwao. 1991. Neither Here nor There:
Why "Dallas" Failed in Japan. *Com-
munication* 12(2):99-110.

Kunda, Ziva and Kathryn C. Oleson. 1997. When Exceptions Prove the Rule: How Extremity of Deviance Determines the Impact of Deviant Examples on Stereotypes. *Journal of Personality and Social Psychology* 72(5):965-79.

Larsen, Steen and Uffe Seilman. 1988. Personal Remindings While Reading Literature. *Text* 8:411-29.

Lichter, S. Robert, Linda Lichter, Stanley Rothman, and Daniel Amundson. 1987. Prime-Time Prejudice: TV's Images of Blacks and Hispanics. *Public Opinion* (July-Aug.):13-16.

Lippmann, Walter. 1922. *Public Opinion*. New York: Free Press.

Marcus-Newhall, Amy, Norman Miller, Rolf Holtz, and Marilyn Brewer. 1993. Cross-Cutting Category Membership with Role Assignment: A Means of Reducing Intergroup Bias. *British Journal of Social Psychology* 32(2):125-46.

Mauer, Kristin L., Bernadette Park, and Myron Rothbart. 1995. Subtyping Versus Subgrouping: Processes in Stereotype Representation. *Journal of Personality and Social Psychology* 69(5):812-24.

Montgomery, K. C. 1989. *Target Prime Time: Advocacy Groups and the Struggle over Entertainment Television*. New York: Oxford University Press.

Murphy, Sheila and J. Gerard Power. 1997. Strangers in Science: Altering Perceptions of Women as Scientists Through Televised Counter-Stereotypes. Manuscript.

Power, J. Gerard, Sheila Murphy, and Gail Coover. 1996. Priming Prejudice: How Stereotypes and Counter-Stereotypes Influence Attribution of Responsibility and Credibility Among Ingroups and Outgroups. *Human Communication Research* 23(1):36-58.

Prentice, Deborah A., Richard J. Gerrig, and Daniel S. Bailis. 1997. What Readers Bring to the Processing of Fictional Texts. *Psychonomic Bulletin and Review* 4(3):416-20.

Schwartz, Norbert and Gerald Clore. 1983. Mood, Misattribution, and Judgments of Well-Being: Informative and Directive Functions of Affective States. *Journal of Personality and Social Psychology* 45:513-23.

Seiter, Ellen. 1986. Stereotypes and the Media: A Re-Evaluation. *Journal of Communication* 36:14-26.

Signorielli, Nancy. 1985. *Role Portrayal and Stereotyping on Television: An Annotated Bibliography of Studies Relating to Women, Minorities, Aging, Sexual Behavior, Health and Handicaps*. Westport, CT: Greenwood Press.

Strange, Jeffrey and Cynthia Leung. In press. How Anecdotal Accounts in News and in Fiction Can Influence Judgments of a Social Problem's Urgency, Causes, and Cures. *Personality and Social Psychology Bulletin*.

Tajfel, Henri. 1982. Social Psychology of Intergroup Relations. *Annual Review of Psychology* 33:1-39.

Tversky, Amos and Daniel Kahneman. 1973. Availability: A Heuristic for Judging Frequency and Probability. *Cognitive Psychology* 5:207-32.

Weber, Renee and Jennifer Crocker. 1983. Cognitive Processes in the Revision of Stereotypic Beliefs. *Journal of Personality and Social Psychology* 45(5):961-77.

Wood, Julia. 1994. *Gendered Lives: Communication, Gender and Culture*. Belmont, CA: Wadsworth.

ANNALS, *AAPSS*, **560**, November 1998

Individual and
Cultural Reality Monitoring

By MARCIA K. JOHNSON

ABSTRACT: What is the relationship between our perceptions, memories, knowledge, beliefs, and expectations, on one hand, and reality, on the other? Studies of individual cognition show that distortions may occur as a by-product of normal reality-monitoring processes. Characterizing the conditions that increase and decrease such distortions has implications for understanding, for example, the nature of autobiographical memory, the potential suggestibility of child and adult eyewitnesses, and recent controversies about the recovery of repressed memories. Confabulations and delusions associated with brain damage, along with data from neuroimaging studies, indicate that the frontal regions of the brain are critical in normal reality monitoring. The author argues that reality monitoring is fundamental not only to individual cognition but also to social/cultural cognition. Social/cultural reality monitoring depends on institutions, such as the press and the courts, that function as our cultural frontal lobes. Where does normal social/cultural error in reality monitoring end and social/cultural pathology begin?

Marcia K. Johnson is professor of psychology at Princeton University. She taught at the State University of New York, Stony Brook, before moving to Princeton in 1985. Her work on memory and reality monitoring has been supported by awards from the Guggenheim and Cattell foundations, a fellowship at the Center of Advanced Study in the Behavioral Sciences, and grants from the National Science Foundation, the National Institute of Mental Health, and the National Institute on Aging.

CONSIDER the relationship between our perceptions, memories, knowledge, and beliefs, on one hand, and reality, on the other (for example, Johnson 1988; Johnson and Sherman 1990). As events are experienced, encoding them into memory is constructive in that our interpretation of those events (even what constitutes an event to begin with) is influenced by our prior knowledge (for example, schemas), expectations (for example, activated goals or agendas), and social context (for example, what others value) (Bartlett 1932; Bransford and Johnson 1973; Schank and Abelson 1977). What we then subsequently ruminate about, and how we ruminate about it, will be determined by schemas, expectations, and social context as well (Bruner 1997; Nelson 1993). Even later, the information we access will depend on what cues are available (Tulving 1983), as well as our goals and the knowledge we bring to bear (Ross 1989; Wilson and Brekke 1994).

The fact that the relationship between cognition and reality is not a one-to-one mapping creates the core epistemological dilemma we face—a dilemma that suffuses our understanding of who we are, our relations with other people, and every judgment and decision we make. Think how different life might be if we never confused what we only thought about doing with what we actually did (no returning to check the stove), if we never disagreed with a significant other about who said what, if we knew exactly where we saw a fact we need for our job, if we never misappropriated another's ideas, if we could trust the accounts of honest eyewitnesses about a crime to be accurate, if the events remembered from our childhood were not influenced by our subsequent experiences, and if we could keep our beliefs about each individual from being contaminated by stereotypes that might not be true of them. We can only barely begin to imagine, I think, the kind of clarity of thought and transparency of our emotions that such factual certainty might engender.

Of course, to lapse into acting as if memory were a perfect representation of actuality is to fall prey to naive realism. Those of us who read cognitive and social psychology, or current papers in history, anthropology, sociology, or literary studies, are likely to be reminded frequently of just how naive, naive realism is. Although protected from naive realism (at least in our professional lives), we run the risk instead of being sucked into the quicksand of a kind of naive constructivism. Naive constructivists act as if all memories, knowledge, and beliefs were equal—as if the fact that there are multiple ways of perceiving, interpreting, and construing made it impossible or fruitless to judge between them. It is a point of view that does not appreciate the functional importance of mechanisms that normally constrain just how far out memories, knowledge, and beliefs can get.

INDIVIDUAL
REALITY MONITORING

It seems unlikely that a cognitive system would be viable if all information from all sources were simply represented in a jumble of amodal, abstract, propositional statements with no clue at all as to their origin. A system that treated, for example, the products of its imagination as equivalent to the products of its perception would likely suffer some evolutionary hardships. My lab has been intrigued by the question of how a cognitive system solves the problems posed by the constructive nature of cognition. We assume that the cognitive system represents information in ways that preserve its history (for example, visual information in visual cortex, auditory information in auditory cortex) (Damasio 1989). Thus the qualities of such information when it is activated, along with various inferential capacities that we have, typically allow us to make better than chance attributions about the epistemological status of our mental experiences (Johnson and Raye 1981). Nevertheless, both the information represented and the processes doing the attribution are imperfect, and thus errors will occur. However, our cognitive system is better off for having this information represented and for having such judgment mechanisms recruited than not. Clear evidence for this is the profound errors and confusions that occur when the capacity for creating these representations or for retrieving and evaluating them breaks down in cases of extreme distraction or stress or from organic brain damage (for example, Johnson 1988, 1991).

Both accurate and inaccurate memory can be understood within a cognitive architecture that specifies the processes recruited when information is encoded, consolidated, accessed, and monitored. Although all of these aspects of encoding and remembering affect the veridicality of memories and beliefs, this last step, the taking of a mental experience to correspond to some class of mental experience (a perception, a memory of an actual event, a prior or current imagination, a good judgment, a reasonable belief), is what we mean by reality monitoring or evaluation and attribution. Whether activated information is taken to be memories, knowledge, or reasonable beliefs is based on its phenomenal properties and its relation to other knowledge and memories. Such monitoring is affected by a number of factors, including the cost of errors, the time available, the person's motivation, and, again, the social context (Johnson and Raye 1981; Johnson, Hashtroudi, and Lindsay 1993).

In laboratory experiments, it is possible to induce people to claim to have seen things they have only imagined and to induce them to claim to have experienced autobiographical events the experimenter only suggested (for example, Johnson, Hashtroudi, and Lindsay 1993; Loftus 1997). More important, however, we can vary conditions to understand the factors that increase and decrease the probability of distortions in memory. In this work we do not necessarily focus only on whether a memory is accurate—we are, in fact, more interested in what leads someone to take it as true, rather than whether it is really true.

We know quite a bit about individual reality-monitoring processes. For example, there appear to be relatively simple, fast, heuristic processes that make attributions about the source of memories based on how familiar they are or based on an assessment of such characteristics as the amount of perceptual and contextual detail they have. For example, on average, memories of perceived events have more perceptual and contextual detail than memories of imagined events. Thus, if a memory is vivid, we tend to believe that it represents a real, perceived event. There are also slower, more systematic processes that attempt to retrieve additional supporting or disconfirming episodic information from memory; that evaluate information for internal consistency; or that compare memories with general knowledge to make plausibility assessments. This sort of systematic processing is particularly susceptible to disruption from stress, operating under short deadlines, and distraction, and such disruptions markedly increase reality-monitoring errors. Both heuristic and systematic processing are important because they provide useful checks on each other. If a vivid memory of a fantasy or dream passes the heuristic check for perceptual detail, it would likely be mistaken for reality unless caught by the more systematic plausibility check. On the other hand, if we took everything that was plausible as a real memory, regardless of whether it had any of the particular details characteristic of event memories, we would also make many more reality-monitoring errors than we do.

In individuals, these reality-monitoring processes are the result of neural interactions between different regions of the brain. Particularly important are medial temporal regions (especially the hippocampal formation) that appear to be central in binding the various elements of experience into complex memories to begin with, and the frontal lobes that appear to be central in both heuristic and systematic retrieval and evaluation of information. For example, patients with brain damage to the frontal lobes sometimes show a clinical symptom called confabulation characterized by untrue statements (sometimes quite fantastic) that the patient believes. One confabulating patient claimed to have played cards at a club away from the hospital the night before with the doctor and head nurse; another claimed to have been killed in World War I and then brought back to life (Stuss et al. 1978). Another claimed to have been a space pirate (Damasio et al. 1985).

In addition, clinical syndromes are sometimes accompanied by what is called anosognosia or anosodiaphoria. Anosognosia is an absence of awareness of deficit. Confabulating patients do not know they are confabulating. Likewise, patients with brain damage in certain regions may deny the paralysis in their arm or that they are blind. Patients with anosodiaphoria know they have a cognitive or physical deficit, but they show a casual disregard for the fact—they do not appear to be disturbed at all by the problem.

Cognitive psychologists have a number of techniques for studying the role of various brain regions in reality monitoring in normal individuals (Johnson and Raye 1998). For example, my lab recently published a study in which we recorded brain activity (event-related potentials) from electrodes placed on the scalp of people as they engaged in memory tasks (Johnson, Kounios, and Nolde 1996). In one study, people saw some pictures of items and imagined others. Later the names of these items were mixed with the names of new items and half the people were asked to indicate which items had been in the previous task and which were new (an old/new recognition task). Other people were asked to indicate whether the items in the previous task had been seen, imagined, or were new (source identification task). The largest difference in brain activity between simply saying that an item was experienced previously (the old/new task) and identifying the source of the memory was recorded at electrodes over the frontal lobes. This is just what we would expect from the breakdown in reality monitoring that occurs from frontal brain damage. We have since used a technique that provides more precise spatial information, functional magnetic resonance imaging, in a similar study. We found activity in right and left prefrontal cortex (PFC) for both old/new recognition and source identification tasks—but the activity was greater in left PFC when participants were engaged in source identification than when they were engaged in old/new recognition (Nolde, Johnson, and D'Esposito in press). We are currently exploring the hypothesis that right PFC is disproportionately involved in heuristic evaluation processes and left PFC (or right and left together) in more systematic evaluation processes (Nolde, Johnson, and Raye in press).

In short, reality-monitoring failures in individuals can occur as a by-product of less than perfect but normal reality-monitoring processes or from more severe, clinically significant disruptions in reality monitoring that are associated with psychopathology or brain lesions. Neuroimaging techniques, in combination with cognitive theories, allow us to explore on-line the brain mechanisms that correspond to psychological processes as individuals engage in reality monitoring.

SOCIAL/CULTURAL REALITY MONITORING

So far I have treated reality monitoring as if it were almost entirely a private mental activity of the individual. Reality-monitoring processes, however, are embedded within an interindividual social context that influences the nature of the events we experience initially and how we interpret them, what we subsequently think about, including how we embellish memories, and the criteria we use later for making attributions about the origin of mental experiences. Furthermore, joint remembering has the potential for co-constructing myths, some of which may be dysfunctional (as when a batterer's victim thinks that the batterer is responding to transgressions of the victim) and some of which may be quite functional (for example, the sense of common history and shared enjoyment from reviewing together photographs of a family vacation that depict the fabulous scenery but not the arguments over when and where to stop for lunch).

Joint remembering also provides the possibility for reducing distortion. I might recognize that your account is more accurate than mine, once I hear it. Even if I do not have a sense that your account is better, if you remember an event quite differently from the way I do, it might appropriately reduce my confidence in an inaccurate memory. Socially isolated individuals, or those embedded in a social context that does not engage in interpersonal reality monitoring or that does so in unconstrained or pathological ways, potentially run the risk of increased reality-monitoring errors. As events are recounted, the interactions between family and friends play a critical and relatively unexplored role in everyday reality monitoring (for example, Middleton and Edwards 1990).

Societies or cultures, like individuals, require reality-monitoring processes to keep their memories and beliefs in line with reality (Johnson 1996). Informal social interactions are important at this more general social level as well—affecting, for example, the spread of rumors, development of urban myths, conspiracy theories, and so forth. Here there are a number of potentially interesting questions. For example, what evaluative processes and criteria do individuals within a given community use in interpersonal reality monitoring? Are there characteristic differences between communities not only in the information they have available but also in how they evaluate it? Just as at the individual level we can ask whether some people are more

susceptible to distortions of reality (for example, people who have vivid images), we can ask whether some groups are at risk for reality-monitoring errors.

In addition to relatively informal social interactions between families and friends, there are more role-based, organized, or institutionalized reality-monitoring functions operating at the social/cultural level—in journalism, the legal system, science, education, therapy, and so forth. These institutions have explicit truth missions. Their members go through credentialing procedures that range from informal apprenticeships to formal training programs followed by licensing exams. Such procedures are designed, for example, to develop an appreciation for multiple perspectives, expertise in procedures for collecting and evaluating evidence, an understanding of objectivity (and its limits), and a sensitivity to the potential impact of motives and biases. Consumers and clients accept this expertise—indeed, they pay for it. It is one thing for a friend to question the accuracy of one's memory (or to encourage belief in it) and another for one's therapist to do so. It is one thing for a fellow citizen to question (or endorse) the account of a politician and another for a journalist to do so. It is one thing for an individual to claim that someone has lied and another for a court to find that a statement was (or was not) libelous. The impact of these institutionally based reality-monitoring activities can be profound for the individual (for example, in the case of interactions with a therapist) and for the society more generally (for example, in the case of a news story reporting a lie by a political candidate).

It is worth considering the functional and structural roles played by various organizations and institutions in this social/cultural reality monitoring. Therapists, journalists, lawyers, scientists, and educators, I want to suggest, are our social/cultural frontal lobes. They perform imperfect but nevertheless critical processes for society as a whole to function well in our complex world. Within each of these institutions, parallels with individual reality monitoring can be seen. For example, consider the heuristic processes used in individual reality monitoring. These typically work, but they can let errors slip through; ordinarily, vivid detail in a memory is more likely to arise from real than imagined events, but using the amount of detail as a heuristic for identifying the origin of information sometimes causes unusually vivid or detailed memories for imagined events to be taken as real. Similarly, a journalist might heuristically assume that the facts given by a scientist or the head of a bureaucracy are correct because ordinarily these are the people who would be likely to know those facts. This works much of the time but not always.

As a potential check to reduce reality-monitoring errors, an individual can engage in more extended retrieval and reasoning, evaluating memories in light of other information. Similarly, journalists have a repertoire of systematic checks—consulting other sources, looking for documents, evaluating the expertise and motives of sources—all the activities of good investigative journalism. Importantly, the products produced by journalists are monitored by editors for newsworthiness, clarity, accuracy, completeness, and fairness. As with a normally functioning individual, mistakes will sometimes get through these systematic self-checks and editorial checks; however, these heuristic and systematic processes should provide constraints that limit the frequency and magnitude of distortions of reality.

For individuals, when these heuristic and systematic processes are not operating normally—when they are disrupted through brain damage, psychopathology, drugs, or other extreme circumstances—we say that the person is confabulatory, delusional, psychotic, or dysfunctional. When analogous processes are not operating in journalism, we call it tabloid journalism (for example, Goode with Hetter 1994). The incursion of tabloid journalism into mainline journalism is like progressive frontal damage. To fail to see it, or to treat it as our inevitable postmodern condition, is cultural anosognosia (unawareness of deficit). To treat it as harmless entertainment is to exhibit cultural anosodiaphoria (unconcern about deficit).

How professions or institutions regulate the practice of their members (and the extent to which they should) is a complex topic (for example, Belsey and Chadwick 1992; Fry 1985; Pippert 1989). Systematic studies comparing the mechanisms that different institutions (for example, print media versus television; therapists versus lawyers) use for within-institution reality monitoring would be intriguing. The media, for example, have an implicit contract with readers and viewers, and lapses are disconcerting. However, people are likely to forgive what they believe to be honest mistakes. Distrust and cynicism are more likely if people believe that the media are careless, biased, or malicious, that is, if they believe that within-institution reality-monitoring processes have broken down.

Don Hewitt, one of the creators of the highly successful CBS newsmagazine show *60 Minutes* was quoted recently (Mifflin 1998) as being concerned about the impact of the success of *60 Minutes* on the quality of television journalism. The increasing number of shows with a newsmagazine format require more and more news stories; one potential consequence is that the standards for what constitutes news have slipped (partly as a result of needing to fill airtime), resulting in a blurring of the line between news and entertainment. The combination of personal journalism (that is, celebrity journalists) and stories that are sensational (for example, celebrity court cases, alleged sexual activities of politicians) has turned news from a financial drain into a moneymaker for networks, which increases the pressure for more moneymaking "news."

Many other stories have appeared in the media in recent years that raise important questions about the procedures for collecting and reporting news—for example, questions about the distorting influence of pay-

ing sources and dramatizing the news with reenactments and music (Tharp and Streisand 1994), the replacement of documentaries with docudramas (Frankel 1997), and the special problems posed by the open access of the Internet (for example, Turner 1996). As professional electronic journalism and Internet news services develop, reality-monitoring issues will be central. For example, Matt Drudge, the producer of an Internet column (the *Drudge Report*), is currently being sued by Sidney Blumenthal, a former journalist and current adviser to President Clinton, for publishing allegations (subsequently retracted) that Blumenthal has abused his wife (Clines 1998). Clines points out that Drudge does not have to answer to any editor regarding the accuracy of his stories, and he quotes Drudge as saying that the erroneous report in the Blumenthal case was "at worst . . . an accurate report of an inaccurate rumor."

As another example of institutionalized reality monitoring, consider therapy. There has been a dramatic rise in the number of cases in which adult individuals believe they have recovered previously repressed memories of childhood sexual abuse. For the moment, set aside the issues of the serious incidence of sexual abuse in our culture, questions that have been raised about the reality of repression or about the therapeutic value of recovering memories. More central to the current thesis is that therapists are engaged in a memory-exploring profession (as are, for example, police officers, lawyers, and child welfare workers) and hence engage in a type of interpersonal reality monitoring in collaboration with clients. Their suggestions and responses have the imprint of authority or expertise as they help frame the pursuit of memories. Certain therapeutic practices used in certain situations may reflect a therapist's inappropriately low criterion vis-à-vis heuristic judgment processes: for example, assuming that eating disorders or difficulties in intimate relations are sure signs of childhood sexual abuse. Other practices reflect a failure of more systematic processes: for example, using hypnosis to uncover repressed memories, exposing patients to many accounts of sexual abuse, or explicitly urging patients to adopt lax criteria in evaluating the veridicality of their memories. Such practices may reflect a failure to consider that these practices themselves can be potential sources of the memories that are presumably recovered—that is, they may induce imagined events that are later taken to be memories of real events (for example, see Lindsay and Read 1994; see also Ceci and Bruck 1993 for similar issues with respect to inducing memories in children suspected to be victims of sexual abuse).

Like journalists, therapists must operate with imperfect reality-monitoring procedures, both as they apply to individual patients' memories and beliefs and as they apply to empirical evidence and clinical case studies about the efficacy of clinical practices. They must also operate within time and economic constraints, for example, making judgments quickly about how to respond to something a client says or to what a client seems to feel.

Within-profession response to the possibility that false memories might be induced by therapy has come in the form of task forces, workshops, published articles, and symposia at major conventions devoted to evaluating current evidence and practice (for example, Pressley and Grossman 1994). Clients have a right to expect that therapists keep up on the relevant theoretical ideas and findings for their field, but even in the best therapeutic practice, there will be overlooked information and honest misjudgments. However, like journalism, there is a point at which therapeutic practice is delusional and dysfunctional, a point at which imperfect but reasonable therapy becomes tabloid therapy. (Of course, just as there are tabloid journalists and tabloid therapists, there are tabloid lawyers, tabloid scientists, tabloid educators, and so on.)

A salient feature of our culture is that cross-institutional reality monitoring takes up some of the slack from failures of within-institution monitoring. Thus journalists monitor politicians, the courts monitor journalists and therapists, university professors in departments of communications monitor journalists, and so forth. A key type of cross-institutional reality monitoring is provided by academic research in, for example, history, sociology, and political science. The expanding field of media criticism evaluates practices, and studies the relation between practices and outcomes (for example, Cappella and Jamieson 1997; Fallows 1996). Similarly, within academia, there has been a burgeoning of therapy criticism (for example, Dawes 1994;

Loftus and Ketcham 1994; Ofshe and Watters 1994; Spanos 1994), which has, in turn, generated a call (Pope 1996) for the critics to raise their own standards of reality monitoring (that is, of unbiased evaluation of evidence).

By far, one of the most powerful sources of cross-institutional monitoring in our culture is provided by the courts. Two such cases illustrate some of the complexities inherent in the issues involved. The first was the suit brought against the journalist Janet Malcolm by the psychoanalyst Jeffrey Masson, claiming libel for a 1983 *New Yorker* article she wrote about him. Masson claimed that Malcolm made up quotations that were unflattering and damaged his professional reputation. This case dragged on for more than 10 years. The Janet Malcolm case is particularly interesting because Malcolm was a talented journalist who skated the line between effective, engaging reporting and what some regard as tabloid practices, and it shows the problem the courts face in deciding what is and what is not a faithful account of events. In 1989, a three-judge panel of the U.S. appeals court in California dismissed the libel suit, ruling 2-1 "that even if Masson did not say those words, Malcolm's inventions were permissible because they did not 'alter the substantive content' of what he actually said, or were a 'rational interpretation' of his comments" (Henry 1989, 49). This ruling was subsequently overturned by the U.S. Supreme Court, and in 1993 a jury concluded that five statements were fabricated and that

Masson was libeled in two of them, but it deadlocked on the damages to be awarded. In 1994, another trial was held and the new jury found that two of the quoted statements were fabricated and one was defamatory. "But it ruled that Ms. Malcolm neither knew that the defamatory quotation was false nor acted with a 'reckless disregard as to its truth or falsity,' the standard public figures like Mr. Masson must meet to win libel judgments" (Margolick 1994). This case has generated much discussion within the media about journalistic practice.

A second case illustrating cross-institutional reality monitoring was brought by Gary Ramona, a father who sued the therapists who had treated his daughter. He claimed that she had been a victim of suggestive therapeutic techniques that led her to have false memories of being sexually abused by him. This case was decided in Ramona's favor, presumably partly on the basis of expert witness testimony that confusions between real and imagined events have been shown in laboratory studies and that the techniques used by the therapists could have induced false memories (Butler 1994). The Ramona case is particularly interesting because it raises the question of whether the courts are the best place to decide what is and what is not acceptable therapeutic practice.

If accurate, the reported costs of both of these cases were staggering—"a fortune in legal fees" in the case of the Masson-Malcolm conflict (Margolick 1994) and $1.7 million in legal costs for Mr. Ramona (Butler

1994). It does not seem too far-fetched an idea that less expensive, more efficient, and equally effective or better mechanisms could be devised for adjudicating issues such as whether journalistic or therapeutic practice meets current acceptable standards. A challenging policy problem would be to try to devise fair, high-quality, and less costly procedures for reality-monitoring the institutions and professionals who are themselves engaged in reality monitoring.

A DANGEROUS ANALOGY?

Does suggesting there might be an analogy between individual and social/cultural reality monitoring invite dangerous overextensions? With an individual, sufficient disruption of biological processes that affect mental functioning can result in involuntary commitment. Might we not invite involuntary commitment of media deemed pathological or invite the outlawing of therapists offering unconventional, but potentially effective, help? Might not the treatment—censorship or stifling professionalization—be worse than the disease? Whatever benefits in improved quality of work come about from credentialing, licensing, submitting one's work to the review of an editor, and so forth may come at the cost of introducing a source of systematic bias from whatever agency or group controls the licensing or review process.

Pointing out the critical function played by mechanisms of reality monitoring at the social/cultural level should not necessarily lead to endorsing violations of our First Amendment rights. Self-censorship (that is, conforming to standards) is the kind of self-discipline that we associate with professional activity. Self-control, self-monitoring, inhibiting impulse, taking into account consequences, seeking and evaluating alternatives—these are functions of the frontal lobes. But the frontal lobes do more than edit and constrain; they also enable the creativity we associate with professional activity: generating possibilities, following clues, discovering relations, challenging the given. Reality monitoring does not necessarily bring the monitor's conclusions into conformity with the party line. Reality monitoring, especially when there are different levels (individual, inter-, and intra-institutional) contributing their heuristic and systematic checks to the overall process, can be a way of discovering flaws in status quo beliefs.

As with individual reality monitoring, at the level of within- and between-institution reality monitoring, rules or practices that completely inhibited all speculative accounts, or accounts that do not conform to institutional definitions of reality, would not, in the end, be functional reality monitoring. Lack of spontaneity, inability to self-initiate, and perseveration of a dominant response are signs of frontal pathology just as is a failure to inhibit bizarre and fantastic responses. A culture, like an individual, must balance evaluative and generative functions.

Social/cultural reality monitoring requires that we identify possible evaluative criteria and procedures within any given domain, agree to use them, and devise a means for changing them when appropriate. These criteria presumably include procedures for challenging the status quo, not simply for ensuring conformity. This is not necessarily easy, and it is certainly not error-proof, but the alternative is confusion, perhaps chaos. At the individual level, reality monitoring underlies sanity. At the social/cultural level, both within- and between-institutional reality monitoring promote trust, and, most important, the conditions necessary for the freedom provided by informed choice.

CONCLUSION

While there is still much to learn, we know a considerable amount about the cognitive psychology of individual reality monitoring—the factors and processes that operate in attributing memories, knowledge, and beliefs to sources. Our understanding of individual reality monitoring will continue to deepen as we conceptualize and characterize the architecture of the cognitive system: how various regions of the brain interact in reality monitoring and the relation between particular symptoms and particular lesions in the system (for example, Johnson and Raye 1998). Similarly, our understanding of social/cultural reality monitoring will deepen as we conceptualize and characterize the complex architecture that interrelates various institutions and organizations as they constrain our understanding of truths in various domains (Johnson 1996). As with individual reality monitoring, it may be especially informative to attempt to specify the relation between symptoms and lesions in individual parts of the system.

Our ordinary commonsense notions about memories and beliefs may not appreciate how constructed our lives are and how difficult it is to establish the truth of what happened. But let us not climb out on that constructivist limb and saw it off (cf. Lichtenberg 1996). Facts matter. It matters whether or not sexual abuse took place. It matters whether or not a journalist misrepresents what a source said. It matters whether or not lawyers purposefully mislead juries about the facts and whether juries and judges are equipped to evaluate the information before them. Furthermore, any relaxation of the reality-monitoring processes within an institution potentially reduces its legitimacy (and therefore efficacy) as a cross-institutional reality-monitoring mechanism. As a culture, we depend on these institutional mechanisms as fundamentally as individuals depend on their cognitive reality-monitoring mechanisms. Although it may be difficult to differentiate permissible interpretation and ordinary errors from pathology at either the individual or the cultural level, there are functional differences, and our challenge is to understand them. For a culture, as for individuals, what matters more than the truth of any one particular memory or belief (which may be impossible to determine) is the mechanisms we have in place for reality monitoring.

References

Bartlett, Frederic Charles. 1932. *Remembering: A Study in Experimental and Social Psychology*. New York: Cambridge University Press.

Belsey, Andrew and Ruth F. Chadwick. 1992. Ethics and Politics of the Media: The Quest for Quality. In *Ethical Issues in Journalism and the Media*, ed. Andrew Belsey and Ruth F. Chadwick. New York: Routledge.

Bransford, John D. and Marcia K. Johnson. 1973. Considerations of Some Problems of Comprehension. In *Visual Information Processing*, ed. William Chase. New York: Academic Press.

Bruner, Jerome. 1997. What Is a Narrative Fact? Paper presented at The Future of Fact: An Annenberg Scholars Conference, Annenberg Public Policy Center, University of Pennsylvania, Feb.

Butler, K. 1994. Memory on Trial. *San Francisco Chronicle*, 24 July.

Cappella, Joseph N. and Kathleen Hall Jamieson. 1997. *Spiral of Cynicism: The Press and the Public Good*. New York: Oxford University Press.

Ceci, Stephen J. and Maggie Bruck. 1993. The Suggestibility of the Child Witness: A Historical Review and Synthesis. *Psychological Bulletin* 113:403-39.

Clines, Francis X. 1998. Gossip Guru Stars in 2 Roles at Courthouse. *New York Times*, 12 Mar.

Damasio, Antonio R. 1989. Time-Locked Multiregional Retroactivation: A Systems-Level Proposal for the Neural Substrates of Recall and Recognition. *Cognition* 33:25-62.

Damasio, Antonio R., Neill R. Graff-Radford, Paul J. Eslinger, Hanna Damasio, and Neal Kassel. 1985. Amnesia Following Basal Forebrain Lesions. *Archives of Neurology* 42: 263-71.

Dawes, Robyn M. 1994. *House of Cards: Psychology and Psychotherapy Built on Myth*. New York: Free Press.

Fallows, James M. 1996. *Breaking the News: How the Media Undermine American Democracy*. New York: Pantheon Books.

Frankel, Max. 1997. One Peep vs. Docudrama. *New York Times Magazine*, 16 Mar., 26.

Fry, Don. 1985. *Believing the News*. St. Petersburg, FL: Poynter Institute for Media Studies.

Goode, Erica with Katia Hetter. 1994. The Selling of Reality. *U.S. News & World Report*, 25 July, 49-56.

Henry, William A., III. 1989. The Right to Fake Quotes. *Time*, 21 Aug., 49.

Johnson, Marcia K. 1988. Discriminating the Origin of Information. In *Delusional Beliefs: Interdisciplinary Perspectives*, ed. Thomas F. Oltmanns and Brandan A. Maher. New York: John Wiley.

———. 1991. Reality Monitoring: Evidence from Confabulation in Organic Brain Disease Patients. In *Awareness of Deficit After Brain Injury*, ed. George P. Prigatano and Daniel L. Schacter. New York: Oxford University Press.

———. 1996. Fact, Fantasy and Public Policy. In *Basic and Applied Memory Research: Theory in Context*, ed. Douglas J. Herrmann, Cathy McEvoy, Christopher Hertzog, Paula Hertel, and Marcia K. Johnson. Vol. 1. Mahwah, NJ: Lawrence Erlbaum.

Johnson, Marcia K., Shahin Hashtroudi, and Stephen D. Lindsay. 1993. Source Monitoring. *Psychological Bulletin* 114:3-28.

Johnson, Marcia K., John Kounios, and Scott F. Nolde. 1996. Electrophysiological Brain Activity and Memory Source Monitoring. *NeuroReport* 7:2929-32.

Johnson, Marcia K. and Carol L. Raye. 1981. Reality Monitoring. *Psychological Review* 88:67-85.

———. 1998. False Memories and Confabulation. *Trends in Cognitive Sciences* 2:137-45.

Johnson, Marcia K. and Steven J. Sherman. 1990. Constructing and Reconstructing the Past and the Future in the Present. In *Handbook of Motivation and Cognition: Foundations of Social Behavior*, ed. E. Tory Higgins and Richard M. Sorrentino. Vol. 2. New York: Guilford Press.

Lichtenberg, Judith. 1996. In Defense of Objectivity Revisited. In *Mass Media and Society*, ed. James Curran and Michael Gurevitch. 2d ed. London: Arnold.

Lindsay, D. Stephen and J. Don Read. 1994. Psychotherapy and Memories of Childhood Sexual Abuse: A Cognitive Perspective. *Applied Cognitive Psychology* 8:281-338.

Loftus, Elizabeth F. 1997. Memory for a Past That Never Was. *Current Directions in Psychological Science* 6:60-65.

Loftus, Elizabeth F. and Katherine Ketcham. 1994. *The Myth of Repressed Memory: False Memories and Allegations of Sexual Abuse*. New York: St. Martin's Press.

Margolick, David. 1994. Psychoanalyst Loses Libel Suit Against a New Yorker Reporter. *New York Times*, 3 Nov.

Middleton, David and Derek Edwards. 1990. Conversational Remembering: A Psychological Approach. In *Collective Remembering*, ed. David Middleton and Derek Edwards. Newbury Park, CA: Sage.

Mifflin, Lawrie. 1998. An Old Hand's View of TV News: Not Good. *New York Times*, 22 Mar.

Nelson, Katherine. 1993. The Psychological and Social Origins of Autobiographical Memory. *Psychological Science* 4:7-14.

Nolde, Scott F., Marcia K. Johnson, and Mark D'Esposito. In press. Left Prefrontal Activation During Episodic Remembering: An Event-Related fMRI Study. *NeuroReport*.

Nolde, Scott F., Marcia K. Johnson, and Carol L. Raye. In press. The Role of Prefrontal Cortex During Tests of Episodic Memory. *Trends in Cognitive Sciences*.

Ofshe, Richard and Ethan Watters. 1994. *Making Monsters: False Memories, Psychotherapy, and Sexual Hysteria*. New York: Charles Scribner's Sons.

Pippert, Wesley G. 1989. *An Ethics of News: A Reporter's Search for the Truth*. Washington, DC: Georgetown University Press.

Pope, Kenneth S. 1996. Memory, Abuse, and Science: Questioning Claims About the False Memory Syndrome Epidemic. *American Psychologist* 51:957-74.

Pressley, Michael and Lisa R. Grossman, eds. 1994. Introduction. *Applied Cognitive Psychology* 8:277-80.

Ross, Michael. 1989. Relation of Implicit Theories to the Construction of Personal Histories. *Psychological Review* 96:341-57.

Schank, Roger C. and Robert P. Abelson. 1977. *Scripts, Plans, Goals, and Understanding: An Inquiry into Human Knowledge Structures*. Hillsdale, NJ: Lawrence Erlbaum.

Spanos, Nicholas P. 1994. Multiple Identity Enactments and Multiple Personality Disorder: A Sociocognitive Perspective. *Psychological Bulletin* 116:143-65.

Stuss, Donald T., Michael P. Alexander, Aubrey Lieberman, and Harvey Levine. 1978. An Extraordinary Form of Confabulation. *Neurology* 28:1166-72.

Tharp, Mike and Betsy Streisand. 1994. Tabloid TV's Blood Lust. *U.S. News & World Report*, 25 July, 46-48.

Tulving, Endel. 1983. *Elements of Episodic Memory*. Oxford: Clarendon Press.

Turner, Richard. 1996. When Rumors Make News. *Newsweek*, 30 Dec., 72.

Wilson, Timothy D. and Nancy Brekke. 1994. Mental Contamination and Mental Correction: Unwanted Influences on Judgments and Evaluations. *Psychological Bulletin* 116:117-42.

ANNALS, *AAPSS*, **560**, November 1998

Struggle in Cyberspace:
Fact and Friction on the World Wide Web

By JAMES E. KATZ

ABSTRACT: The Internet and World Wide Web have transformed the way local cultures produce and maintain solidarity regarding what should be accepted as facts. These technologies provide a level playing field—it is no longer the case that those with the most massive resources will have the biggest audience. Indeed, many small sites command huge followings. The Internet and the Web allow for the quick dissemination of information, both false and true; unlike newspapers and other media outlets, there are often no quality control mechanisms on Web sites that would permit users to know what information is generally recognized fact and what is spurious. On the Internet and the Web, facts more easily escape from their creator's or owner's control and, once unleashed, can be bandied about. Groups that wish to control what is perceived as fact will find the Internet a threat. Those groups that hail competition between outlooks will welcome what the Web hath wrought.

Professor James E. Katz studies how the Internet and World Wide Web have been changing the way we live and communicate. Before coming to Rutgers, he was director of social science research at Bellcore. Earlier in his career, he was on the faculties of the University of Texas and Clarkson University and won fellowships to the Massachusetts Institute of Technology and Harvard. Katz is the author of several books, and his writings have been translated into five languages.

P OLLSTERS working for the National Geographic Society and
National Science Foundation find
that many of the so-called facts we
Americans believe are true—be they
about whether the planet Earth revolves around the sun, which two nations signed the Strategic Arms Limitation Talks (SALT) Treaty, or where
in the world the United States is—
are actually incorrect. Even the best
and brightest among us are ignorant
of vast stretches of history, science,
culture, and the arts. Indeed, many
of the facts that we individually know
and recite are simply assertions that
have been passed along to us from
accepted authorities (such as parents
and friends and, occasionally, experts). Only most infrequently will
we be skeptical enough to verify what
is presented to us as fact.

People—with the exception of
postmodernists—do not like being reminded of this limiting condition of
reality. Solipsism, as witnessed
through Plato's eyes, has been galling
thinkers for over two millennia. We
would prefer to go on with our quotidian existence than wrestle with un-
knowns. (Moreover, many cognitive
psychologists from Herbert S. Simon
onward argue that this is just as well
for everyone's sake.)

FACTS ARE CULTURALLY
PRODUCED AND ENFORCED

The cultural production and control of knowledge—or facts, as we call
them here—deserve a closer look, especially from the perspective of how
these processes are being affected by
expanding capabilities of networked
computers. The rapid and cheap
movement of information allowed by
the Internet and related technologies
poses some intriguing challenges
for the more traditional forms of what
we might term the sociology of
knowledge.

Until the spread of radio and television programming a few decades
ago, the production and interpretation of facts had been largely locally
controlled. The significance of the entire process can be summed up by
pointing to the importance governments have placed on the broadcasting of propaganda to the populations
of their opponent powers, and the
major efforts the opponent powers
have invested in interfering with the
broadcasts attest to that importance.
Yet, even in the Old Testament, concern over foreign ideas and the importation of them as a way to erode
or weaken an enemy were discussed
prominently. More recent and perhaps more dramatic is the instance of
the importation from Switzerland
into Russia of Lenin by the Germans
during World War I. Lenin, by the
way, made the trip in a sealed railroad car. The dimension of hermeti-
cally segregating a dangerous ide-
ologue seems inescapable. From still
more recent memory, I note that the
Shah of Iran was undermined in substantial part by audiocassettes of
Ayatollah Khomeini's speeches that
were smuggled into that country.

But what can be easily won may
not be so easily held. This can be as
true of converts to a viewpoint as it is
of territories held through garrisons.
As Niccolò Machiavelli reminds, "The
nature of the people is variable, and
though it is easy to persuade them, it

is difficult to hold them to that persuasion. So it is necessary to take such measures that, when they believe no longer, *they can be made to believe by force*" (1940, 22, revised translation by author, emphasis added). Indeed, considerable force has been used over the centuries to persuade and maintain the belief structures of local societies. Nazi Germany, Pol Pot's Cambodia, and Stalinist Russia are but a few examples.

A BRIEF HISTORY
AS TO THE MATTER OF FACT

Although space precludes an exhaustive recapitulation of the way force has been used to make facts, it is worth pointing out some of the traditional characteristics of facts and their substratum belief structures. Among the salient characteristics are the following:

1. Local control. Those who were dominant in the local area could exercise their power to limit the access and information flows from the outside.

2. Expensive information. Costs, particularly financial costs of access, were substantial. It was difficult even to acquire information about how to look for additional information. As is well known, as the cost of something rises, less of it will be used, and information and competing explanations are no exception to this rule.

3. Geographical limitation. Distance from the source drastically diminishes the availability of information. In the past, it was often nec-

essary to travel to the relevant location to peruse documents, and often the documents could be viewed only with special permission by special people under special circumstances.

4. Historical bias. Competing interpretations of past events were often unavailable, and the more distantly they occurred in the past, the less accessible they were.

5. Manipulation by opinion leaders and elites. History is written by those who live to write it. Plato, writing in *The Republic*, held that truth should be made to serve the state; it is advice that has been heeded even by those who have never read Plato.

6. Codes supplanted. Considerable effort has been devoted to supplanting previous codes and creating and maintaining new official versions. Much of the Balkan peninsula is now caught up in this process, with predictably horrifying consequences.

The growing availability of the Internet is altering all these conditions. The World Wide Web and associated technologies pose a direct threat to those who have used more traditional processes and technologies for controlling the movement and dissemination of information (as well as misinformation). Steps have been taken by Singapore and China (the latter nicknamed "The Building of the Great Firewall of China") to limit the material that can be viewed by denizens of their respective countries. In 1997, a Singaporean man was fined the equivalent of $55,000 for improperly downloading offensive offshore materials. The United States has also attempted to pass legislation limiting what materials can be seen over the Internet. (The U.S. Supreme Court overturned the Communications Decency Act in 1997.)

Among the consequences for the facts of our time, and for those of the future, are that equal time is given to any viewpoint; false information spreads quickly; true information spreads quickly; and facts more easily escape from their creator's or owner's control. Let us briefly survey each of these consequences in turn.

Equal time to any viewpoint

Organizational size does not necessarily translate into a large Internet presence. Indeed, the bookseller amazon.com grew from nothing to a major merchant with a handful of staff in a matter of months. More pertinent for our interests is the way in which political organizations can use the Internet to countervail their opponents. For instance, one can go to the Web site of Britain's ruling party and learn about all the good things they have done for their country and, for that matter, Ireland. With a mere click of a mouse, an interested individual can go to Sinn Fein's Web site and learn about the evils of that ruling party.

More disturbing are the hate groups that are increasingly populating the Web. They range from neo-Nazis to pederast groups, and everything in between. Any kind of lie can be told, and, with the Web authoring tools so readily available, an undocumented lie can be made to look as real as the most carefully documented research finding.

Fast spread of false information

Urban legends, those more than believable stories passed by word of mouth, have found a new speed and impact via the Internet. These, in my personal experience, have included an alleged commencement address at the Massachusetts Institute of Technology by author Kurt Vonnegut, Jr. (nice speech, but not his) (Schmich 1997), which was also reported as a Harvard commencement address,[1] as well as false notices that the Internet would be shut down on 30 June ("to clean out old email messages"). Much more malicious is the continually resurfacing rumor that if one tries to help another motorist drive more safely, one is putting one's life in danger. The specifics of this rumor are that it is a gang initiation rite to drive at night with one's car lights out. When a courteous motorist flashes his or her lights at the aspiring gang member, to alert of the presumed mistake, the would-be gang member follows the motorist home and shoots him or her to death in the driveway. Supposedly this is part of a gang initiation ritual.

Such facts can be troubling to large numbers of people. The *Philadelphia Inquirer* of 27 February 1997 reported, for example, that scores of area workers were frightened when they read in their E-mail of a "well organized, well funded" ring that stole kidneys from unwary business travelers. The scenario, described to

Mobil Oil workers among others, was as follows:

The crime begins when a business traveler goes to a lounge for a drink at the end of the workday. A person in the bar walks up as they sit alone and offers to buy them a drink. The last thing the traveler remembers until they wake up in a hotel room bathtub, their body submerged to their neck in ice, is sipping the drink. There is a note taped to the wall instructing them to not move and to call 911. A phone is on a small table next to the bathtub for them to call. The business traveler calls 911, who have become quite familiar with this crime. The business traveler is instructed by the 911 to very slowly and carefully reach behind them and feel if there is a tube protruding from their lower back. The business traveler finds the tube and answers yes. The 911 operator tells them to remain still, having already sent paramedics to help. The operator knows that both of the business travelers' kidneys have been harvested. . . . This is not a scam or . . . a science fiction novel, it is real. It is documented and confirmable.

Of course, the contact numbers provided are not working numbers. The consequences of false facts such as these can be painful, including massive amounts of wasted effort and loss of peace of mind.

Fast spread of true information

The Internet can also make obscure facts widely known. A popular Web site is "The Smoking Gun" (http://www.thesmokinggun.com), which has posted Federal Bureau of Investigation memos about Lucille Ball and Frank Sinatra, the arrest report sheet of Clinton nemesis Linda Tripp, and George Burns's at- tempt at smuggling goods into the United States. Matt Drudge, in his inside-Washington scoop column, has repeatedly embarrassed the Clinton administration.

Escape from creator's or owner's control

Governments, of course, will seek to control what is going on over the Internet. But at the same time, the Internet can erode the government's ability to control information, foreign policy, and its domestic population. The Internet was used to call into question the probity of the Federal Bureau of Investigation when Pierre Salinger, former presidential press secretary, revealed documents that he had found on the Internet that turned out to be fakes. The Central Intelligence Agency and other agencies have had their Web sites hacked (that is, broken into, or improperly accessed by outsiders attacking from remote computer terminals); in some cases the hackers would change the agency logo or write embarrassing graffiti over the agency emblem. Such damage can range even to stealing and publicizing state secrets. This was done in the wake of India's 1998 atom bomb tests. Beginning in May, hackers breached the Bhabha Atomic Research Center in Bombay, India's most sensitive nuclear weapons research facility. Their sophisticated attack not only profoundly embarrassed India's government but made public secret data from the tests as well (see, for example, http://www.antionline.com/Special Reports/milworm/story3.html). This action also raised apprehension about the security and proliferation of nuclear information, especially those in developing countries.

CONCLUSION

While there is much ballyhoo about how the Internet will improve education and make all our lives better, it is quite apparent that the Internet poses new problems for how we traditionally create, consider, and act on facts. The public policy problems of governments, and for famous people in general, are likely to be enormous. These include loss of control, reintroduction of embarrassing chapters of history, and the investment of more effort in image making and preservation. It can also allow more numerous and cacophonous voices, which in turn could make it harder to reach agreement between fractious groups.

At the same time, more ideas can be circulated, and more viewpoints can be expressed. According to Seymour M. Lipset and colleagues (1956), multiple stakes in multiple venues helps the spread and preservation of democracy. If what is true for a typographer's union is also true for countries (and, indeed, this seems to be the case), then ultimately cyberspace bodes well for the future, both of people and of facts.

Note

1. The spurious speech also was reported as a "Quote of the Day" on Wired news service.

References

Lipset, Seymour M., Martin Trow, and James Colemen. 1956. *Union Democracy: What Makes Democracy Work in Unions and Other Organizations?* Garden City, NY: Doubleday.

Machiavelli, Niccolò. 1940. *The Prince.* Trans. Luigi Ricci. New York: Random House.

Schmich, Mary. 1997. Vonnegut? Schmich? Who Can Tell in Cyberspace? *Chicago Tribune*, 3 Aug.

Book Department

INTERNATIONAL RELATIONS AND POLITICS

DeLEON, PETER. 1997. *Democracy and the Policy Sciences*. Pp. xii, 160. Albany: State University of New York Press. Paperbound, $18.95.

Peter DeLeon's book continues his project of contextualizing the development of policy analysis as a significant feature of the public arena in the late twentieth century. Whereas *Advice and Consent* (1988) mapped how the academic discipline and the everyday practice of policy analysis had developed in not always congruent fashion in recent years, *Democracy and the Policy Sciences* offers a more theoretically sustained attack on policy analysis in the dominant mode.

The development of policy analysis as applied economics is DeLeon's object of critique. Here he follows in the footsteps of others and effectively highlights the rationalistic and objectivistic biases of today's dominant policy analysis paradigm. He goes further, however, than many critics who came before him and offers his readers something distinctive. DeLeon's succinctly written, if sometimes dense, narrative opens the door to a worldview that will be very different for many practitioners of policy analysis. Yet it will be one that actually enables them, if they let it, to start to put the politics back into public policy analysis, right where it belongs. In other words, DeLeon's text does require some effort on the part of its intended audience. Yet, if that audience is willing to stretch a little and grow in the process, the returns to policy analysis and public policymaking can be great. Regardless of what one might think about reading in another idiom or having to digest another vocabulary, this book does something more than make the valid, if shopworn, points about how policy analysis in the dominant mode can often be exclusionary and conservative. It specifies a real alternative—one that is already being practiced.

DeLeon not only critiques the "positivism" of the dominant paradigm but also introduces readers to the world of "postpositivism." DeLeon elaborates how postpositivism's appreciation of the socially constructed and discursively constituted character of policy reality engenders his alternative program of a more politicized "participatory policy analysis." This alternative program appreciates the ineliminably contestable nature of policy reality, the unavoidable role of subjective values in policy analysis, and the impossibility and undesirability of expunging politics from the analysis as well as the making of public policy. Grounded in the theoretical investigations of interpretivists, hermeneuticists, critical theorists, and postmodernists, this participatory policy analysis would be centrally committed to enabling more people, from more diverse points of view, to say more thoughtful things about what public policy ought to be like.

In these bleak times of profoundly conservative public policymaking buttressed by objectivistic policy analyses, reading DeLeon is one way to begin the process of building an appreciation for the need for an alternative approach. Taking his text seriously can help make participatory policy analysis a more common practice. With this text in hand, we might even begin to dare to think that policy analysis might begin to be tolerant of competing perspectives and that public policymaking might become democratically accountable. It would be even better if DeLeon and many other proponents of postpositivistic approaches would forgo extensive arguments on why such approaches are needed and instead spend more time actually implementing them. Nonetheless, DeLeon's book is very convincing in suggesting that for any of these alternatives to become reality, we need to end scientific policy analysis as we have known it and start ushering in its participatory alternative.

SANFORD SCHRAM

Bryn Mawr College
Pennsylvania

DUNN, DELMER D. 1997. *Politics and Administration at the Top: Lessons from Down Under.* Pp. x, 194. Pittsburgh, PA: University of Pittsburgh Press. $45.00. Paperbound, $19.95.

Delmer Dunn's important new book is a shorter, Australian version of Hugh Heclo's classic *Government of Strangers*— really more a government of friends in this case. Interviewing 38 Australian cabinet ministers, ministerial staff members, and career executives in 1992 and 1996, Dunn explores their interrelationships in search of lessons for American political appointees and their career executives. The Australian national government presents an interesting case for comparison because its "Washminster" system combines American-style federalism and bicameralism with British responsible parliamentary government. Dunn's work is particularly interesting because, during the study period, parliamentary elections brought a center-right coalition to power, ending 13 years of Labor rule and giving the national bureaucracy an entirely new set of ministers to follow.

As in other studies of Western national governments, Dunn finds that relations between career executives and political appointees in the Australian higher civil service exhibit exchange and a division of labor. Career executives offer expertise and continuity. Politicians—in this case, cabinet ministers and their staffs—offer political accountability and brokering skills. A mix of political accountability and bureaucratic expertise is achieved with a relatively small number of political appointees engaged in long-term relationships with career officials. Indeed, "the average minister in Australia manages his or her constituency services and runs the department . . . with fewer staff members than the typical U.S. Senator." Notably, there were few pressures to increase the number of political appointees even after the first party change in a decade.

Dunn makes a good case that American political appointees need to establish and communicate their objectives. If career executives do not know what appointees want, they cannot help them get it. Further, both career and political officials must respect neutral competence. Both politicians and those in the academy need to resurrect—but also remake—the politics-administration dichotomy, and Dunn has interesting ideas about how to do so.

Dunn sometimes underestimates the difficulties of applying lessons from a smaller and less conflict-prone polity. In particular, the shadow cabinet system of parliamentary government ensures that Australian political appointees have far better preparation than their American counterparts. Still, *Politics and Administration at the Top* is a provocative and insightful work that should be read by scholars and practitioners.

ROBERT ANTHONY MARANTO

Federal Executive Institute
Charlottesville
Virginia

FRANCK, THOMAS M. 1995. *Fairness in International Law and Institutions.* Pp. xxxvi, 500. New York: Oxford University Press. No price.

Fairness in International Law and Institutions is a critical examination of the fairness toward both states and persons of contemporary international law. In Thomas Franck's view, international law and institutions are today sufficiently mature to make it reasonable to demand that they serve as instruments of fairness. In short, the probationary period is over. Through the lens of fairness, Franck masterfully critiques the international legal topics that are typical grist of a survey course in public international law.

The bulk of this compact 500-page work is divided between a discussion of the fairness of international law and institutions, on one hand, and a discussion of the international law of distributive justice, on the other. In part 1, Franck defines "fairness" as a composite of two independent variables, legitimacy (order)

and distributive justice (change). Fairness discourse becomes the integration of these two, oftentimes competing, variables. Part 2 treats the international law of human rights and self-determination. Part 3 addresses international legal institutions, focusing on the role of the U.N. secretary-general and the Security Council in maintaining peace and security. Included in this discussion is an analysis of the laws of war, the right of self-defense, and collective security measures. Part 3 also critiques the International Court of Justice as an institution of procedural and substantive fairness.

Part 4 turns the discussion to the role of international law and institutions in distributive justice. Here Franck's focus is on international economic law (trade, investment, and preferential treatment of developing countries) and international environmental law.

Part 5 concludes with Franck's thoughts on how to shape a global discourse on fairness so that both states and persons have a voice. His modest proposal is to remake the U.N. General Assembly in the image and likeness of the U.S. Congress. The General Assembly would become a bicameral body. One chamber would represent the countries of the world and would maintain the current U.N. "one state, one vote" principle. The other chamber would represent the people of the world, whose representatives would be elected under a system of universal suffrage, in numbers based on a negotiated allocation of seats corresponding to population size. By giving the people of the world an independent voice, the virtual stranglehold that states have over the development of international law and its institutions as instruments of fairness would be broken.

KEVIN C. KENNEDY

Michigan State University
East Lansing

JOHNSON, JAMES TURNER. 1997. *The Holy War Idea in Western and Islamic Traditions.* Pp. ix, 185. University Park: Pennsylvania State University Press. $45.00. Paperbound, $16.95.

This is an elegant little book. James Turner Johnson is the foremost expert on the history and conceptual underpinnings of the just-war tradition in the West. For the past ten years, along with his colleague John Kelsay, he has expanded his scope by studying the ideology of war in Islam. This is the fourth book comparing the Western and Islamic concepts of war between them, and it succeeds brilliantly in articulating the categories through which ideological justification for war is conceptualized in the West and in Islamic civilization.

Johnson sets out to compare how the two civilizations have historically defined the interrelationship of religion, statecraft, and war. He largely refrains from commenting on the current standoff between Western and Islamic values on these issues but concentrates on the historical and conceptual underpinnings of today's ongoing crisis.

The first chapter traces the different historical trajectories through which the ideologies of warring traveled between the two civilizations. Although holy war ideas made up a number of important strands of the Western fabric, they had to compete with a set of secular principles that came to be referred to as just-war theory, and by the beginning of the modern period, the holy war idea was rejected in the West. Under Islam, however, where for historical reasons religion was understood from earliest times as properly integral to the political order (no rending between Caesar and God), the ethical regulation of warring took place wholly within the framework of religion. The second chapter examines the idea of holy war, both in the West and in Islam,

and ends with a comparison of the concerns of the holy war construct with that of just war.

Chapter 3 concentrates on the question of justification for going to war, and here Johnson compares the Augustinian division between *civitas terrenae* (earthly city) and *civitas dei* (city of God) with the Islamic *dar al-harb* (abode of war) and *dar al-islam* (abode of peace). In a most interesting discussion, he compares the theological thrust of the Christian model (right belief) with the juridical thrust of the Islamic (right behavior) and extrapolates how the different emphases affected the subsequent models through which justification to war developed. Chapter 4 treats the authority required for authorizing holy war under Christendom and Islam, while chapter 5 covers the conduct of war within the holy war paradigms. The final chapter provides a fascinating discussion of the impact of holy war ideas on the practice of statecraft in both civilizations.

This book succeeds in bringing to our attention the important role of religion in the political order, not only under Islam but also in the West and even in our own day. This is an excellent example of how a study of premodern history and ideas sheds important light on attitudes, ideals, and behaviors of the present.

REUVEN FIRESTONE

Hebrew Union College—Jewish
 Institute of Religion
Los Angeles
California

MICHAELS, JUDITH E. 1997. *The President's Call: Executive Leadership from FDR to George Bush.* Pp. x, 348. Pittsburgh, PA: University of Pittsburgh Press. $50.00. Paperbound, $22.95.

Judith E. Michaels's new book, *The President's Call*, is a veritable encyclopedia of information on presidential appointments. It is by far the most comprehensive study to date in this field. It examines a wide variety of topics including presidential strategies for controlling the bureaucracy, the qualities presidents look for in their appointees, how appointees perceive their interactions with presidents and other actors in the political process, and how appointees perceive the civil servants and other individuals with whom they interact at the bureaucratic level.

It is in providing the appointees' view of the bureaucratic process that Michaels makes her greatest contribution. Using data from a study of Senate-confirmed political appointees conducted during the Bush presidency, Michaels demonstrates that many of the truths we commonly teach about the bureaucracy may no longer be valid. For example, she ably demonstrates that most political appointees are satisfied and work well with the career bureaucracy. This was true even during the Reagan and Bush years. She also demonstrates that the bureaucracy during the Bush presidency cannot be described as "a government of strangers," which again runs contrary to common wisdom on the subject. She also makes a very strong case for why political appointees and career civil servants should work together rather than in a conflictual environment. Michaels also identifies the most common sources of tension and stress among appointees, as well as the most rewarding aspects of their job. Michaels even addresses the thorny subject of what constitutes success for any political appointee. Finally, she breaks the analysis down by different types of political appointees (for example, inspector generals, members of independent regulatory commissions, cabinet secretaries, deputy secretaries, assistant sec-

retaries, and so forth). Through this process, we get a nuanced portrait of how political appointees at different levels within the bureaucracy view and interact with the political and bureaucratic processes.

While the work is comprehensive, my only criticism is that it lacks a unifying theme. Certainly, themes develop throughout the course of the book, but it would have been a stronger work if it had been written with a clear theme in mind. Still, this is a masterful work, one that certainly will be compared to the other top works in the political appointment literature.

RICHARD W. WATERMAN

University of New Mexico
Albuquerque

SCARROW, SUSAN E. 1996. *Parties and Their Members: Organizing for Victory in Britain and Germany.* Pp. vii, 277. New York: Oxford University Press. $72.00.

Susan Scarrow has given us much to think about in *Parties and Their Members*. Her book explores the fate of mass-membership parties in Germany and Great Britain to ascertain if party members have in fact become less relevant to European political parties at the end of the twentieth century. Scarrow gives a comprehensive overview of political party theory regarding membership parties and finds a general consensus that contemporary political parties have moved beyond wanting to increase party membership because they rely so much on mass-based technology to contact potential voters that they no longer need the efforts of formally enrolled party members (who, in contrast to ordinary party supporters, pay dues and forswear allegiance to other parties) to engage in mobilization for them. Scarrow wants to see if, in fact, party leaders in the major parties in Britain and Germany have given up on members; she pursues this question by looking at the inclusiveness of the parties' membership policies, the centralization of their decision-making processes, and the mediation channels between leaders and members.

In an extensive consideration of the fund-raising, communications, electoral mobilization, and inter-election activities of the German Christian Democratic Union and Social Democratic Party and the British Labour and Conservative parties, Scarrow finds that none of the four parties has abandoned the membership party model. In fact, all four parties have found new ways for their members to help them retool their electoral strategies in a changed campaign environment. Just at the moment when some believe that mass communications have made party members obsolete, Scarrow shows that other party concerns, such as their own legitimacy and the problem of alienating informed voters through mass communications appeals, make membership more valuable than ever. Revisiting her three dimensions of party outreach to members, Scarrow concludes that all parties under consideration have adopted their membership strategies to be more inclusive (to increase party membership), less centralized (to promote local participation), and less mediated (to allow greater control of the leadership by the membership) than in previous eras (with the exception of the British Conservative Party, which has had these characteristics for a longer period of time). This indicates that members have assumed different positions of importance in contemporary European parties.

Scarrow's book is exceptionally well written and clearly presents her arguments and cases, which reflect exhaustive research on the topic. Scholars of political parties everywhere will benefit from the suggestion that we think of how parties use their core supporters within the demands of mass technology elections, not despite them.

ROBIN KOLODNY

Temple University
Philadelphia
Pennsylvania

STAUDT, KATHLEEN A. and WILLIAM A. WEAVER. 1997. *Political Science and Feminisms: Integration or Transformation?* Pp. xv, 193. New York: Twayne. $28.95.

Women's studies has sought to integrate women into all disciplines by using existing paradigms and to transform the methods and basic questions addressed, as needed. Political science is viewed here as a particularly "masculine" discipline whose focus has been on those (mostly men) who govern.

Political scientists Staudt and Weaver present an intellectual history of the discipline and the development of women's studies within each of the six traditional subfields: political theory, comparative politics, international relations, American politics, public law, and public administration. They provide a well-grounded review of the contributions of these feminist scholars, who have often challenged the current norms of neutrality, rationality, objectivity, and individualism. Yet the study is empirical in that the authors draw upon a random survey of department chairpersons and extensive analyses of conference programs, leading textbooks, top journals, and exemplary course syllabi for inclusion of women and research on women.

Although Staudt and Weaver conclude that gender research is often ignored by all except those who do such work, they argue that some subfields have been more receptive. Scholars of American politics, public administration, and political theory have integrated women into studies of voting behavior, personnel management, and justice and equity. Comparative politics and public law, being more global and interdisciplinary, have been more transformative. A feminist international relations, the last to emerge, has faced the greatest challenge in a subfield focused on nation-states and wars and unwilling to concede the centrality of gender-related variables such as population growth and literacy.

The audience for this book will be primarily political scientists, for whom this will be a supplement to books on "the state of the discipline" published by the American Political Science Association. Women's studies scholars should ponder some provocative ideas found here. For example, if women's studies is ignored by others in the discipline, perhaps the titles of such studies should not signal gender content. Further, to include sex as just another variable in statistical analyses is to put women's studies at risk; if women are not different from men, then sex and gender can be ignored. The book also is accessible to those interested in current controversies in higher education. In particular, those who studied political science between 1960 and 1980 will find that the classic works of that period are now widely criticized (but specialists in U.S. politics are still resented as ethnocentric dominators of the discipline).

JANET K. BOLES

Marquette University
Milwaukee
Wisconsin

SUSSMAN, GERALD. 1997. *Communication, Technology, and Politics in the Information Age.* Pp. xiii, 317. Thousand Oaks, CA: Sage. $56.00. Paperbound, $27.95.

Struggling mightily to find hope for a brighter world in the age of the information highway, Gerald Sussman looks to the voice of the people to overcome the power of corporate capitalists and lead us to the bright uplands of a socially conscious world.

In his eloquent listing of the problems, Sussman joins a long line of critics, made up mostly of disappointed scholars, journalists, and former champions of technology, champions who saw technology as the savior to emancipate human beings from the power of the transnational capitalists he sees as controlling humankind politically, economically, socially, and linguistically. What is needed, however, is more than the few "cracks" he sees in the "empire of power" erected by corporations, the government, the military, and the media. So far, he sees only a few "blips," in the form of new communication and information tools: an alternative press, public access cable television, and the Internet. It would have been nice if Sussman had told us how the commonwealth of ordinary people active in alternative media might acquire the economic tools they need to wrest power from "the hegemony of political economic power" that he speaks of.

But let us not quibble. Sussman has written a fine book, much of it offering sound historical background, much of it citing the numbing statistics that illustrate the might of the corporate world, the government (including its military and police), and the mass media conglomerates.

At the heart of Sussman's book is a strong effort to smash the image of technology, which he sees as a new kind of state religion in the United States. He points out the many labor-saving benefits of the fruit of technology but argues that technology threatens something more serious: a totalitarian society. Along the way, he speaks out against surveillance technology that threatens turning the country into a police state. He speaks of "vast wastelands" that include not only television, public as well as private, but also newspapers, magazines, and movies, all the wastelands boosted by the deregulation of corporations.

So much criticism has already been directed at the power of the men at the peak of the corporate culture, especially the global media, that one is led to wonder whether a new contribution is necessary. Yet, if knowledge and awareness can help, Sussman's book provides some small hope in his analysis of the power of language.

As food for contemplation, the book points to how language is used by the hegemony he identifies at the top of the heap. By giving the word "technology" all the attributes of a human being, we remove it from political reality. Real thought and serious analysis are frustrated when inanimate instruments such as technology, computers, and robots are anthropomorphized.

When useful new machines are created, Sussman notes, we tend to credit technology; when the results are bad, we still blame technology. Notice, Sussman says, that human beings are thus removed from the equation. It is as if political choices are gone. What we need, Sussman asserts, are those very political choices. Going a bit further, he writes, "The grammar of technological determinism hides the human agents precisely to disguise the political economic and repressive aspects and identities of empowered institutions and interests acting through their technocratic instruments."

This distorted use of language, in Sussman's analysis, is perhaps the chief weapon in the propaganda arsenal of those who wield hegemonic power to maintain their power base. Can the Internet and its buddies overmaster this?

J. HERBERT ALTSCHULL

Johns Hopkins University
Baltimore
Maryland

AFRICA, ASIA, AND
LATIN AMERICA

VATIKIOTIS, MICHAEL R. J. 1997. *Political Change in Southeast Asia: Trimming the Banyan Tree*. Pp. xiv, 230. New York: Routledge. $69.95. Paperbound, $19.95.

Michael Vatikiotis is Bangkok bureau chief of the *Far Eastern Economic Review*. In that capacity, he has written countless articles as well as books including *Indonesian Politics Under Suharto* (1993). He is well situated to analyze the kinds of change, political and economic, that Southeast Asia is undergoing. He is concerned especially about whether Western-style democracy will replace the contemporary authoritarianism that is justified in Southeast Asia in the name of social order and economic development. The subtitle of the present book, *Trimming the Banyan Tree*, is a metaphor for this political change. Nothing is able to grow under the sacred banyan tree unless major trimming takes place: loosening of collective bonds and opening space for rising aspirations of the new middle classes.

Timing is everything. Unfortunately, *Political Change in Southeast Asia* arrived at precisely the time when the Southeast Asian economic miracle had become the Southeast Asian economic mirage. Vatikiotis, who had written that

Southeast Asia would enter the new century with wealth and confidence, did not foresee the debacle faced by Thailand, in particular, as well as, less drastically, by Malaysia, Indonesia, and the Philippines. In his defense, no scholars or journalists predicted the enormity of the crisis faced by Southeast Asia as a result of currency devaluation, the precipitous fall of the stock market, high inflation, rising unemployment, falling exports, and pervasive malaise. Southeast Asia ignored the danger signs: an inflexible exchange rate with the American dollar; the rising values of the dollar vis-à-vis the Japanese yen; competition for exports from Vietnam and other nations with cheap labor; and empty condominiums, office buildings, and hotels. All of the "Asian values"—such as discipline, hierarchy, face, and community—came to naught in the crisis situation. Instead, corruption, incompetence, and cronyism prevailed, unlimited by effective state institutions accountable to the people. The incompetent administrations of Chavalit Yongchaiyut and his predecessor Banharn Silipa-Archa in Thailand are the quintessential examples of what went wrong.

Despite the fact that a major part of his book is already out of date, there is much to be gained by reading it. Sometimes the reading is rough because Vatikiotis crams so much material in each chapter. For example, the prologue includes discussion of westernization in Thailand, the rise of the middle class, civil war in Cambodia, political development Southeast-Asian-style, theories of economic growth, strong government, bureaucratic authoritarianism, military rule, problems of leadership succession, the rise of nongovernmental organizations, and urbanization. The prologue then continues with summaries of the contemporary political situations in all 10 of the Southeast Asian nations, an

analysis of "continuity and change," and ethnicity. Each of the chapters continues in the same vein—too much disparate material that is difficult to assimilate. But the effort is worthwhile because Vatikiotis presents a fascinating summary of changes in a vibrant area of the world: how Southeast Asian countries have preserved, recovered, and adapted traditional models of political power in the face of extraordinary pressure from the West. He concludes that the region offers an example worth emulating.

CLARK D. NEHER

Northern Illinois University
DeKalb

UNITED STATES

ANDERSEN, KRISTI. 1996. *After Suffrage: Women in Partisan and Electoral Politics Before the New Deal.* Pp. viii, 191. Chicago: University of Chicago Press. $38.00. Paperbound, $13.95.

Ever since American women won the vote in 1920, one question has dominated discussions of the aftermath: what difference did it make? In answering, most commentators look at a narrow range of variables, such as how many women voted, how they voted in relation to men, and whether the women's vote led to concrete political results. They usually conclude that woman suffrage was a relatively minor event. After all, only a few women voted, and most of these voted with their husbands; moreover, the general course of American politics after 1920 did not change.

In *After Suffrage*, Kristi Andersen, a political scientist at Syracuse University, shifts the direction of this discussion. First, she critiques the conclusions reached by previous scholars, showing how they either misinterpreted or used insufficient data. Then she provides examples of how women's votes became a factor in public policy. Most important, she reframes the discussion by arguing that scholars should look at a broader issue: how woman suffrage affected the conception and practice of women's citizenship. Once this question is asked, she argues, scholars will see how suffrage led to more significant changes in American political life than previously acknowledged.

Locating her query in the postsuffrage decade, to her mind the "critical period in the transformation of the relationship between gender and citizenship," Andersen points to how suffrage not only doubled the electorate but also allowed women to "renegotiate the boundaries" of sex-typed political roles. Eventually, women's functioning in these roles not only became "an accepted part of American politics" but also forced political parties to change their rules. In the process, women also changed their own and American political culture. Excluded from political power for so long, women had achieved political ends before suffrage but primarily through pressure group politics. After suffrage, they brought this form of political agitation into the foreground of American political life, thereby contributing further to a decline of party influence begun at the end of the previous century and changing women's own expectations of themselves as agents of political change. These were far from negligible results for an institutional change dismissed by others as insignificant.

Written clearly and concisely, this book is accessible to students, although its brevity means that Andersen had to leave some aspects of the larger political context insufficiently explained and developed. As a synthesis of the scholarship on a number of important and provocative issues, however, it should be both informative and stimulating to all students of U.S. political history.

ELISABETH ISRAELS PERRY
Vanderbilt University
Nashville
Tennessee

CEASER, JAMES W. 1997. *Reconstructing America: The Symbol of America in Modern Thought*. Pp. x, 292. New Haven, CT: Yale University Press. $30.00.

At a time when the United States has become the only superpower of the world and beneficiary of a constellation of favorable economic circumstances, it is instructive to be reminded that there remains a centuries-old tradition of hostility to this country and what it stands for. This hostility transformed America, in the eyes of many intellectuals, into a symbol of everything that is wrong with the contemporary world. Many of these intellectuals have been distinguished and influential: "the terms employed to describe America . . . draw on the ideas of some of the world's most acclaimed thinkers, and the elevation of Disney to an object of high philosophical inquiry ranges from the work of the Frankfurt School's Theodor Adorno . . . to that of Jean Baudrillard" (8-9). At a time when we are regularly cautioned to respect different cultures,

of no other country today could one say things routinely charged against America without being accused of something far worse than cultural insensitivity. Can one imagine, for example, a famous intellectual calling the people of Zimbabwe "obese" or those of Ecuador "idiotic" or those of Cambodia "uncultured"? (248)

It is especially tempting in the post-Communist era to ignore and forget these beliefs and attitudes. The book here reviewed not only examines their distant and largely forgotten roots; it also links them to the current forms of hostility to the West and modernity, more familiar in the context of multiculturalism. Most important, anti-Americanism (a term Ceaser avoids although it is the essence of "the symbol of America in modern thought") is closely linked to the rejection of the French Enlightenment, Western rationality, and modernity.

This is a complex, demanding, but ultimately highly rewarding book. The inquiry spans two centuries, and, correspondingly, much of the discussion is historical, consisting of the close scrutiny of the writings of various authors, not all of them likely to be familiar to contemporary readers. Given the intellectual-historical character of this study, the title is not too helpful; without the subtitle, it would leave the reader at a loss, without a clue to the topic. "Reconstructing America" by itself could refer to all sorts of political or sociological projects and ideas, from mass transportation to low-cost housing and the revitalization of the nuclear family. Moreover, there is not that much in the book that actually addresses "reconstruction," that is, arguments on behalf of the "real America" and contrasting it with its symbolic misrepresentations. The book is basically an explication and critique of long-standing misperceptions and denigrations of America, stretching from the eighteenth century to the present and uniting critics abroad with those at home.

Criticism abroad, the book suggests, established the negative conceptions of America and influenced domestic critiques. Since the 1960s—it seems to me—the roles have been reversed, however: critics abroad seem to take their cues from indigenous American social critics, finding ample ammunition in their pronouncements as well as in American mass culture, the latter certainly being a tempting target. The domestic critics and critiques play a modest part in the book; references to them are scattered and few. While Ceaser has undertaken a historical study, it would have been of great interest to learn about the contribution American intellectuals have made to the prevailing symbolic image of America, or about the relationship between the foreign and domestic sources of this image. Ceaser may rightly respond that that would have been a different book.

The tone of the volume is clearly and (for me) admirably set by the first paragraph of the book, which is well worth citing:

If it were acceptable in a work of modern scholarship to rise with indignation in the defense of one's own country, I would begin this book with a simple call to arms: it is time to take America back from the literary critics, philosophers and self-styled postmodern thinkers who have made the very name "America" a symbol for that which is grotesque, obscene, monstrous, stultifying, stunted, leveling, deadening, deracinating, deforming, rootless, uncultured, and—always in quotation marks—"free" . . . .

But given the strictures that bind us inside the academy such a declaration of patriotism or profession of support for one's own is out of the question—unless, of course, it is made on behalf of a group that proclaims itself to be marginalized, victimized or oppressed.

Throughout the volume, Ceaser seeks to show both what America has come to symbolize in modern thought (the components of the aversion and hostility) and the spiritual ancestry of and inspiration for present-day hostility to America. In doing so, he provides a wealth of information that is likely to be unfamiliar even to many well-educated readers. The more distant roots of anti-Americanism have been unknown and implausible partly because of the historical record, so clearly at odds with them, in particular the fact that since its earliest days vast numbers of people have avidly sought to enter this much-maligned country, as they do to this very day. The well-articulated and strongly felt anti-Americanism has been the attribute of intellectuals and aspiring intellectuals, at home as well as abroad, and not of ordinary people.

This volume focuses on these symbolic misrepresentations among French and German intellectuals. It shows with great clarity that the themes of hostility have remained remarkably stable over the centuries. But there is also much historical novelty here. How many even among educated Americans would know, for example, about the so-called degeneracy thesis of two centuries ago, which held not so much that American society was degenerate but that the flora and fauna were: "this thesis which dominated advanced scientific thinking in Europe during the second half of the 18th century . . . held that animals in America were inferior in variety, strength and beauty to those found in Europe." This inferiority also applied to humans: "the American Indian was a lesser being than the European or for that matter the Asian or African." The degeneracy theory "contended that everything that was transported from the Old World to the New—from plants to animals, and again to humans—became stunted" (19).

Such ideas were upheld by, among others, Georges Louis Leclerc and Cornelius de Pauw, hardly household names for the American reader. Their writings are examined at some length. But although the biological origins and aspects of the idea of degeneracy have long been discarded,

its basic conclusion has been widely embraced. In . . . philosophy, history and literary criticism the word "America" has become a symbol of disfigurement, disease and distortion. . . . [Whereas] the 18th century scientists went only so far as to charge the American mind with mediocrity and unoriginality . . . intellectuals in the 20th century identified America as "a crime against humankind" and as the "site of catastrophe." (43)

(It may be recalled that the native critics of America in the 1960s and 1970s liked to spell the name of the country "Amerika," thereby suggesting its links with things German and Nazi German.) Ceaser also discusses the critical responses to the degeneracy thesis put forward by Benjamin Franklin, Thomas Jefferson, Alexander Hamilton, and George Washington.

The ideas of Arthur de Gobineau (1816-82), the French philosopher-historian who pioneered racialist thinking about America, are among those examined at length since it was he (and other thinkers at the time) who regarded America as "the place where the meaning of race in human history was being played out" (106). Ceaser shows elements of a peculiar continuity between Gobineau's preoccupation with race as a determinant of culture and polity and more recent thinking about these matters:

racialist thinking has reemerged at the vanguard of modern intellectual discourse under the aegis of . . . multiculturalism, . . . [which] has made racial categories the common currency of contemporary thought. While this school claims in one breath that the source of difference in society is cultural, in the next it closely links these societies to biological and especially racial groups. (107)

The reader also learns about the dispute between Gobineau and Tocqueville. The latter, not surprisingly, was critical of Gobineau's conviction that race was the prime determinant of social and political institutions.

Critics of America often contrasted unfavorably the American Revolution with the French, perceiving the former as more prosaic and limited in its objectives: "The American Revolution made its peace . . . with the lower side of human nature . . settling for man as he was" whereas "the French Revolution relied on and kept alive the notion of a 'higher possibility' . . ." (77)—that is to say, it had a utopian component many intellectuals found appealing.

Among French authors, the ideas of Jean Baudrillard, a contemporary French writer, postmodernist, and prominent figure in France, are given particular attention. While less vitriolic than some other critics, he, too, sees Americans as "savages" and "primitives" (232), as people "devoid of any aesthetic sense," "lacking entirely in identity" (236), with no sense of history, as rootless, tasteless suburbanites living in "a mass society where quantity is what counts." Worse than that, they inhabit "the land of the living dead" (235).

Among the less familiar German critics of America, we are introduced to Nikolaus Lenau, a romantic poet who visited this country in 1832-33. He saw Americans as rootless and America as "a country in which the bond among people is based on rational calculation of personal interest and not on some more fundamental, natural (in the sense of organic and preexisting) connection" (170). The famous poet Heinrich Heine, who never visited, was even more severe in his judgments, voicing sentiments all too familiar today regarding America as a "gigantic prison of freedom" and a country where "the most extensive of all tyrannies, that of the masses, exercises its crude authority" (171). German critics of the United States also included Nietzsche, for whom it represented "the coming future in its most disfigured form" (171-73), and the lesser-known but influential Arthur Moeller van den Bruck (1876-1925). Likewise, Rainer Maria Rilke, the famous German poet (1875-1926), was impressed by the standardization, homogeneity, and spiritual emptiness in American culture.

Such observations bring us to the contemporary critiques of America as a threat to high culture and cultural traditions. These were expressed by Oswald Spengler, Ernst Jünger, and especially Martin Heidegger. Spengler, it turns out,

was a forerunner of the more recent believers in a moral equivalence between the United States and the Soviet Union, emphasizing the shared materialism of both and concluding that "both regimes are mass societies that effectively operate as tyrannies" (179). Even Max Weber found the unappealing aspects of modernity (the "iron cage" image) culminating in America. As he saw it, this was a social system "where the pursuit of wealth, stripped of its religious and ethical meaning, tends to become associated with purely mundane passions" (185).

It was Heidegger, Ceaser argues, who did the most to associate America with the most repugnant aspects of modernity and who fashioned it "as a symbol that has ever since connected the themes of desolation, horror and homelessness to America . . . the symbol of the crisis of our age . . . [and] the supreme impediment to spiritual reawakening" (187). For him, as for many of his fellow intellectuals at the time and up to the present, "Americanism came to represent modernism in its most advanced, and usually most grotesque form" (186), the global center and source of inauthenticity. Like Spengler, he was a proponent of the moral equivalence thesis. Heidegger's beliefs created a momentous legacy, Ceaser believes; "filtered through the writings of intellectuals, [he] has exercised a profound influence on the actual world" (211). These ideas show up (vulgarized or not) in countless college courses, books, articles, television commentaries, and sermons in this country today.

Another theme in the book concerns the part played by political science in the definition and images of America. Ceaser argues that the negative images of America are largely products of literary studies and sensibilities and that they rest, to a great degree, on the denial of the importance and autonomy of political phenomena. This helps to explain the popularity and influence of the moral equivalence thesis (which overlooked and denied key political differences between the United States and the Soviet Union and which endured from the 1960s until the collapse of the Soviet Union):

the sad truth is that many of the best minds of our time have obscured the importance of the political question, skipping quickly over the differences among regimes and affixing blame for the horrors of our era on the West, or America, or Enlightenment civilization. . . . Such are the irresponsible distortions that follow from the failure to include political phenomena as a distinct part of reality. (161)

At a time when the aversion of many academic intellectuals to Western ideas of rationality has reached new heights (even to include rejections of science) especially in the context of postmodernism and multiculturalism, the nagging question remains, What precisely do some intellectuals find so troubling and repellent in modernity, rationality, and the ideals of the French Enlightenment? It seems to me that the attack on modernity (as symbolized by the United States) stems from two major and related impulses. One is the apprehension toward modernity incarnated in urban-industrial mass society: leveling, homogenizing, impersonal, bureaucratic, anti-individualistic, routinized, and hostile to spontaneity, nature, and whatever is natural. The second is the aversion to modernity perceived as the destroyer of meaning: prosaic, commercial, deadening, and bereft of spiritual values and gratifications. It is revealing of the incoherence of many of these critiques that they lament at once both the homogenizing, anti-individualistic aspects of modernity and its subversion of genuine community, not recognizing that there is an inherent tension—indeed, conflict—between the value placed on the individual and the veneration of community.

By implication, this excellent book helps the reader to understand that the negativity inspired by America as symbol of modernity and Western rationality reflects an unwillingness to accept and come to terms with a world from which (in the words of Weber) the gods have retreated and in which harmony between incompatible desires and values is unattainable no matter how angry and resentful this may make those who pursue such harmonies and unities.

PAUL HOLLANDER

University of Massachusetts
Amherst

GIMPEL, JAMES. 1996. *National Elections and the Autonomy of American State Party Systems*. Pp. xi, 241. Pittsburgh, PA: University of Pittsburgh Press. $45.00. Paperbound, $19.95.

In 1956, the eminent political scientist V. O. Key published *American State Politics*, a volume that sought to explain the contrasting characteristics of political party systems as they operate in the various American states. Now, 40 years later, political scientist James Gimpel has published a volume that follows in Key's tradition. As was the case for Key, the major stimulus for Gimpel's undertaking was a fascination with the politics of one particular region of the United States. For Key, that region was the South; for Gimpel, that region is the West, a region in which he was raised. He defines it as the 11 contiguous states west of the Dakotas.

Despite the title of the book, Gimpel's major focus is on these western states. While two chapters are devoted to state party systems in the East and Midwest (New York and New Jersey; Ohio and Pennsylvania), four chapters are devoted to the "Desert Southwest" (New Mexico and Arizona), the Pacific Northwest (Washington and Oregon), California, and Idaho. Thus the volume might well carry the subtitle *Western Politics*, paralleling Key's earlier regional study, *Southern Politics* (1949).

The justification for Gimpel's more general title becomes apparent in the introductory two chapters, where he compares the party systems of the western states with those of the eastern and midwestern states. Key had advanced the generalization that the politics of the American states are invariably molded by national politics. That is, state party systems are not autonomous; voters form loyalties to the Democratic or Republican Party because of the issues over which presidential elections are fought, and those same two party labels, as well as the coalitions of interests that they represent, continue to prevail when voters have to choose between Republican and Democratic candidates running for state-level offices.

Gimpel's purpose is to demonstrate that while this generalization has been true for the eastern and midwestern states, it has not been true for the West. Whatever their party loyalties may be in presidential elections, when it comes to voting at the state level, western voters have been influenced more by the appeal of individual candidates or state-related issues. What's more, Gimpel argues, eastern and midwestern voters in recent years have begun to show the same behavior. To support his overall thesis, Gimpel presents tables showing the percentage of the respective parties' votes for the offices of president, governor, senator, and congressman, focusing on the extent to which the pattern of partisan votes cast for state-level offices parallels the pattern recorded for the office of president. Despite the problems associated with interpreting such data, most of which Gimpel acknowledges, readers will be rewarded by a provocative, well-argued thesis.

HOWARD A. SCARROW

State University of New York
Stony Brook

PEMBERTON, WILLIAM. 1997. *Exit with Honor: The Life and Presidency of Ronald Reagan.* Pp. xv, 312. Armonk, NY: M. E. Sharpe. $29.95.

William Pemberton has digested scores and perhaps hundreds of books about Ronald Reagan to create, in this engagingly written volume, a useful overview of the origins and career of the fortieth president. Even veteran Reagan watchers will find nuggets here about Reagan's early life, Nancy Reagan's often pivotal role in his presidency, and the simplicity—some might say, the vacuity—of Ronald Reagan's worldview. Pemberton's book is likely to be adopted as an undergraduate-level or graduate-level primer on Reagan for courses in modern history, the American presidency, and related topics.

The book is less hagiographic than its title might suggest. It reports some of the more disturbing aspects of Reagan's presidency, including the president's readily observable mental decay, which set in at least as early as his 1984 campaign. Similarly, despite the recent wave of idealized accounts of Reagan's role in the dissolution of the USSR, Pemberton concludes that upheaval should instead be traced primarily to an economic and ideological crisis within the Soviet Union, for which Reagan's administration cannot in truth claim responsibility.

Despite its strengths, the book has several important conceptual gaps. The first is the lack of attention given to George Bush in discussing the infighting and clandestine operations spawned in part by Reagan's declining mental abilities. Much of the Iran-contra affair and the later debacle in U.S. relations with Iraq should be traced to the vice president, the documentary record shows.

Second and more fundamentally, Pemberton consistently evaluates the administration's legacy from the standpoint of those at the center of contemporary power, rather than through the eyes of people on the periphery. For millions of people who lost ground during the Reagan years, his administration is likely to be seen as considerably more brutal and less honorable than Pemberton's depiction of it.

The book nevertheless retains much of the sunny optimism of Reagan himself. When the president left office in 1989, Americans were economically better off and living in a safer world than when he assumed power, Pemberton writes. Reagan's message had reaffirmed for many that "America was God's chosen nation" and that nostalgic but socially sanctioned beliefs about culture, sexuality, and international power actually were true. As veteran presidential adviser Paul Nitze commented with unintended irony, Reagan should be viewed as a "very superior president on the main issue," namely, "eloquently defending the value system of the United States."

CHRISTOPHER SIMPSON

American University
Washington, D.C.

POLLACK, SHELDON D. 1996. *The Failure of U.S. Tax Policy: Revenue and Politics*. Pp. xi, 321. University Park: Pennsylvania State University Press. $29.95.

Professor and tax attorney Sheldon D. Pollack is hardly alone in his criticism of the U.S. tax system. Congressional hearings in the summer of 1997 exposed bureaucratic ineptness, agent amorality, and harassment of taxpayers and led to a major restructuring of the Internal Revenue Service. The Republicans are poised to make taxation a major issue in the 1998 elections, even voting in November 1997 for a study (funded with $30 million in taxpayers' money) to find out if people think their tax system is fair.

Unlike the congressional hearings, Pollack's focus is on the tax code as a whole and the major players who influence it: tax lawyers, lobbyists, presidential contenders, members of congressional revenue committees, and (increasingly) the media. He identifies three main "failures" of the tax code: its monumental complexity, its instability, and the partisan political purposes for which it has been used, which all too often have little to do with raising revenue. He also notes the empty symbolism underlying much of the rhetoric of tax reform: "the political interests of policymakers may very well be served best by acting in Congress to increase the complexity of the tax laws and at the very same time campaigning for reform and simplification before their constituents." His critique of the reigning academic paradigm of incrementalism is apt, since it has been blamed for both too much and too little change in an evolving tax system where significant innovation has occurred. These points are amply illustrated by Pollack's detailed account of the 1986 tax reform. He is critical of the "highly partisan, ideologically motivated tax policies" that intruded into the congressional process during the 1980s. Pollack's model of tax innovation stresses the importance of military crisis, but, as he notes, this descriptive model is of little help in predicting future changes.

Whose interests are served by the rhetoric of tax simplification? Pollack, in a postscript on Steve Forbes's flat-tax proposals, roundly criticizes them as both simple and wrong-headed. Pollack wisely points out that any major shift in tax policy would impose significant "transition costs": businesses would have to adopt new accounting methods; the Treasury would have to review the entire body of tax law to close off new loopholes; states whose tax systems were linked to the Internal Revenue Code would have to make major revisions. Social institutions ranging from home mortgages to symphony orchestras and universities would have to consider new methods of financing. But tax attorneys should do well trying to make sense of a new system for their clients.

SUSAN HANSEN

University of Pittsburgh
Pennsylvania

SHERRY, MICHAEL S. 1995. *In the Shadow of War: The United States Since the 1930s.* Pp. xii, 595. New Haven, CT: Yale University Press. $40.00. Paperbound, $18.00.

Michael Sherry is best known for his masterful book, *The Rise of American Air Power: The Creation of Armageddon* (1987), a history and critique of strategic bombing through the end of World War II. Anyone who picks up *In the Shadow of War* expecting a work of that quality, however, will be disappointed. Sherry's thesis is that, in the 1940s, America became militarized and remained so throughout the Cold War. This is hardly a novel proposition. It was a central theme of the Eisenhower presidency and, although not a very popular idea at first, gained wider acceptance in the 1960s and has been the subject of many books.

Despite his gifts as a historian, Sherry contributes little that is new to this literature. One may admire his thoroughness and share his indignation, while failing to see what Sherry has learned that inspired him to write more than 500 pages of text. There are some good things in Sherry's book. Given his knowledge of World War II, he is at his best when discussing the "military Keynsianism" of the period and the growing intimacy between arms and commerce. In addition, he shows President Roosevelt to have been a more sophisticated analyst of national security requirements than is generally recognized.

Sherry is at his weakest in dealing with Eisenhower, the one president who said out loud and repeatedly that America was in danger of becoming a garrison state, and who did something about it. On the one hand, Sherry knows this and gives Ike some credit for holding the line on defense spending. On the other, Ike failed to demilitarize the nation, and therefore his limited successes "made possible a further accommodation to militarization, if only by lessening its burdens a bit." To Sherry, when Presidents Truman and Kennedy increased defense spending, they promoted militarization, but when Eisenhower reduced it, he also boosted militarization. This is bad history and poor logic.

Sherry ends on a dubious note, proclaiming the end of militarization at a time when defense spending remains astonishingly high for a country with no serious enemies. In addition, he credits the excesses of militarization with making people more cynical about government, even though defense seems to be one of the few government institutions that Americans still respect. In this otherwise critical book, optimism finally wins out over common sense.

WILLIAM L. O'NEILL

Rutgers University
Highland Park
New Jersey

SHESOL, JEFF. 1997. *Mutual Contempt: Lyndon Johnson, Robert Kennedy, and the Feud That Defined a Decade.* Pp. xl, 591. New York: W. W. Norton. $32.50.

This aptly titled book is the first study devoted exclusively to the Lyndon Johnson–Robert Kennedy feud, which culminated in Kennedy's challenge of the Johnson presidency in 1968. It easily supersedes works that deal with the conflict in a broader context. Concentrating on the 1959-68 period, it contends that Johnson and Kennedy had come to hate one another as a result of differences relating to personality, issues, and politics. Each brought out the worst in the other partly because of their stark differences, despite some remarkably similar traits. The much older Johnson had risen from the poverty-ridden hill country of central Texas as a wheeler-dealer politician, who learned to massage differences in Congress to achieve legislative successes. The Harvard-educated Kennedy came from wealth, was the brother of a martyred president, disliked politicians, and saw things in terms of black and white. Yet both imagined themselves as underdogs; both were thin-skinned, volatile, and overly ambitious.

Shesol's study reveals how extensive their clashes were, beginning with Kennedy's 1959 visit to the LBJ ranch, where his futile attempt at deer hunting caused Johnson to comment, "Son, you've got to learn to handle a gun like a man." It includes differences relating to the vice presidential nomination in 1960, Johnson's role in the Kennedy administration, the accession of Johnson to the presidency in 1963, the rejection of Robert Kennedy for the vice presidency in 1964, and Kennedy's evolving problems with the Johnson administration over domestic policy and the Vietnam war. Both men sometimes became victims of misperceptions fed by underlings, the press, and their own paranoia. Both showed vindictiveness—Robert, in the way he treated Vice President Johnson, and LBJ, while president, in the way that he used his power. Even immediately after Robert Kennedy's death, Johnson occasionally displayed a pettiness that negated his thoughtfulness toward the Kennedy family.

Shesol reveals the complexity of the Johnson-Kennedy differences, which might obscure the basis for their difficulties. More than anything, Robert Kennedy's hatred of Johnson had much to do with the latter's challenge of John Kennedy for the nomination in 1960. For such political disloyalty Robert Kennedy never forgave Adlai Stevenson. With Johnson, nothing weighed more than Kennedy's intense opposition to him for the vice presidency in 1960. To make matters worse, RFK mistreated Vice President Johnson afterward. Everything else in terms of causation is almost superfluous. Later President Johnson had good reason to fear Robert Kennedy as one who held claim to the Kennedy legacy. What will probably always be unclear, however, is the extent to which differences caused the two to shade policy positions in ways that they might not have done—most notably relating to Vietnam. Their disagreements, Shesol claims, have evolved into the present-day clashes between "Old" and "New" Democrats.

Shesol, a Rhodes scholar, has provided a thoughtfully written, well-researched, entertaining, and judicious study that will hold the attention of anyone interested in recent American political history.

JAMES N. GIGLIO

Southwest Missouri
  State University
Springfield

SOCIOLOGY

FORDHAM, SIGNITHIA. 1996. *Blacked Out: Dilemmas of Race, Identity and Success at Capital High*. Pp. xiv, 411. Chicago: University of Chicago Press. No price.

Blacked Out is a sophisticated, insightful analysis of the behavior and psyche of black students at Capital High, a secondary school in Washington, D.C.

In a prologue critical of anthropology as producing the written word (ethnography) that "remains the civilized weapon that maintains the status quo in a postmodern form of colonialism," Signithia Fordham explains her own use of ethnography as a medium of representation. She claims a "split selfhood": neither quite an anthropological self, which she holds as "rigidly scripted," nor an "other" self—the black self constructed by whites. She says of herself:

I am an anthropologist. I am also racially identified as African-American. I am involuntarily diasphoric—a wanderer. Therefore, I embody and reflect this "halfie" status, both in terms of the anthropological self and the Black self. In constructing this ethnography, I became keenly aware of the duality of my "split selfhood," of the imperative to use data based on watching and the violence attendant on trying to "make a way out of no way" in my chosen profession.

The author strikes a note, in this characterization of herself, to which any anthropologist sensitive to the dilemmas of being a watcher will resonate. Louise Spindler and I have been watchers in five quite different cultures, and from the start of our fieldwork in the late 1940s to the present, we have always been uncomfortable in the role of watcher, have felt quite marginalized whether studying another culture or living in our own, and have been utterly fascinated by the whole experience.

Fordham's "split selfhood" is what makes her ethnography of Capital High so unusual and so penetrating. She goes far beyond the now usual reflexivity required of ethnographers. She projects, intentionally, her "split selfhood" in her analysis. Nothing is quite as it seems. All protestations, policies, and propositions have a nether side. Nothing is black or white (nothing racial implied) but appears in many shades of gray. This is the way Fordham wrote her book, and that is why it is so satisfying.

The black self requires academic underachievement for success in the imagined black community. Academic success, when achieved, is a weapon to support the black self. Teachers and school officials are seen as foreign seers, but they are kept at arm's length and their wisdom eschewed. The black fictive kinship system requires that skills and expertise be used to connect to the imagined black community. "This is the only value or prestige a 'gift' or skill has for the individual, the only way he or she can become wise, something other than an 'educated fool.' "

Fordham carries resistance theory further than other analysts do by moving into the black psyche to treat with such dynamics as those previously expressed. The book as a whole is an analysis of the resistance of black students to the "makeover" they see as the purpose underlying school-sanctioned learning—an effort of the larger society to reconstitute their black identity.

Signithia Fordham says much more than I have been able to convey in this short review. Reading the book will inform you.

GEORGE D. SPINDLER

Stanford University
California

LAVIN, DAVID E. and DAVID HYLLE-GARD. 1996. *Changing the Odds: Open Admissions and the Life Chances of the Disadvantaged.* Pp. ix, 292. New Haven, CT: Yale University Press. No price.

During the fall of 1970, in response to pressures supporting an increase in access to college enrollment, the City University of New York (CUNY) adopted an admissions policy guaranteeing college entrance to all city high school graduates. This policy shift dramatically expanded minority access to CUNY, increased the size of that year's freshmen class (up 75 percent from the previous year), and more widely distributed the city's high school graduates among the CUNY colleges. Lavin and Hyllegard's book brings this story up to date, using data gathered from official CUNY records and a sample survey of 1970-72 open-admissions students conducted in 1984. The book also provides a clear and fluidly written account of the history of open admissions and the changes that have taken place in the policy, changes that have been extensive and increasingly conservative in political orientation, a process continuing even now.

In this well-crafted and important book, the basic question Lavin and Hyllegard pose for themselves, and one that makes this book's story more than a local curiosity, is, To what degree did the open-admissions policy facilitate social mobility for disadvantaged students? The answer they derive from their data to this fundamental question is clear and challenges all who are skeptical of the possibilities of educational policy for changing the odds of the poor to achieve stable, middle-class lives. Open admissions more than tripled the number of blacks who earned bachelor's and master's degrees; the number of Hispanic bachelor's degrees more than doubled and their M.A. rate almost doubled. White, mostly working-class students also benefited in substantial numbers, although that development is little known outside of the university itself. In tune with the city's rapidly changing economy, these college graduates were able to take advantage of the new occupational opportunities. Overwhelmingly they found employ-

ment, and they found it in white-collar positions. In one calculation of the economic benefit of open admissions, Lavin and Hyllegard assert that "for one year of the 1980's we estimate that former open-admissions students earned almost $67 million more than they would have earned if CUNY's program had never been instituted."

Lavin and Hyllegard argue that the policy has had ripple effects as these educationally and economically better-off graduates transmit their new advantages to their own children. Nevertheless, the policy shift was no panacea; the analysis shows that the policy had important limitations for poor, minority students and that past disadvantages of inadequate academic preparation led to slower rates of achievement as students needed to pass through non-credit remedial courses, had lower graduation rates, and experienced weaker payoffs in the labor force than was the case for the generally better-prepared white students.

Thus the policy produced substantial gains but has been challenged as both political ideology and financing have changed. The book ends by considering these gains in the light of current circumstances. The cutbacks at CUNY in recent years have resulted in a weakening of the policies of the early 1970s, even compared to the policies of the mid-1970s, when tuition was imposed at the university. Noting that CUNY's students are even more disadvantaged today than they were in 1970, Lavin and Hyllegard caution against further cutbacks in the policy. The city's labor force has become very precarious for anyone without at least some college, and there will be less opportunity for college-level education for many city high school graduates if CUNY reduces its accessibility.

FLOYD M. HAMMACK

New York University
New York City

MARTIN, SUSAN EHRLICH and NANCY C. JURIK. 1996. *Doing Justice, Doing Gender: Women in Law and Criminal Justice Occupations*. Pp. xi, 270. Thousand Oaks, CA: Sage. $38.95. Paperbound, $17.95.

Two patterns characterize women's experiences in the paid labor force: being segregated in female-dominated occupations and being relegated to the lower echelons of male-dominated occupations. The effects of these patterns are aptly reflected in the familiar phrases "gender wage gap" and "glass ceiling." Despite dramatic increases in the number of women in the paid labor force, numerous policies aimed specifically at ending discriminatory practices, and over 30 years of feminism, gender bias in the workplace is alive and well.

While the disparities in earnings and career trajectories between women and men have been explained in terms of biology, structural/organizational constraints, socialization practices, human capital, paternalism, capitalism, and blatant sexism, none of these explanations has been able to tell us why the disparities have been impervious to our corrective efforts. Fortunately, in *Doing Justice, Doing Gender*, Martin and Jurik offer an alternative explanation. What is compelling about their analysis, though, is that it is framed in an ultra-male context—the criminal justice system. The relevance of this context should not be minimized since, whether one is looking at the perpetrators of crime or those who administer justice, the world of criminal justice is distinguished by its maleness. In fact, the entire culture of criminal justice is permeated by maleness and is thus an ideal context for examining why women have yet to be accepted and integrated as coworkers.

The primary reason why women's integration has been so elusive, Martin and Jurik tell us, is related to the way biological sex is socially interpreted. In other words, being a female or male is not simply a function of biological sex but is an identity that emerges through a social process. Being a female or male is socially produced, and it is largely for this reason that policies aimed at ameliorating gender bias have not achieved their intended goals. Policy cannot end discriminatory practices so long as people believe that being female is a handicap. Gender bias is not typically deliberate but occurs because of the prevailing values that get attached to being female or male. These beliefs take shape and meaning through our relationships and interactions with others. These social processes form the essence of "doing gender," a term that refers to the process of making gender meaningful in our everyday interactions with others.

Martin and Jurik apply the conceptual framework of doing gender to their analysis of women's employment history in law enforcement, the law, and corrections. They focus on five aspects of the social production of gender in justice work: historical changes in labor queues; gendered work cultures; men doing gender; the gendered logic of justice; and women doing gender. To their credit, they also apply this framework to race and class. For example, when gender is combined with race, Martin and Jurik describe how minority women are doubly stigmatized and consequently further marginalized. The process works similarly for class distinctions.

Although the number of women in law enforcement, law, and corrections has increased since Title VII, women still constitute a conspicuous minority of those working in these areas. Martin and Jurik do an excellent job of documenting just how the career trajectories of women differ from those of men in these fields and why. The only shortcoming I find in the book is with the authors' assertion that none of the three fields shows signs of becoming "feminized" (a code word for "ghettoized," or the decrease in the market value of an occupation when women become the numerical majority). On the contrary, there is mounting evidence that the legal profession is becoming ghettoized. In fact, Hagan's research, which the authors cite, on the dual career tracks of lawyers as well as recent *National Law Journal* survey results and statistics from the National Center for State Courts and the American Bar Association all indicate a widening of the gap between women's and men's career tracks. Although the number of men in law overall is shrinking, men are clustered in the plum positions while women occupy the rest, and the gap between the two is widening. The numerical shifts and the widening of the gap strongly point to a pattern of what I would call stratified feminization.

A stronger case for this process can be made if specialty area is examined. For example, the judiciary is one of the most prestigious branches of law and it is highly stratified by gender. Although women have made some inroads, they are mostly confined to lower courts while men monopolize the higher courts. The judiciary, like the law, is a two-tiered system. Consider, for example, that although women account for almost 40 percent of the students in law schools and 20 percent of lawyers, they comprise only 7 percent of the law-trained judges in state courts. At the federal level, of the 753 full-time judges, women comprise only 7 percent. When we consider the effects of gender and race, we see that out of the 50 states and the District of Columbia, only 16 states have African American women serving on their courts. The lack of progress in breaking through to the upper echelons of the court system is distressing considering that it has been over a hundred years since the first woman justice of the peace was appointed. I wish Martin and Jurik had drawn sharper parallels between the patterns noted in Reskin and Roos's *Job Queues and Gender Queues*, particularly in banking, and law since there are signs in law of a stratified feminization process.

Martin and Jurik present a well-argued and well-documented analysis of the way doing gender works, and the contributions far outweigh any shortcomings. *Doing Justice, Doing Gender* is an important addition to the literature on occupations, gender studies, and women and criminal justice.

PHYLLIS COONTZ

University of Pittsburgh
Pennsylvania

POTUCHEK, JEAN L. 1997. *Who Supports the Family: Gender and Breadwinning in Dual Earner Marriages.* Pp. ix, 249. Stanford, CA: Stanford University Press. Paperbound, $16.95.

With the influx of married women and women with children into the paid labor force, researchers have tried to understand what factors lead women to seek paid employment. Do they work primarily to enhance their family earnings or to pursue careers and/or income equality with men? Research findings suggest that most married women have difficulty balancing paid work and family work. Yet, for the most part, women enjoy working in preference to being housewives. Middle-class women, with opportunities for education, tend to be career oriented, while working-class women tend to engage in paid work primarily for the money they earn and which their families increasingly need.

Jean Potuchek, in her book *Who Supports the Family*, takes these issues a significant step further by analyzing the relationship between married women's paid work and their self-perception as breadwinners. Her book is based on a study of 153 randomly chosen dual-earner couples in the Lewiston-Auburn area of Maine.

Potuchek suggests that women who see themselves as breadwinners tend to embody characteristics of women often described as career oriented. They tend to be younger, more educated, recently married, and childless; they earn paychecks more equal to those of their husbands. Yet she finds that only 15 percent of the wives in her sample considered themselves to be "co-breadwinners" with their husbands; only 26 percent of their husbands considered their wives to be co-providers.

Not only career-oriented or professional women see themselves as co-breadwinners. Instead, a wide variety of factors lead women to see themselves this way. These factors, Potuchek argues, can be best understood through the use of gender construction theory, an approach that assumes that gendered attitudes and behavior about work roles are not merely the fixed product of early socialization. Instead, they emerge in response to social interaction and the ways in which individual experience is influenced by external social constraints.

As gender inequality continues to persist in the workplace, the good-provider role continues to be accorded to men, who, at the same time, must also take responsibility for providing. Nevertheless, if the breadwinner role is still a male preserve, as women's paid employment has become increasingly legitimated, this gender boundary has become increasingly permeable and open to challenge by working wives.

Today, married women's sense of authority for defining their paid work as breadwinning or not emerges from the complex and constantly changing social circumstances of each family. Women's self-definition in terms of earning is typically a response to negotiations between husband and wife in the context of changing employment situations and each spouse's notion of his or her own and the other's responsibility for paid work and care for home and children.

Potuchek demonstrates how ongoing contention and cooperation exists among husbands and wives about these issues—along traditional as well as nontraditional lines. She concludes by pointing out that as long as sex segregation of the labor force and sex discrimination continue to enforce a lower waged female workforce, the same forms of contention and cooperation are likely to continue.

Jean Potuchek has written an important book. In addition to providing a wealth of detail about the lives and conflicts of the population she studied, *Who Supports the Family* is well-conceptualized and skillfully researched, employing both quantitative and qualitative methods. It makes an important contribution to the literature about women's responses to the available roles in the paid workforce.

ELLEN ROSEN

Nichols College
Dudley
Massachusetts

ECONOMICS

KRAUSE, ELLIOTT A. 1996. *Death of the Guilds: Professions, States and the Advance of Capitalism, 1930 to the Present.* Pp. xi, 305. New Haven, CT: Yale University Press. $37.50.

A major comparative study of the professions is long overdue, and Elliott Krause has supplied one. Five countries (the United States, Britain, France, Italy, and Germany); four professions in each country (medicine, law, the academy, engineering); and four dimensions of control in each profession (over their own associations, over the workplace, over the market, and relations with the state): Krause travels a huge terrain and, for the most part, travels it in style. Unfortunately, however, it is not always clear in what direction he is headed.

The professions, according to Krause, are fundamentally continuous with the guilds of the Middle Ages and Renaissance. Although Krause is rightly insistent on acknowledging both variations among professions and among nations, he argues that their "guild power" is generally in decline, giving way not only to capitalism but also to states themselves increasingly involved in the direction of economies. This is fine as far as it goes but, even as a very basic framework, may be misleading.

In emphasizing the medieval origins of the professions, Krause obscures the extent to which the nineteenth- and early-twentieth-century revival of professionalism (at least in the United States and Britain, the two cases I know best) was a precursor of neither capitalism nor the modern state but a self-consciously liberal alternative to both. In particular, Anglo-American professionalism was a means of protecting certain core values—health, justice, knowledge, and, to a much lesser extent, technology—from the uncertainties of the market and the dangers of a state that was, in any event, probably inadequate to safeguard them. Krause explains the decline of professionalism as part of a master narrative of modernity: capitalism (along with the state as an agent of capitalism) has, in Krause's phrase, "finally caught up with the last guilds." A more compelling explanation—one supported by the mass of material Krause reviews but underconceptualized in his text—is that the rise of welfare states has not only extended state control over the professions in the name of social justice but has undermined their legitimacy as semi-private guarantors of key values, leaving them vulnerable, at moments of Reaganism and Thatcherism, to the incursions of markets. If the professions in France and Germany have suffered less in recent years than those in the United States and Britain, it is not because they are more powerful but because, in far more statist regimes, they had never assumed the same importance in the infrastructure of liberalism.

These reservations notwithstanding, *Death of the Guilds* is a valuable compendium, extraordinary in its range and filled with insights about particular professions and their national contexts.

ROBERT ZUSSMAN

University of Massachusetts
Amherst

LEWIS, LIONEL S. 1996. *Marginal Worth: Teaching and the Academic Labor Market*. Pp. vii, 162. New Brunswick, NJ: Transaction. $29.95.

This book attempts to analyze in some detail the often heard complaint that teaching is sorely neglected in American colleges, that teachers devote more of their energies to research than to teaching and are seldom rewarded for excellent teaching.

The general thrust of the book is seemingly not new, but Lionel Lewis has collected considerable evidence that bears out some of the disparaging remarks heard outside the university. Lewis has collected substantial quantitative information about salary rewards for teaching as well as anecdotal material from university administrators about how the teaching function is looked upon and how it figures into tenure and promotion decisions. One of the leading conclusions to come out of the study is that while the teaching function is universally praised on campus and said to be at the heart of the educational mission, in actual fact it is not highly esteemed and is poorly rewarded.

Anyone interested in the question of the way teaching is valued and rewarded in the American university will find much useful information here. If the book has a defect, it is probably a lack of any historical context for the subject. The early universities that were developed in Europe in the Middle Ages were dedicated to some kind of community of learners. As Alfred North Whitehead once said, the original justification for a university was to "preserve the connection between knowledge and the zest for life by uniting the young and old in an imaginative consideration of learning."

When the great American research universities arose in the late nineteenth century, this ideal went out the window. Universities became research tanks, with students as second-class citizens—passive receivers at the end of a pipeline. When, after World War II, the universities were expected to pump the multitudes through the pipeline, it was inevitable that teaching (true interaction between individuals) would become a peripheral and degraded function.

The American university today (and there is some resistance, of course) consists of distinct and separate cultures, with students mostly coming to have a good time, polish their social skills, enjoy liberation from their parents, with the promise of a better job at the end of their ordeal. Professors live mostly in another world, the world of their academic specialty. In the schism between these two worlds lies the principal reason for the diminished importance of teaching.

GEORGE H. DOUGLAS

University of Illinois
Urbana

OTHER BOOKS

ALLOTT, MARGARET and MARTIN ROBB, eds. 1998. *Understanding Health and Social Care*. Pp. ix, 318. Thousand Oaks, CA: Sage. $68.50. Paperbound, $27.50.

ANDREW, JOHN A., III. 1998. *Lyndon Johnson and the Great Society*. Pp. ix, 211. Chicago: Ivan R. Dee. $24.95.

ARMITAGE, DAVID, ed. 1997. *Bolingbroke: Political Writings*. Pp. xliv, 305. New York: Cambridge University Press. $64.95. Paperbound, $24.95.

BAILEY, F. G. 1998. *The Need for Enemies: A Bestiary of Political Forms*. Pp. xiv, 223. Ithaca, NY: Cornell University Press. $39.95. Paperbound, $15.95.

BEITMAN, BERNARD D. 1998. *The Psychotherapist's Guide to Cost Containment: How to Survive and Thrive in an Age of Managed Care*. Pp. xiii, 161. Thousand Oaks, CA: Sage. Paperbound, $23.50.

BRADEN, SIDANI. 1997. *Evaluating Nursing Interventions: A Theory-Driven Approach*. Pp. x, 190. Thousand Oaks, CA: Sage. $46.00. Paperbound, $21.95.

BRANTS, KEES, JOKE HERMES, and LIESBET VAN ZOONEN, eds. 1998. *The Media in Question: Popular Cultures and Public Interests*. Pp. vi, 184. Thousand Oaks, CA: Sage. $79.95. Paperbound, $32.95.

BURSTEIN, PAUL. 1998. *Discrimination, Jobs, and Politics: The Struggle for Equal Employment Opportunity in the United States Since the New Deal*. Pp. xlii, 247. Chicago: University of Chicago Press. Paperbound, no price.

CLOR, HARRY M. 1996. *Public Morality and Liberal Society: Essays on Decency, Law, and Pornography*. Pp. x, 235. Notre Dame, IN: University of Notre Dame Press. No price.

CLOUD, DANA L. 1998. *Control and Consolation in American Culture and Politics: Rhetorics of Therapy*. Pp. xxiii, 192. Thousand Oaks, CA: Sage. $45.00. Paperbound, $19.95.

COLAS, DOMINIQUE. 1997. *Civil Society and Fanaticism: Conjoined Histories*. Pp. xxx, 480. Stanford, CA: Stanford University Press. $65.00. Paperbound, $21.95.

COLEMAN, CHARLES J., THEODORA T. HAYNES, and MARIE T. GIBSON McGRAW, eds. 1997. *Labor and Employment Arbitration: An Annotated Bibliography, 1991-1996*. Pp. vii, 163. Ithaca, NY: Cornell University Press. $35.00.

DAVIDSON, ROGER H., SUSAN WEBB HAMMOND, and RAYMOND W. SMOCK, eds. 1998. *Masters of the House: Congressional Leaders over Two Centuries*. Pp. xi, 345. Boulder, CO: Westview Press. $69.00. Paperbound, $30.00.

DOMINGUEZ, JORGE I. and JAMES A McCANN. 1996. *Democratizing Mexico: Public Opinion and Electoral Choices*. Pp. xvi, 269. Baltimore, MD: Johns Hopkins University Press. $45.00.

ELKIN, JUDITH LAIKIN. 1998. *The Jews of Latin America*. Pp. xv, 339. New York: Holmes & Meier. $45.00. Paperbound, $19.50.

EVERETTE, E. DENNIS and ROBERT W. SNYDER. 1998. *Covering Congress*. Pp. xviii, 170. New Brunswick, NJ: Transaction. Paperbound, $21.95.

FARMER, HELEN S. 1997. *Diversity and Women's Career Development*. Pp. xvi, 344. Thousand Oaks, CA: Sage. $54.00. Paperbound, $24.95.

FERNANDEZ-MADRID, FELIX. 1998. *Che Guevara and the Incurable Disease*. Pp. viii, 163. Pittsburgh, PA: Dorrance. $16.00.

FREEDMAN, SAMUEL G. 1998. *The Inheritance: How Three Families and the American Political Majority Moved from Left to Right*. Pp. 464. New York:

Touchstone Books. Paperbound, $15.00.

GOLDSTENE, PAUL N. 1997. *Revolution, American Style: The Nineteen-Sixties and Beyond.* Pp. xiii, 136. Novato, CA: Chandler & Sharp. Paperbound, $12.95.

GOONESEKERE, SAVITRI. 1998. *Children, Law and Justice: A South Asian Perspective.* Pp. 420. Thousand Oaks, CA: Sage. $39.95.

GRAHAM, SARA HUNTER. 1996. *Woman Suffrage and the New Democracy.* Pp. xviii, 234. New Haven, CT: Yale University Press. No price.

GRAY, JOHN. 1995. *Enlightenment's Wake: Politics and Culture at the Close of the Modern Age.* Pp. ix, 203. New York: Routledge. Paperbound, $16.99.

HAMES, TIM and NICOL RAE. 1996. *Governing America: History, Culture, Institutions, Organization and Policy.* Pp. ix, 339. New York: Manchester University Press. $75.00. Paperbound, $24.95.

HEYMAN, NEIL M. 1997. *World War I.* Pp. xxiii, 257. Westport, CT: Greenwood Press. $39.95.

HILTEBEITEL, ALF and BARBARA D. MILLER, eds. 1998. *Hair: Its Power and Meaning in Asian Cultures.* Pp. xvi, 297. Albany: State University of New York Press. No price.

HILTY, JAMES W. 1997. *Robert Kennedy: Brother Protector.* Pp. xii, 642. Philadelphia: Temple University Press. $34.95.

HOFFMANN, STANLEY, ed. 1998. *Judith N. Sklar: Political Thought and Political Thinkers.* Pp. xxvi, 402. Chicago: University of Chicago Press. Paperbound, no price.

HOFFMANN, STANLEY and DENNIS F. THOMPSON, eds. 1998. *Judith N. Sklar: Redeeming American Political Thought.* Pp. xvii, 209. Chicago: University of Chicago Press. $38.00. Paperbound, $13.95.

HOOGVELT, ANKIE. 1997. *Globalization and the Postcolonial World: The New Political Economy of Development.* Pp. xvi, 291. Baltimore, MD: Johns Hopkins University Press. $45.00. Paperbound, $17.95.

ILCHMAN, WARREN F. and NORMAN T. UPHOFF. 1998. *The Political Economy of Change.* Pp. xxxvi, 316. New Brunswick, NJ: Transaction. Paperbound, $24.95.

INKELES, ALEX. 1998. *One World Emerging: Convergence and Divergence in Industrial Societies.* Pp. xix, 423. Boulder, CO: Westview Press. $39.00.

JOSEPH, K. J. 1998. *Industry Under Economic Liberalization: The Case of Indian Electronics.* Pp. 245. New Delhi: Sage. $29.95.

KABRA, KAMAL NAYAN. 1998. *Development Planning in India: Exploring an Alternative Approach.* Pp. 251. New Delhi: Sage. $32.00.

KALLEN, HORACE M. 1998. *Culture and Democracy in the United States.* Pp. lxix, 339. New Brunswick, NJ: Transaction. Paperbound, $29.95.

KATZ, MARK N. 1997. *Revolutions and Revolutionary Waves.* Pp. xiii, 171. New York: St. Martin's Press. $45.00.

KICKERT, WALTER J. M., ERIK-HANS KLIJN, and JOOP F. M. KOPPENJAN, eds. 1997. *Managing Complex Networks: Strategies for the Public Sector.* Pp. xviii, 206. Thousand Oaks, CA: Sage. $40.00. Paperbound, $13.95.

KLAUSEN, JYTTE and LOUISE A. TILLY. 1997. *European Integration in Social and Historical Perspective.* Pp. xvi, 322. Lanham, MD: Rowman & Littlefield. $64.00. Paperbound, $22.95.

LUSZTIG, MICHAEL. 1996. *Risking Free Trade.* Pp. x, 180. Pittsburgh, PA: University of Pittsburgh Press. $49.95. Paperbound, $22.95.

MARTY, MYRON A. 1997. *Daily Life in the United States, 1960-1990: Decades of Discord.* Pp. xix, 371. Westport, CT: Greenwood Press. $45.00.

McGUIGAN, JIM, ed. 1998. *Cultural Methodologies.* Pp. vii, 215. Thousand Oaks, CA: Sage. $65.00. Paperbound, $26.95.

McKNIGHT, GERALD D. 1998. *The Last Crusade: Martin Luther King, Jr., the FBI, and the Poor People's Campaign.* Pp. v, 192. Boulder, CO: Westview Press. $25.00.

McLEOD, JOHN. 1998. *Narrative and Psychotherapy.* Pp. xi, 180. Thousand Oaks, CA: Sage. $65.00. Paperbound, $24.95.

McQUIRE, SCOTT. 1998. *Visions of Modernity.* Pp. vi, 279. Thousand Oaks, CA: Sage. Paperbound, $24.95.

MICHIO, MURAMATSU. 1997. *Local Power in the Japanese State.* Pp. xxi, 182. Berkeley: University of California Press. $45.00. Paperbound, $16.95.

MONTGOMERY, JOHN D., ed. 1997. *Values in Education: Social Capital Formation in Asia and the Pacific.* Pp. x, 199. Hollis, NH: Hollis. $29.95.

MURAKAMI, YASUSUKE. 1996. *An Anticlassical Political-Economic Analysis: A Vision for the Next Century.* Pp. xxix, 476. Stanford, CA: Stanford University Press. $60.00.

MURDOCK, STEVE H. 1995. *An America Challenged: Population Change and the Future of the United States.* Pp. xxiii, 253. Boulder, CO: Westview Press. No price.

NASH, GEORGE H. 1996. *The Life of Herbert Hoover: Master of Emergencies, 1917-1918.* Pp. xiii, 656. New York: Norton. $45.00.

NORTON, KINGSLEY and GILL McCAULEY. 1998. *Counselling Difficult Clients.* Pp. x, 153. Thousand Oaks, CA: Sage. $55.00. Paperbound, $21.95.

PEBLEY, ANNE R. and LUIS ROSERO-BIXBY, eds. 1997. *Demographic Diversity and Change in the Central American Isthmus.* Pp. xiv, 736. Santa Monica, CA: Rand. Paperbound, $30.00.

RICH, DAVID Z. 1997. *Crisis Theory.* Pp. ix, 234. Westport, CT: Praeger. $59.95.

ROBERTSON, JOHN, ed. 1997. *Andrew Fletcher: Political Works.* Pp. xlix, 243. New York: Cambridge University Press. $64.95. Paperbound, $24.95.

ROSE, TANIA, ed. 1998. *Dispatches from the Revolution: Russia, 1916-1918.* Pp. xii, 181. Durham, NC: Duke University Press. $49.95. Paperbound, $15.95.

ROTBLAT, JOSEPH, ed. 1998. *Nuclear Weapons: The Road to Zero.* Pp. xii, 331. Boulder, CO: Westview Press. $65.00.

ROZELL, MARK J. and CLYDE WILCOX, eds. 1997. *God at the Grass Roots, 1996: The Christian Right in the 1996 Elections.* Pp. x, 285. Lanham, MD: Rowman & Littlefield. $60.00. Paperbound, $22.95.

RUBIN, BARNETT R. 1995. *The Search for Peace in Afghanistan: From Buffer State to Failed State.* Pp. xi, 190. New Haven, CT: Yale University Press. No price.

SASSEN, SASKIA. 1996. *Losing Control? Sovereignty in an Age of Globalization.* Pp. xvi, 148. New York: Columbia University Press. $24.95.

SCATES, SHELBY. 1997. *Warren G. Magnuson and the Shaping of Twentieth-Century America.* Pp. x, 360. Seattle: University of Washington Press. $27.50.

SCHLEICHER, DAVID and BRENDON SWEDLOW, eds. 1998. *Federalism and Political Culture: Aaron Wildavsky.* Pp. xx, 138. New Brunswick, NJ: Transaction. $29.95.

SCHMERTZ, ERIC J., NATALIE DATLOF, and ALEXEJ UGRINSKY, eds. 1997. *Ronald Reagan's America.* Vol.

1. Pp. xiv, 425. Westport, CT: Greenwood Press. $72.50.

SCHMERTZ, ERIC J., NATALIE DATLOF, and ALEXEJ UGRINSKY, eds. 1997. *Ronald Reagan's America.* Vol. 2. Pp. xii, 883. Westport, CT: Greenwood Press. $72.50.

SCHNEIDER, RONALD M. 1996. *Brazil: Culture and Politics in a New Industrial Powerhouse.* Pp. xvi, 255. Boulder, CO: Westview Press. Paperbound, no price.

SCHRAM, SANFORD F. and PHILIP T. NEISSER, eds. 1997. *Tales of the State: Narrative in Contemporary United States Politics and Public Policy.* Pp. vii, 270. Lanham, MD: Rowman & Littlefield. $65.00. Paperbound, $22.95.

SHAH, A. M., B. S. BAVISKAR, and E. A. RAMASWAMY, eds. 1997. *Social Structure and Change: Development and Ethnicity.* Vol. 4. Pp. 261. New Delhi: Sage. $32.00.

SHAIN, YOSSI and AHARON KLIEMAN, eds. 1997. *Democracy: The Challenges Ahead.* Pp. xiii, 237. New York: St. Martin's Press. $65.00.

SHARMA, K. L. 1997. *Social Stratification in India: Issues and Themes.* Pp. 218. New Delhi: Sage. $28.00.

SHELLEY, FRED M., J. CLARK ARCHER, FIONA M. DAVIDSON, and STANLEY D. BRUNN. 1996. *Political Geography of the United States.* Pp. xiv, 364. New York: Guilford. $47.95. Paperbound, $24.95.

SHUKLA, MADHUKAR. 1997. *Competing Through Knowledge: Building a Learning Organisation.* Pp. 334. New Delhi: Sage. $36.50.

SINGELIS, THEODORE M., ed. 1998. *Teaching About Culture, Ethnicity, and Diversity: Exercises and Planned Activities.* Pp. xii, 255. Thousand Oaks, CA: Sage. Paperbound, $24.95.

SINGER, S. FRED. 1997. *Hot Talk, Cold Science: Global Warming's Unfinished Debate.* Pp. x, 110. Oakland, CA: Independent Institute. Paperbound, $14.95.

SINGH, RAJENDRA, ed. 1998. *Grammar, Language, and Society: Contemporary Indian Contributions.* Pp. 366. Thousand Oaks, CA: Sage. $45.00.

SMALL, MELVIN. 1996. *Democracy and Diplomacy: The Impact of Domestic Politics on U.S. Foreign Policy, 1789-1994.* Pp. xix, 200. Baltimore, MD: Johns Hopkins University Press. Paperbound, no price.

SNAPP, J. RUSSELL. 1996. *John Stuart and the Struggle for Empire on the Southern Frontier.* Pp. xii, 238. Baton Rouge: Louisiana State University Press. $42.50.

SNIDERMAN, PAUL M., JOSEPH F. FLETCHER, PETER H. RUSSELL, and PHILIP E. TETLOCK. 1996. *The Clash of Rights: Liberty, Equality, and Legitimacy in Pluralist Democracy.* Pp. xi, 291. New Haven, CT: Yale University Press. Paperbound, no price.

SOYINKA, WOLE. 1996. *The Open Sore of a Continent: A Personal Narrative of the Nigerian Crisis.* Pp. vi, 170. New York: Oxford University Press. $19.95.

STADLER, MICHAEL A. and PETER A. FRENSCH, eds. 1997. *Handbook of Implicit Learning.* Pp. xi, 636. Thousand Oaks, CA: Sage. $75.00.

STAVRAKIS, PETER J., JOAN DeBARDELEBEN, and LARRY BLACK, eds. 1997. *Beyond the Monolith: The Emergence of Regionalism in Post-Soviet Russia.* Pp. xii, 259. Baltimore, MD: Johns Hopkins University Press. $45.00.

STEINBERG, LAURENCE. 1997. *Beyond the Classroom: Why School Reform Has Failed and What Parents Need to Do.* Pp. 223. New York: Touchstone Books. Paperbound, $12.00.

STEINMO, SVEN. 1996. *Taxation and Democracy: Swedish, British, and American Approaches to Financing the Modern State.* Pp. xvii, 280. New

Haven, CT: Yale University Press. $40.00. Paperbound, $17.00.

STOREY, JOHN, PAUL EDWARDS, and KEITH SISSON. 1997. *Managers in the Making: Careers, Development and Control in Corporate Britain and Japan.* Pp. viii, 262. Thousand Oaks, CA: Sage. Paperbound, $26.50.

STRIKWERDA, CARL. 1997. *A House Divided: Catholics, Socialists, and Flemish Nationalists in Nineteenth-Century.* Pp. xv, 454. Lanham, MD: Rowman & Littlefield. $62.50. Paperbound, $23.95.

TONRA, BEN, ed. 1997. *Amsterdam: What the Treaty Means.* Pp. viii, 224. Dublin: Institute of European Affairs. Paperbound, no price.

TREXLER, RICHARD C. 1995. *Sex and Conquest: Gendered Violence, Political Order, and the European Conquest of the Americas.* Ithaca, NY: Cornell University Press. $29.95.

URBAN, GEORGE R. 1998. *Radio Free Europe and the Pursuit of Democracy: My War Within the Cold War.* Pp. x, 322. New Haven, CT: Yale University Press. $30.00.

WELSCH, WOLFGANG. 1997. *Undoing Aesthetics.* Pp. x, 209. Thousand Oaks, CA: Sage. $69.95. Paperbound, $23.95.

WELTMAN, JOHN J. 1995. *World Politics and the Evolution of War.* Pp. xii, 263. Baltimore, MD: Johns Hopkins University Press. Paperbound, no price.

WIARDA, HOWARD J. 1996. *Iberia and Latin America: New Democracies, New Policies, New Models.* Pp. x, 118. Lanham, MD: Rowman & Littlefield. $52.50. Paperbound, $21.95.

WISEMAN, JOHN A. 1996. *The New Struggle for Democracy in Africa.* Pp. vi, 200. Brookfield, VT: Ashgate. No price.

WITT, STEPHANIE L. and SUZANNE McCORKLE, eds. 1997. *Anti-Gay Rights: Assessing Voter Initiatives.* Pp. vi, 200. Westport, CT: Praeger. $55.00.

WITTNER, LAWRENCE S. 1998. *Resisting the Bomb: A History of the World Nuclear Disarmament Movement.* Pp. xiv, 641. Stanford, CA: Stanford University Press. $65.00. Paperbound, $24.95.

WRIGHT, JOHNSON KENT. 1997. *A Classical Republican in Eighteenth-Century France: The Political Thought of Mably.* Pp. vii, 261. Stanford, CA: Stanford University Press. No price.

YAMAMURA, KOZO, ed. 1998. *A Vision of a New Liberalism? Critical Essays on Murakami's Anticlassical Analysis.* Pp. vii, 312. Stanford, CA: Stanford University Press. $49.50.

YANG, BENJAMIN. 1997. *Deng: A Political Biography.* Pp. xix, 331. Armonk, NY: M. E. Sharpe. $59.95. Paperbound, $21.95.

YEATTS, DALE E. and CLOYD HYTEN. 1997. *High-Performing Self-Managed Work Teams: A Comparison of Theory to Practice.* Pp. xvii, 378. Thousand Oaks, CA: Sage. $58.00. Paperbound, $27.95.

ZACHARIAH, K. C. and S. IRUDAYA RAJAN, eds. 1998. *Kerala's Demographic Transition: Determinants and Consequences.* Pp. 367. New Delhi: Sage. $39.95.

ZALEWSKI, MARYSIA and JANE PARPART, eds. 1997. *The "Man" Question in International Relations.* Pp. vii, 219. Boulder, CO: Westview Press. $59.00. Paperbound, $18.95.

ZARTMAN, I. WILLIAM and J. LEWIS RASMUSSEN, eds. 1997. *Peacemaking in International Conflict: Methods and Techniques.* Pp. ix, 412. Washington, DC: United States Institute of Peace Press. Paperbound, no price.

ZIMMERMAN, JOSEPH F. 1997. *The Recall: Tribunal of the People.* Pp. viii, 194. Westport, CT: Praeger. $55.00.

INDEX

Special Issues of the **Journal of Language and Social Psychology**

The Language of Equivocation

Journal of Language and Social Psychology
Volume 17, Numbers 1 / March 1998
Volume 17, Number 2 / June 1998
Single Issue: Individual $20 / Institution $75

4 ways to order and share the best scholarship in your field

■ Back Issues

Make sure you didn't miss any important articles that you need for your own practice, research or classroom. Back issues are available at 20% discount. To order, call Sage Customer Service at (805) 499-9774 or email: order@sagepub.com.

■ Reprints

Customize your instructional materials to fit your classroom and symposia needs with powerful, new ideas from leading scholars in the field. Reprints make cost-effective additions to your course materials and conference packets. They are convenient and easy to obtain. To order multiple copies of a recent article, call Sage Reprint Services at (805) 499-0721, Ext 7535 or email: reprint@sagepub.com.

■ Special Issues

Occasionally an entire issue is devoted to a single relevant topic, viewing it at length and in depth. The pertinent information in these Special Issues is something you will refer to again and again. Sage offers discounts of up to 60% on multiple copies for classroom adoption. For more information on multiple-copy prices call (805) 499-0721, ext. 7528 or email: adopt_jnl@sagepub.com.

■ Sample Copies

Sample copies (up to two) may be obtained on request directly from Sage Publications, by calling Sage Customer Service at (805) 499-9774 or e-mail:jsamples@sagepub.com.

SAGE PUBLICATIONS, INC.
2455 Teller Road, Thousand Oaks, CA 91320
Tel: (805) 499-0721 ■ Fax: (805) 499-0871
Visit us at http://www.sagepub.com